QUEER DATA

BLOOMSBURY STUDIES IN DIGITAL CULTURES

Series Editors
Anthony Mandal and Jenny Kidd

This series responds to a rapidly changing digital world, one which permeates both our everyday lives and the broader philosophical challenges that accrue in its wake. It is inter- and trans-disciplinary, situated at the meeting points of the digital humanities, digital media and cultural studies, and research into digital ethics.

While the series will tackle the 'digital humanities' in its broadest sense, its ambition is to broaden focus beyond areas typically associated with the digital humanities to encompass a range of approaches to the digital, whether these be digital humanities, digital media studies or digital arts practice.

Titles in the series

THE TROUBLE WITH BIG DATA
by Jennifer Edmond, Nicola Horsley, Jörg Lehmann and Mike Priddy

Forthcoming titles

HUMAN EXPLOITS, CYBERPUNK AND THE DIGITAL HUMANITIES
by Aaron Mauro

AMBIENT STORIES IN PRACTICE AND RESEARCH
Edited by Amy Spencer

METAMODERNISM AND THE POSTDIGITAL IN THE
CONTEMPORARY NOVEL
by Spencer Jordan

QUEER DATA

USING GENDER, SEX AND SEXUALITY DATA FOR ACTION

Kevin Guyan

BLOOMSBURY ACADEMIC
LONDON • NEW YORK • OXFORD • NEW DELHI • SYDNEY

BLOOMSBURY ACADEMIC
Bloomsbury Publishing Plc
50 Bedford Square, London, WC1B 3DP, UK
1385 Broadway, New York, NY 10018, USA
29 Earlsfort Terrace, Dublin 2, Ireland

BLOOMSBURY, BLOOMSBURY ACADEMIC and the Diana logo
are trademarks of Bloomsbury Publishing Plc

First published in Great Britain 2022
Reprinted in 2022 (three times)

For legal purposes the Acknowledgements on p. viii constitute
an extension of this copyright page.

Cover design: Eleanor Rose
Cover photographs: Pussy Power placard at march in support of women and
LGBTQ rights, London, January 2017 © Daniel James Homewood / SOPA Images /
LightRocket via Getty Images; July 2017 Pride in London Parade © David Cliff /
SOPA Images / LightRocket via Getty Images; marcher dressed as Marilyn Monroe,
at Gay Pride march, London, July 1994 © Steve Eason / Hulton Archive /
Getty Images; Torn paper © Nikola Vukojevic / iStock / Getty Images Plus

Bloomsbury Publishing Plc does not have any control over, or responsibility
for, any third-party websites referred to or in this book. All internet addresses given
in this book were correct at the time of going to press. The author and publisher
regret any inconvenience caused if addresses have changed or sites have ceased to
exist, but can accept no responsibility for any such changes.

A catalogue record for this book is available from the British Library.

A catalog record for this book is available from the Library of Congress.

ISBN: HB: 978-1-3502-3073-6
       PB: 978-1-3502-3072-9
       ePDF: 978-1-3502-3074-3
       eBook: 978-1-3502-3075-0

Series: Bloomsbury Studies in Digital Cultures

Typeset by Integra Software Services Pvt. Ltd.
Printed and bound in Great Britain

To find out more about our authors and books visit www.bloomsbury.com
and sign up for our newsletters.

To exist is to resist,

with or without data.

CONTENTS

ACKNOWLEDGEMENTS

Queer Data is dedicated to those not in the room when decisions are made about them. People at the sharp end of administrative practices, assigned a category but denied a say. Individuals not counted accurately and individuals not counted at all. *Queer Data* is for everyone who has had to provide (yet more) data as proof of injustice in the hope that the system will change, if not now but in the future. *Queer Data* is for those asked to provide data to prove their existence.

I wish to note particular thanks to Kirstie English, Ashlee Christoffersen, Emma Ritch, Vic Valentine, Jess Moody, Gary J. Gates and Kath Browne for notes and reflections on draft chapters. Feedback received on the draft manuscript during blind peer review was also helpful in shaping the final version of the text. In addition, the support and enthusiasm of Paula Kennedy at Emerald and Laura Cope and Ben Doyle at Bloomsbury Academic helped transform *Queer Data* from a collection of ideas into a published work. I am also grateful for the many conversations shared with colleagues at Advance HE and Equality Challenge Unit about data, identities and inequality in higher education. My ideas were also shaped through insights from many researchers, practitioners and activists, engaged in the use of data for action in the UK and around the world, who took time to speak to me about their work. This includes students, attendees, co-panellists and organizers at events hosted by Queer Code Scotland, Princeton University's Queer Politics Seminar, the Irish Sexualities and Genders Research Network, the University of Stirling, UK Data Service and the Data 4 Good Festival.

Writing this book was only possible because of the support and solidarity from my grandparents and parents: Jim and Grace Marnoch, Isobel Guyan, Craig and Alison Guyan. And lastly, my husband Andrés Ordorica – my partner for long writing days, coffee breaks and discussions about how to change the world for the better.

My examination of the design of the sexual orientation question in Scotland's 2022 census, discussed in Chapters 3 and 5, is derived in part from an article published in the Journal of Gender Studies, 2021, © Taylor & Francis, available online: http://www.tandfonline.com/10.1080/09589236. 2020.1866513.

ABBREVIATIONS

AI	Artificial intelligence
BAME	Black, Asian and minority ethnic
CTEEA	Culture, Tourism, Europe and External Affairs committee
EDI	Equality, diversity and inclusion
EHRC	Equality and Human Rights Commission
EIA	Equality impact assessment
EU	European Union
GEO	Government Equalities Office
GIRES	Gender Identity Research & Education Society
GRA	Gender Recognition Act
GRC	Gender Recognition Certificate
ICAO	International Civil Aviation Organisation
LGBTQ	Lesbian, gay, bisexual, trans and queer
MP	Member of Parliament
MSP	Member of the Scottish Parliament
NRS	National Records of Scotland
NSO	National Statistical Office

Abbreviations

OECD   Organisation for Economic Co-operation and
Development

ONS   Office for National Statistics

UN   United Nations

INTRODUCTION: DATA AND DIFFERENCE

Queer data is a tension. On one hand, it freezes in time and space particular ideas about what it means to identify as lesbian, gay, bisexual, trans and/or queer. It establishes these meanings as categories, which are fed into counting machines and used as the basis for decision-making. This construction and deployment of categories are at odds with the *queering* of data, which critically questions the foundations upon which these categories stand, the value granted to some identities above others and who *actually* benefits from the collection, analysis and use of data about LGBTQ people. Queer data is more than a study of individuals that sit outside the categories of heterosexual or cisgender. It is equally a brash, confrontational and in-your-face challenge to conventional understandings of how data and identities intersect – how people respond to queer data is either their problem or their wake-up call. As an approach to data and identities, queer data disrupts the binaries of male/female, heterosexual/homosexual and cis/trans and asks us to reconsider the notion that 'numbers speak for themselves'. When data captures the lives and experiences of LGBTQ people, numbers do not speak for themselves – they always speak for someone. As I will argue, decisions made about who to count, what to count and how to count are not value-neutral but bring to life a particular vision of the social world.[1] Queer data exposes the decisions made about data, from collection to its use for action, to ensure that data about LGBTQ people is used to construct a social world that values and improves the lives of LGBTQ people.

Gender, sex and sexuality data is having a particular moment in the UK with increased interest from those outside of academic contexts and those engaged in data practices in the public, private and voluntary sectors.[2] Some

---

[1] I use the term 'social world' to underscore that perceptions of reality are contested, contextual and shaped by our actions rather than something objective that exists beyond us.

[2] A constellation of activities related to gender, sex and sexuality data occurred between 2019 and 2021, including the Scottish Government's formation of a Sex and Gender in Data Working Group, proposals to reform the Gender Recognition Act in the Scottish and UK Parliaments, and debate about approaches to the collection of diversity monitoring data in public, private and voluntary sector organizations.

of this interest relates to the UK's 2021 and 2022 censuses, which, for the first time, capture data about the population's sexual orientation, gender identity (England and Wales) and trans status/history (Scotland), discussed in Chapter 3. The addition of these questions marks a landmark moment for LGBTQ representation and the potential for improved evidence to address inequality. Yet, participation in the census, and other data collection exercises, is a double-edged sword as they require LGBTQ people to engage in practices that flattens the diversity of experiences and design-out certain lives. This data dilemma, the potential benefits of being counted versus the risk of being counted in ways that are inaccurate or further entrench inequality, might seem relatively new. However, there exists a long history of political and social struggles over the design of classification systems that present themselves as 'purely technical' but promote a biased account of the social world.[3] Several studies have investigated the implications of this data dilemma for women, indigenous communities and people of colour.[4] María Lugones has described how mechanisms of 'heterosexuality, capitalism, and racial classifications' were forged by colonial powers as a 'colonial/modern gender system' that has since shaped contemporary ideas about identity classifications.[5] Lauren E. Bridges has also explained that histories of naming and categorization 'have long been entangled in histories of sovereignty, colonialism, subjugation and exploitation'.[6] Critical race theorists, such as Richard Delgado and Jean Stefancic, have similarly argued that races operate as 'categories that society invents, manipulates, or retires when convenient'.[7] Although 'invented' as a category, the effects of race on social relations and people's life opportunities are material and multiple.[8] *Queer Data* expands on feminist, postcolonial and critical race scholarship to explore how,

---

[3] Geoffrey C. Bowker and Susan Leigh Star, *Sorting Things Out: Classification and Its Consequences* (Cambridge: The MIT Press, 1999), 196.

[4] Scholarship includes Catherine D'Ignazio and Lauren F. Klein, *Data Feminism* (Cambridge: The MIT Press, 2020); Maggie Walter and Chris Andersen, *Indigenous Statistics: A Quantitative Research Methodology* (Walnut Creek: Routledge, 2013); Ruha Benjamin, *Race after Technology: Abolitionist Tools for the New Jim Code* (Medford: Polity, 2019).

[5] María Lugones, 'Heterosexualism and the Colonial/Modern Gender System', *Hypatia* 22, no. 1 (2007): 187.

[6] Lauren E. Bridges, 'Digital Failure: Unbecoming the "Good" Data Subject through Entropic, Fugitive, and Queer Data', *Big Data & Society* 8, no. 1 (1 January 2021): 2.

[7] Richard Delgado and Jean Stefancic, *Critical Race Theory: An Introduction* (London: New York University Press, 2001), 7.

[8] Zeus Leonardo, 'Through the Multicultural Glass: Althusser, Ideology and Race Relations in Post-Civil Rights America', *Policy Futures in Education* 3, no. 4 (1 December 2005): 409.

among LGBTQ individuals, those who stand to benefit from 'being counted' also risk engaging with technologies that might normalize categories and practices that hamper rather than help the wider LGBTQ population.

The topic of difference has energized the work of LGBTQ researchers, practitioners and activists since, at least, the middle decades of the twentieth-century. Although this work addressed themes such as social mobilization, political organization and cultural representation, the experiences of people we might now describe as LGBTQ have historically eluded data collectors and analysts, an absence I explore in Chapter 1.[9] In rare instances where data about individuals that transgressed normative ideas about gender, sex or sexuality was captured in datasets, it predominantly featured as a means to pathologize or stigmatize, record acts understood as criminal or deviant, or differentiate individuals from the normative majority. Knowing more about the membership and contours of an identity group can inform decisions made about the allocation of resources, changes in legislation, access to services and protections under the law. Gathering evidence of a problem is one of the key methods used to advance the rights of marginalized groups in the UK. For example, public bodies are required to publish relevant and proportionate information that demonstrates their compliance with the duties described in the 2010 Equality Act.[10] This includes the collection, analysis and publication of employees and service users' data, as it relates to nine protected characteristics: age, disability, gender reassignment (trans status), marriage and civil partnership, pregnancy and maternity, race, religion and belief, sex and sexual orientation. Heightened data competence can therefore ensure data is used to improve the lives and experiences of LGBTQ people rather than only serve the interests of, what Catherine D'Ignazio and Lauren F. Klein describe as, the three S's: science (universities), surveillance (governments) and selling (corporations).[11] As a contested and political practice, the collection, analysis and presentation of data about LGBTQ people are partly constructed through administrative

---

[9] John Grundy and Miriam Smith, 'Activist Knowledges in Queer Politics', *Economy and Society* 36, no. 2 (May 2007): 301.

[10] The Equality Act has three general duties: eliminate unlawful discrimination, harassment and victimization; advance equality of opportunity between people who share a protected characteristic and those who do not; foster good relations between people who share a protected characteristic and those who do not, noted in Equality and Human Rights Commission, 'Public Sector Equality Duty', 26 March 2021.

[11] D'Ignazio and Klein, *Data Feminism*.

decisions made at each stage of this journey, as I discuss in Chapter 2. The production of meaning and subsequent distribution of life chances have the effect of reflecting an incomplete account of LGBTQ lives and experiences to the outside world and among LGBTQ people, whose sense of self is informed by this partial reflection. To minimize the risk of mistakes being made, LGBTQ people need to lead this work and seize control of data that impacts their lives, rather than trust that others will understand, or care enough to understand, experiences that sit beyond their personal frames of reference.

For this reason, *Queer Data* is unapologetic in its focus on the use of data for action that improves the lives of people about whom the data relates. With a focus on events in the UK, *Queer Data* offers an accessible introduction to the interplay between queer theory and gender, sex and sexuality data.[12] Peppered with examples from my work as an equality, diversity and inclusion researcher in Scotland and engagement in the design process of recent UK censuses, *Queer Data* encourages researchers, practitioners and activists to think about data differently and ask critical questions such as 'Why do we collect data this way?', 'Whose interests does data serve?' and 'Why do we collect data at all?' *Queer Data* charts a practical path through this tension that acknowledges data's potential to recreate simplified, stereotypical and exclusionary rules but also operates as a tool to gather evidence, document inequality and bring about change. The conflictual ingredients of queer data therefore require researchers to adopt a mixed approach that elevates the stories of LGBTQ people but also exposes the constructed structures upon which all minority *and* majority identity characteristics stand. By demonstrating that data about cis and heterosexual people also has a history – shaped by social, cultural, economic and political factors – queer data ensures that LGBTQ people are not further marginalized or defined as the 'other' by the research tools used to investigate their lives and experiences.[13]

---

[12] Recent studies that have also explored the intersection of queer theory and gender, sex and sexuality data include Kath Browne and Catherine J. Nash, eds., *Queer Methods and Methodologies: Intersecting Queer Theories and Social Science Research* (Farnham: Ashgate, 2010); D'Lane Compton, Tey Meadow, and Kristen Schilt, eds., *Other, Please Specify: Queer Methods in Sociology* (University of California Press, 2018); Amin Ghaziani and Matt Brim, eds., *Imagining Queer Methods* (New York: New York University Press, 2019).

[13] For discussion of queer theory's disruption of the centre and the margins, see Arlene Stein and Ken Plummer, '"I Can't Even Think Straight" "Queer" Theory and the Missing Sexual Revolution in Sociology', *Sociological Theory* 12, no. 2 (1994): 178.

Count me in

This book is for those interested in research and policy about data and identity who might not necessarily describe themselves as an academic, scholar or statistician. This reflects my background. I live in Edinburgh, Scotland and – for five years – worked as a researcher in the higher education sector. *Queer Data* is based on my experiences of collecting, analysing and using a variety of data related to the identity characteristics of staff and students. My job involved providing advice and guidance to university staff, mainly practitioners working in human resources or EDI teams, on the use of data to identify how staff and students are impacted differently in terms of access, participation and success. From these experiences, I know there are many other diversity and inclusion leads, equality activists, data analysts, research officers and policy managers engaged in on-the-ground work with gender, sex and sexuality data keen to incorporate critical ideas into everyday practices. I started to write this book in response to misconceptions I came across related to data about LGBTQ staff and students. University practitioners, tasked with the responsibility to collect data, contacted me to ask how to undertake meaningful analysis of a minority group when the numbers were 'too small'? What was the rationale for collecting data on identity characteristics other than gender or race? Did they have any business asking staff and students about their sexual orientation? It also became clear to me that, both inside and outside higher education, a small number of campaign groups had weaponized gender, sex and sexuality data in an attempt to roll back the rights of LGBTQ people.[14] This was particularly evident in the spread of misinformation and fearmongering about self-identification and proposed reform of the 2004 Gender Recognition Act in the Scottish and UK Parliaments (legislation intended to simplify the process by which trans people gain legal recognition of their lived gender, through a Gender Recognition Certificate, and change the sex marker on their birth certificate).[15] In one instance, those opposed to

---

[14] For example, LGB Alliance campaigned against the inclusion of materials on 'gender identity' in school lessons on relationships and sex education, see LGB Alliance, 'Schools Crisis? Which Crisis?', LGB Alliance.

[15] The UK Government has described the current system for legal gender recognition as 'bureaucratic and intrusive', while the Scottish Government has labelled it 'intrusive and onerous', in Government Equalities Office, 'LGBT Action Plan: Improving the Lives of Lesbian, Gay, Bisexual and Transgender People' (London: Government Equalities Office, 2018), 22; Scottish Government, 'Review of the Gender Recognition Act 2004: Analysis of Responses to the Public Consultation Exercise' (Edinburgh: Scottish Government, 2018), 23.

the reform of the GRA distributed leaflets that falsely claimed 82 per cent of UK voters were against the proposals, although this claim was subsequently described as 'Mostly false' by the fact-checking news service The Ferret.[16] Accompanied by conspiratorial ideas that proponents of a 'sex-denialist transgender ideology' had captured control of policymaking in Scottish and UK political institutions, campaign groups used data to position trans lives as a legitimate topic of debate, a concern I explore in more detail in Chapter 7.[17] With data about gender, sex and sexuality increasingly understood as a hot topic, its use to delegitimize the lives and experiences of trans people highlights how a greater focus on data can also cause harm to the people about whom the data relates.

I felt frustrated that a general lack of data literacy meant that people rarely looked beyond the headline numbers. I started to write in response. My writing started as a series of blog posts on the practice of EDI work in large public, private and voluntary sector organizations (such as local government, universities, businesses and charities); specific developments in Scotland related to the design of the census; and the Scottish Government's formation of a Sex and Gender in Data Working Group.[18] There was something timely about this work as censuses in England and Wales, Scotland and Northern Ireland asked questions about people's sexual orientation and trans/gender identity for the first time.[19] Decisions made about these census questions were important as censuses do more than simply populate a national dataset for researchers and policymakers, a topic I discuss in Chapter 3. As an exercise conducted every ten years in the UK, they also establish norms for diversity monitoring and data collection that other major organizations tend to follow. Censuses show how data about LGBTQ people goes beyond the identification of problems. It also means something for LGBTQ people. Being included, whether in a list of identity options on a diversity monitoring form or a national census, is an act of registration. Seeing yourself reflected in a data collection exercise can positively shape how you perceive your own identity.[20] It is a means to fight

---

[16] Alastair Brian, 'Claim of 82 Per Cent Opposition to Transgender Self-ID Is Mostly False', *The Ferret*, 2 July 2019.
[17] Jane Clare Jones and Lisa MacKenzie, 'The Political Erasure of Sex: Sex and the Census', 2020, 7–8.
[18] See Scottish Government, 'Sex and Gender in Data Working Group'.
[19] A trans/gender identity question is only asked in censuses in Scotland, England and Wales.
[20] Browne, 'Queer Quantification or Queer(y)ing Quantification: Creating Lesbian, Gay, Bisexual or Heterosexual Citizens through Governmental Social Research', 233.

back against opponents working to silence and erase particular lives: if you appear on the form, it is harder to claim you do not exist. Queer data is also a thorn in the side for liberal figures who understand the addition of more categories or use of inclusive language as mission accomplished. These actions are just the beginning and overlook the construction of gender, sex and sexuality categories, the relationship between these concepts, the mismatch between how people self-identify and how they are perceived by others and the fluidity of gender, sex and sexuality to change across time and space.[21] As discussions about the collection of gender, sex and sexuality data continue to grow among those outside of academic communities, *Queer Data* provides an accessible introduction to these issues, highlights the potential benefits and dangers of data practices for LGBTQ people, and encourages readers to take action.

What is queer data?

Rob Kitchin describes data as 'the raw material produced by abstracting the world into categories, measures, and other representational forms – numbers, characters, symbols, images, sounds, electromagnetic waves, bits – that constitute the building blocks from which information and knowledge are created.'[22] Queer data is more than using data to tell stories about the lives and experiences of LGBTQ individuals: the presentation of data is also an opportunity for LGBTQ people to see themselves reflected, although this mirror image is never a truly accurate representation. In 2016 the Office for National Statistics estimated that 2.5 per cent of the UK population aged sixteen or above identified as lesbian, gay, bisexual or a sexual orientation 'other' than heterosexual.[23] The Government Equalities Office also estimated that between 200,000 and 500,000 trans people live in the UK, though Gender Identity Research & Education Society has argued that the number of people who are 'likely to be gender incongruent to some degree' is more likely

---

[21] Laurel Westbrook and Aliya Saperstein, 'New Categories Are Not Enough: Rethinking the Measurement of Sex and Gender in Social Surveys', *Gender & Society* 29, no. 4 (1 August 2015): 537.

[22] Rob Kitchin, *The Data Revolution: Big Data, Open Data, Data Infrastructures & Their Consequences* (Los Angeles: SAGE Publications, 2014), 1.

[23] Government Equalities Office, 'National LGBT Survey: Research Report' (Manchester: Government Equalities Office, 2018), 14.

around 650,000 or 1 per cent of the UK population.[24] Since August 2019 the polling company YouGov has tracked responses from a sample of just under 2,000 UK adults to the question how do you identify your sexuality on a scale of zero to six, where zero is 'completely heterosexual' and six is 'completely homosexual'. When presented with a scale, in January 2021 just 66 per cent of adults described themselves as 'completely heterosexual'.[25] Data, from sources such as the ONS and YouGov, enables individuals to position their personal experiences within a larger, social tapestry. Feeling part of a community can mobilize people to recognize a shared struggle and take action to change the status quo.[26] Data about LGBTQ lives is not something that people stumble upon, already existing and awaiting discovery – it is produced through the ideas and actions of people in different cultural contexts and historical moments.

Queer data brings together two distinct, though related, strands. Firstly, gender, sex and sexuality data particularly (though not exclusively) as it relates to the lives and experiences of individuals who identify as LGBTQ. My use of the expression 'gender, sex and sexuality' focuses on how researchers and analysts might deploy these terms in data projects, and adopts the following definitions:

- First, gender is used to describe a person's social and personal identity as a man, woman, something between or beyond these concepts; how this is expressed to the outside world; and how this is perceived by others. Gender is enacted in day-to-day life through norms, roles and relationships; those who break from these expectations often face stigma, discrimination or exclusion, depending on the cultural and social context. An individual's gender expression may not conform with their gender identity, just as gender may not correspond with a person's sex assigned at birth or information presented on legal or official documents. Some people may not identify with any gender.

---

[24] The GEO noted that no robust measure of the trans population in the UK exists. Their estimate is therefore based on studies from other countries that indicate between 0.35 per cent and 1 per cent of the population are likely to identify as trans. The GIRES figure is cited in Terry Reed, 'Written Evidence Submitted by GIRES to the Transgender Equality Inquiry', 2015, 2.
[25] YouGov, 'How Brits Describe Their Sexuality', 21 January 2021.
[26] Writing about the history of gay and lesbian activism in the United States, Jeffrey Escoffier notes, 'homosexual emancipation is not possible without a politics of knowledge', in Jeffrey Escoffier, *American Homo: Community and Perversity* (London: Verso, 2018), 118.

- Second, sex is an identity based on primary and secondary sex characteristics, such as genitalia, reproductive functions, hormones, breasts and facial hair. In the UK, the term 'sex' encapsulates concepts that include biological characteristics, legal status (for example, the sex marker on an individual's birth certificate) and a person's lived identity (in other words, how they self-identify and present themselves to others). Although distinct, concepts of gender and sex rely on each other for meaning: sex is not exclusively biological (as it is understood through gendered ideas about bodies), just as gender is not exclusively a social or cultural phenomenon (how we experience our gendered bodies is informed by sex). As Judith Butler argues in *Bodies That Matter: On the Discursive Limits of Sex*, physical bodies do not exist outside of the social meanings we ascribe to them.[27] A queer approach to data is therefore not invested in the erasure or overwriting of sex as a category. In particular, the collection, analysis and use of data about sex (as it relates to biological characteristics) are important in many specific situations such as matters related to sex-specific health conditions. However, consideration of the sexed body in isolation is never enough. People's everyday lives are impacted by how ideas about bodies intersect with power structures in the social world to create and deny life opportunities according to constructed notions of sex and gender. My definition of sex therefore accommodates the binary poles of female/male as well as space between and beyond those poles, for example intersex and non-binary people.

- Third, sexuality is inclusive of identities, attractions and actions that are sexual and/or romantic and directed towards people of the same sex or gender, a different sex or gender, multiple sexes or genders, or no sexes or genders. Data about sexuality can take many forms, such as information about the proportion of men who have sex with men to the number of women married to other women.

The terms presented here are intended to be descriptive rather than prescriptive. How someone defines their gender, sex or sexuality can vary from person to person and, for some people, is experienced as something

---

[27] Judith Butler, *Bodies That Matter: On the Discursive Limits of 'Sex'* (New York: Routledge, 1993), chap. Introduction.

fluid and context-specific that can change over time.[28] Furthermore, my use of distinct terms should not obscure how gender, sex and sexuality are contingent on each other to establish meaning nor should readers assume that concepts exist frozen in time and space. Gender modality, which describes the correspondence or lack of correspondence between one's current sex/gender and their sex/gender assigned at birth, is a term that encapsulates trans and cis identities, as well as ways of identifying beyond the trans/cis binary. Florence Ashley, a transfeminine jurist and bioethicist, explains how gender modality 'recognises the difference between, say, trans and cis women, while at the same time recognising that this difference is not one that makes trans women any less or worse women [...]. Whereas trans and cis women have a different gender modality, they share the same gender identity: woman'.[29] Movement between and beyond genders and sexes, as well as changes in an individual's sexuality during the course of their life, requires a fluid approach. This approach must also accommodate linguistic, cultural and conceptual particularities that emerge in different spaces, as well as accounting for absences (such as asexuality and agender) in the collection, analysis and use of gender, sex and sexuality data. Furthermore, it is not possible to unpick attributes related to gender, sex and sexuality from wider intersectional experiences that mark and shape our everyday lives. As observed by Karen Celis et al., 'gender is never just about sex but varies by race, ethnicity, nation, class, and a variety of other dimensions of social life'.[30] My use of the LGBTQ acronym is therefore a simplified shorthand. Similarly, my use of the expression 'LGBTQ people' should be read as inclusive of the diverse and multiple peoples that constitute each dimension of the acronym. While paying heed to Lee Edelman's claim that 'queerness cannot define an identity, it can only ever disturb one', I include Q in the

---

[28] For discussion, see Judith Butler, *Gender Trouble: Feminism and the Subversion of Identity* (New York: Routledge, 1990); Anne Fausto-Sterling, 'The Five Sexes: Why Male and Female Are Not Enough', *Sciences* 33 (1 January 1993): 20–4; Amanda Bittner and Elizabeth Goodyear-Grant, 'Sex Isn't Gender: Reforming Concepts and Measurements in the Study of Public Opinion', *Political Behavior* 39, no. 4 (1 December 2017): 1021; Anna Lindqvist, Marie Gustafsson Sendén, and Emma A Renström, 'What Is Gender, Anyway: A Review of the Options for Operationalising Gender', *Psychology & Sexuality* Online (18 February 2020): 4.
[29] Florence Ashley, '"Trans" Is My Gender Modality: A Modest Terminological Proposal', in *Trans Bodies, Trans Selves*, ed. Laura Erickson-Schroth, 2nd ed. (Oxford: Oxford University Press, 2021), 2.
[30] Karen Celis et al., 'Introduction: Gender and Politics: A Gendered World, a Gendered Discipline', in *The Oxford Handbook of Gender and Politics*, ed. Georgina Waylen et al. (Oxford: Oxford University Press, 2013), 1.

acronym to recognize the wider range of gender and sexual identities (such as asexual, gender-fluid, pansexual and polysexual) not explicitly included under the LGBT umbrella, as well as those who identify their gender, sex and/or sexuality as 'queer'.[31]

Queer, as an identity label, differs from its use in the second strand of queer data, which examines the *queering* of research methods. Building on Edelman's definition of queerness, Laura Doan draws a distinction between 'queerness-as-being' and 'queerness-as-method' in her historical investigation of same-sex relations between women in early twentieth-century Britain.[32] Doan provides a framework that brings together data *about* LGBTQ people and the *queering* of approaches deployed to collect, analyse and use this data. A queer approach presents more questions than answers. It asks how categories such as 'gay', 'lesbian', 'trans' (and 'queer') emerge, what marks the borders of these categories, who do they exclude and how are they contested?[33] In their edited collection *Queer Methods and Methodologies: Intersecting Queer Theories and Social Science Research*, Kath Browne and Catherine J. Nash describe queer research as 'any form of research positioned within conceptual frameworks that highlight the instability of taken-for-granted meanings and resulting power relations'.[34] In the more recent edited collection *Other, Please Specify*, CJ Pascoe describes 'a queer social science' as 'a method in tension with itself' that 'suggests ways to bring the experiences of "actual people" into dialogue with queer theory'.[35] The clash between queer theory and actual people forces us to consider who is the intended beneficiary of data about LGBTQ people. Most LGBTQ people already know that homophobia, biphobia and transphobia exist and permeate the structures of everyday life. Whether it is a feeling of discomfort that happens when you travel on public transport, the fear of being misgendered when you meet someone for the first time or the

---

[31] Lee Edelman, *No Future: Queer Theory and the Death Drive* (Durham: Duke University Press, 2004), 17.

[32] Laura Doan, *Disturbing Practices: History, Sexuality, and Women's Experience of Modern War* (Chicago: The University of Chicago Press, 2013), viii–ix.

[33] Ki Namaste, 'The Politics of Inside/Out: Queer Theory, Poststructuralism, and a Sociological Approach to Sexuality', *Sociological Theory* 12, no. 2 (1994): 224.

[34] Kath Browne and Catherine J. Nash, 'Queer Methods and Methodologies: An Introduction', in *Queer Methods and Methodologies: Intersecting Queer Theories and Social Science Research*, ed. Kath Browne and Catherine J. Nash (Farnham: Ashgate, 2010), 4.

[35] CJ Pascoe, 'What to Do with Actual People?: Thinking through a Queer Social Science Method', in *Other, Please Specify: Queer Methods in Sociology*, ed. D'Lane Compton, Tey Meadow, and Kristen Schilt (Berkeley: University of California Press, 2018), 301, 302.

use of gender-neutral terms such as 'spouse' or 'partner' to avoid having to out yourself. For LGBTQ people with first-hand experiences, data is not necessary to prove the existence of these problems.

Furthermore, who is involved in decision-making about gender, sex and sexuality data? The state is a key operator in the generation of data, through administrative sources such as tax records and exercises such as the census, and the use of data to provide services to citizens.[36] Around the world, Yoan Mantha and Simon Hudson's analysis of articles published in leading journals for research into artificial intelligence found that of the 4,000 researchers published, 88 per cent were men.[37] In UK universities, in the 2018/19 academic year just 18.4 per cent of computer science students were women.[38] This means that the next generation of data scientists will likely be overwhelmingly male and design future projects, based on their own experiences of the social world, that default to a male subject.[39] D'Ignazio and Klein describe this phenomenon as a privilege hazard, where those in dominant positions are blinded by their social, political and economic interests and unable to see problems that exist for people different from themselves.[40] Yet, in the global tech sector, there are notable examples of gay men in powerful positions, such as Tim Cook (Chief Executive Officer of Apple) and Peter Thiel (Co-founder of Paypal and Director on the board of Facebook).[41] Meaningful change therefore needs to go beyond the logic of more (gay, male) faces in high places and instead reconfigure how those who design data practices and systems conceptualize gender, sex and

[36] Kitchin, *The Data Revolution*, 114.
[37] Yoan Mantha and Simon Hudson, 'Estimating the Gender Ratio of AI Researchers Around the World', Element AI Lab, 2018.
[38] Advance HE, 'Equality in Higher Education: Student Statistical Report' (London, 2020).
[39] See Caroline Criado-Perez, *Invisible Women: Exposing Data Bias in a World Designed for Men* (London: Chatto & Windus, 2019). The Leverhulme Centre for the Future of Intelligence also identified the lack of diversity in the AI workforce as a key issue in the design and implementation of equitable technology, in Clementine Collett and Sarah Dillon, 'AI and Gender: Four Proposals for Future Research' (Cambridge: The Leverhulme Centre for the Future of Intelligence, 2019), 26.
[40] D'Ignazio and Klein, *Data Feminism*.
[41] Furthermore, a 2020 survey conducted for Ukie, the trade association for the UK's games and interactive entertainment industry, found that while 70 per cent of the workforce identified as male, 21 per cent also identified as LGBTQ+. We therefore should not assume that those working in fields related to data are disproportionately heterosexual or cis, in Mark Taylor, 'UK Games Industry Census: Understanding Diversity in the UK Games Industry Workforce' (Ukie, February 2020), 8, 9.

sexuality data so that 'data about us' becomes synonymous with 'data for us', as described in more depth in Chapter 7.

Expanded interest in data about LGBTQ people, among researchers and the general population, has brought with it increased scrutiny of the borders of gender, sex, sexuality and trans identities. The policing of these categories, often by people who do not identify as LGBTQ, tends to foreground biological characteristics, legal documents or sexual practices that fail to acknowledge how identities gain value through the meanings attached to them by society and the uneven distribution of power. Much of this focus involves the concept of self-identification, discussed in Chapter 6. This is where an individual is understood as best-placed to describe their identity characteristics rather than the state, a medical practitioner nor any other 'expert witness'. For opponents of a queer approach to data, self-identification and the fluidity of LGBTQ identities are framed as problems: queer data is understood as postmodern, political and anti-scientific.[42] Gender, in particular, is singled out as something based on social factors such as upbringing, environment, culture and history. This ignores the body of scholarship that demonstrates how social factors impact most, if not all, markers of identity (including sex).[43] A queer approach to data problematizes the authority to categorize LGBTQ people – whether through practices, identities, communities or something else entirely – and who determines if identity claims are valid and an 'accurate' representation of the social world.

Although *Queer Data* foregrounds the lives and experiences of LGBTQ people, the *queering* of methods has implications for all data collection, analysis and presentation, whether or not it relates to LGBTQ individuals. Importantly, the application of 'queer methods' to categories such as 'cis' and 'heterosexual' can disrupt assumptions and biases that have traditionally positioned these identities as default, ahistorical, natural or normal. The

---

[42] For a discussion of sex and gender in survey design, see Alice Sullivan, 'Sex and the Census: Why Surveys Should Not Conflate Sex and Gender Identity', *International Journal of Social Research Methodology* 23, no. 5 (2 September 2020): 7; Andi Fugard, 'Should Trans People Be Postmodernist in the Streets but Positivist in the Spreadsheets? A Reply to Sullivan', *International Journal of Social Research Methodology* 23, no. 5 (25 May 2020): 525–31; Sally Hines, 'Counting the Cost of Difference: A Reply to Sullivan', *International Journal of Social Research Methodology* 23, no. 5 (2 September 2020): 533–8.

[43] See Judith Lorber, 'Believing Is Seeing: Biology as Ideology', *Gender and Society* 7, no. 4 (1993): 568–81; Linda Nicholson, 'Interpreting Gender', *Signs* 20, no. 1 (1994): 79–105; Anne Fausto-Sterling, *Sexing the Body: Gender Politics and the Construction of Sexuality* (New York: Basic Books, 2000).

fusion of data *about* LGBTQ people and the *queering* of methods used to collect, analyse and present this data becomes something more than the sum of its constituent parts. Queer data emerges as the product of tension between categories and anti-categories, assimilation and difference, intrinsic qualities and social constructs, and individuals and populations.

Different types of data

This book explores the *queering* of quantitative and qualitative data. Quantitative data is numerical data that, as the name suggests, can be quantified and analysed using a range of statistical methods. When we talk about quantitative data we usually discuss statistics such as the number of students in UK higher education who disclosed that their gender identity is different from that assigned at birth (13,245 in the 2018/19 academic year) or the proportion of Members of Parliament in Westminster who openly identify as lesbian, gay, bisexual or pansexual (8.6 per cent, as of July 2021).[44] The collection of quantitative data allows for different types of statistical analyses, which might include the calculation of averages (for example, the mean age of LGBTQ staff in an organization), cross-tabulations (when two or more pieces of data are analysed together, such as the proportion of students who are Indian and bisexual) or more advanced analyses that can identify statistical significance (whether or not a finding was the result of chance). Browne has described a lack of critical engagement between users of quantitative methods and those involved in the field of queer studies, as 'quantitative methods require the use of categories' whereas a queer approach 'often eschews the use of labels and definitional fixities in favour of fluid discussions of practices, lives and relegating processes'.[45] Laurel Westbrook et al. explain that 'quantitative methods have long been characterized as both positivist and reductionist, and thus unable to represent systems of oppression such as sexuality, gender, and race with complexity and nuance'.[46] David Gillborn et al. have also discussed how methods used to collect quantitative data, such as surveys, 'can reproduce human bias' and 'should lead us to treat

---

[44] Advance HE, 'Equality in Higher Education', 301; John Peart, 'LGBT MP', LGBT MP, 2021.
[45] Browne, 'Queer Quantification or Queer(y)Ing Quantification', 231, 248.
[46] Laurel Westbrook, Jamie Budnick, and Aliya Saperstein, 'Dangerous Data: Seeing Social Surveys through the Sexuality Prism', *Sexualities* Online (10 February 2021): 2.

quantitative analyses with at least as much caution as when considering qualitative research and its findings'.[47] The operation of quantitative methods, particularly in large-scale exercises such as national censuses, can mask design decisions about how to categorize groups and who to count.

Qualitative data, in contrast, is about qualities: information that does not involve numbers or numerical data. Qualitative data includes transcripts from interviews or focus groups, open-text responses in surveys and sources such as images, song lyrics, film and television dialogue. Analysis of qualitative data can present rich findings and insights into how and why things have happened. Unlike quantitative data, qualitative data does not require a large sample of participants to conduct analysis and provide meaningful results. For example, whereas a survey requires a certain number of people to respond, a one-to-one interview needs just one researcher and one participant. Analysis of qualitative data can take many forms. This might include thematic analysis, where a source is reviewed to identify key themes, or statistical analysis, where qualitative concepts (such as satisfaction) are transformed into quantitative data using a scale of response options (for example, where respondents select an option between 'very dissatisfied' and 'very satisfied').

Quantitative and qualitative methods often overlap. Aside from the transformation of qualitative concepts into quantitative data, qualitative data can help 'plug the gaps' and explain the 'why' of quantitative data trends. For example, we know that one-third of LGBT people in the UK aged sixty-five and over drink alcohol almost every day.[48] However, this data alone does not explain why a difference might exist between LGBT people and the general population. To better understand this issue we need to use qualitative data to help answer the question of why, which could involve running focus groups, conducting one-to-one interviews or analysing open-text survey responses. Feminist scholars, such Ann Oakley and Donna Haraway, are central to how we understand the use of research methods to collect data about the social world. Oakley, for example, championed the use of both quantitative and qualitative methods to ensure research findings

---

[47] David Gillborn, Paul Warmington, and Sean Demack, 'QuantCrit: Education, Policy, "Big Data" and Principles for a Critical Race Theory of Statistics', *Race Ethnicity and Education* 21, no. 2 (4 March 2018): 159.

[48] Stonewall, 'LGBT in Britain – Health Report' (London, November 2018), 16.

distinguish between personal experience and collective oppression.[49] Haraway, along with Sandra Harding and Linda Alcoff, devised an approach called standpoint theory, which highlighted the importance of disclosing the limits of researchers' knowledge.[50] Both approaches involve reflexive considerations of the interplay between researcher and participant, the strengths and weaknesses of 'insider' and 'outsider' research, and the biases and assumptions that researchers bring to their studies – themes explored in more detail in Chapter 5.

The power of queer data

Gender, sex and sexuality data can help address many of society's inequalities. Data enables us to know how many people identify with a particular identity group, this group's experience of services such as healthcare and education, and relative levels of advantage and disadvantage (which involves comparing data for one group against another group or a defined benchmark). Data can expose the effects of patriarchy, misogyny, homophobia, biphobia and transphobia on the systems and structures we rely upon to navigate our everyday lives. Whether it's differences in the use of transport networks, perceptions of crime or success in education, data is central to the diagnosis of a problem and decisions made about how to respond.

Discussions about identity data in the UK tend to focus on headline statistics about a small number of issues, for example, the difference in average pay between men and women or the gap in educational qualifications awarded to people from different racial groups. The reasons for this focus are multiple, including longer histories of collecting data on gender and race and legal requirements for organizations to report particular information.[51] Although data about the gender pay gap or race awarding gap are hugely important, and has focused attention on these inequalities, those engaged in the collection, analysis and use of data about identity characteristics (myself

---

[49] See Ann Oakley, 'Paradigm Wars: Some Thoughts on a Personal and Public Trajectory', *International Journal of Social Research Methodology* 2, no. 3 (January 1999): 247–54.
[50] For a more detailed account of how Haraway, Harding and Alcoff's scholarship relates to data practices, see D'Ignazio and Klein, *Data Feminism*.
[51] For example, since 2017 all employers in England, Scotland and Wales with 250 or more employees are required to publish and report data on the average pay gap between male and female employees.

included) have only tapped a tiny fraction of the potential insights available. Although LGBTQ people equally experience disadvantage because of their gender and/or race, it is less common to see headline statistics related to a person's sexual orientation or whether they are cis or trans. I am particularly surprised when I see intersectional analysis of data about sexual orientations or cis/trans identities and other identity characteristics such as race, ethnicity, age, disability, religion or belief. An intersectional approach to analysis can identify particularities and new challenges. For example, without disaggregated data and an intersectional lens, we would not know that in the UK:

- Half of Black, Asian and minority ethnic LGBT people (51 per cent) have experienced discrimination or poor treatment from others in their local LGBT community because of their ethnicity. This number rises to three in five Black LGBT people (61 per cent).[52]

- Four-fifths of older LGBT people do not trust professionals to understand their culture or lifestyle.[53]

- Just under one in five LGBT people (18 per cent) were concerned that the Covid-19 pandemic would lead to substance or alcohol misuse. This figure was higher among BAME LGBT people (20 per cent) and disabled LGBT people (23 per cent).[54]

- 51 per cent of LGBT people living in Scotland's rural areas have personally experienced prejudice or discrimination for being LGBT.[55]

- Just one in four LGBT people of faith (25 per cent) think their faith community is welcoming of trans people.[56]

Intersectional LGBTQ data tells a nuanced story that better reflects the messy and overlapping experiences of people's everyday lives. Approaches to data collection and analysis are fundamental to the use of queer data to raise awareness, demonstrate where problems exist, challenge misinformation, galvanize communities and hold decision-makers to account. But this can

---

[52] Stonewall, 'LGBT in Britain - Home and Communities' (London, 2018), 5.
[53] Age UK, 'Combating Loneliness Amongst Older LGBT People: A Case Study of the Sage Project in Leeds' (London, 2018), 1.
[54] LGBT Foundation, 'Hidden Figures: The Impact of the Covid-19 Pandemic on LGBT Communities in the UK' (Manchester, May 2020), 6.
[55] Rebecca Crowther, Scott Cuthbertson, and Vic Valentine, 'Further Out: The Scottish LGBT Rural Equality Report' (Edinburgh: Equality Network, 2020), 11.
[56] Stonewall, 'LGBT in Britain - Home and Communities' (London, 2018), 5.

only be achieved in a meaningful way, which brings everyone on board, when intersectionality is embedded throughout the life journey of data, from its collection to its use for action.

The dangers of queer data

'Visibility is a trap', warned Michel Foucault in his account of how power operates in a panoptic prison, where prisoners are unsure when they are being watched and therefore adapt behaviours as if they are always under surveillance.[57] Although the collection of data and its use for positive representations have brought benefits for many LGBTQ people, this should not preclude critical examination of dangers that can emerge from shining light on gender, sex and sexuality data. In my work with universities, as with other large organizations, I saw how practitioners tasked with data collection could lose sight of what data meant and focus attention on fixing the numbers rather than the problems the data was intended to represent. I also grew sceptical of the unchallenged assumption that the use of data to increase the visibility of marginalized groups was always a positive endeavour. In Scotland, more data exists about LGBTQ people than ever before but this has not meant that the lives of all LGBTQ people have necessarily improved. In fact, as demonstrated in data on hate crimes where sexual orientation or transgender identity was an aggravating factor, the number of charges recorded has continued to increase.[58] In their account of how visual representations of trans people have impacted society, Reina Gossett et al. explain, 'We are living in a time of trans visibility. Yet we are also living in a time of anti-trans violence'.[59] More than twenty years prior, in her description of how Black women are seen and not seen, Evelynn Hammonds noted that 'visibility in and of itself does not erase a history of silence nor

---

[57] Michel Foucault, *Discipline and Punish: The Birth of the Prison*, 2nd ed. (New York: Vintage Books, 1995), 200.

[58] Between 2018–19 and 2019–20, the number of hate crime charges related to sexual orientation increased by 24 per cent to 1,486 and the number of charges related to transgender identity increased by one to 41, noted in Crown Office and Procurator Fiscal Service, 'Hate Crime in Scotland, 2019–20', 12 June 2020.

[59] Reina Gossett, Eric A. Stanley, and Johanna Burton, 'Known Unknowns: An Introduction to Trap Door', in *Trap Door: Trans Cultural Production and the Politics of Visibility*, ed. Reina Gossett, Eric A. Stanley, and Johanna Burton (Cambridge: The MIT Press, 2017), xv.

does it challenge the structure of power and domination, symbolic and material, that determines what can and cannot be seen'.[60] Furthermore, efforts to prove the existence of homophobia, biphobia and transphobia (to a predominantly cis, heterosexual audience) require the use of finite resources and the physical, mental and emotional labour of researchers, practitioners and activists. If the burden of proof is higher for LGBTQ people than the general public, and it remains unclear whether the collection of evidence *actually* initiates meaningful change, the utility of a data-based response to fighting injustice is called into question.

Scholars have challenged responses to injustice that present the actions of individuals as removed from wider social contexts.[61] Data practices play a role in this sleight of hand. For example, Ruha Benjamin describes how a focus on the biases of individuals, rather than the data systems they work within, means that 'individuals are treated as glitches in an otherwise benign system'.[62] Data collection methods can compound the focus on individuals as removed from wider structures of power. For example, the collection of data via discrete survey entries or one-to-one interviews might frame an individual's negative experiences as something exceptional and unrelated to social issues such as education, law enforcement or poverty. As a response to problems identified by the research, minor tweaks are made to existing structures rather than a radical overhaul of the entire system. Rinaldo Walcott warns that these gestures towards social transformation, such as initiatives to improve diversity or inclusivity, can defuse attempts to radically change structural conditions that perpetuate the subordination of certain groups.[63]

Taking into account these critiques, the use of data to increase and diversify representations of LGBTQ people promises much but, on its own, is not an outcome that necessarily addresses injustice. In other words, a society with more data about LGBTQ people is not automatically a society that is better for LGBTQ people. In spaces where a queer approach to categorization clashes with the requirements of data to count, such as legal decisions about rights, some LGBTQ lives are valued at the expense of others.

---

[60] Evelynn Hammonds, 'Black (W)Holes and the Geometry of Black Female Sexuality', *Differences: A Journal of Feminist Cultural Studies* 6, no. 2–3 (1994): 141.
[61] For example, Jessie Daniels' detailed account of research into race and racism on the internet notes the tendency of studies to present racism as a problem of individuals' behaviour rather than something structural or institutional, in Jessie Daniels, 'Race and Racism in Internet Studies: A Review and Critique', *New Media & Society* 15, no. 5 (August 2013): 709.
[62] Benjamin, *Race after Technology*, 87.
[63] Rinaldo Walcott, 'The End of Diversity', *Public Culture* 31, no. 2 (1 May 2019): 394.

Dean Spade discusses this problem in his critical reading of legal equality approaches as a response to homophobia, biphobia and transphobia in the United States.[64] A legal equality approach involves granting rights to LGBTQ people so that they align with the existing rights of cis, heterosexual people. Recent examples of this approach include the expansion of the definition of marriage to include same-sex couples and demands for LGBTQ people to serve openly in the armed forces. Rather than seek to change or abolish existing institutions, which have historically excluded LGBTQ people, legal equality campaigners fight for entry into these institutions. However, when successful, access only tends to favour those considered most 'deserving' – in other words, the interests of cis, white, affluent gay men and lesbians.[65] Spade's account of legal equality approaches has implications for the collection, analysis and use of data about LGBTQ people. Participation in data collection exercises, such as national censuses, requires LGBTQ people to follow already-established rules that risk only counting those deemed 'deserving' (by cis, heterosexual standards) and further excludes the most marginalized.[66] By showing how the lives of the most 'deserving' have improved, practices and systems that perpetuate homophobia, biphobia or transphobia can continue to function relatively unscathed.

Data is not reality. Data is a record of the social world mediated through decisions made about what or whom to include and exclude. Queer data is not a passive reflection of the social world but is a productive force that, when handled correctly, can strengthen the efforts of researchers, practitioners and activists to create conditions that enable LGBTQ people to lead full, authentic lives. As an approach, queer data does not prescribe the lives people should lead but can, through the creation of a robust evidence base, construct the conditions that allow people to shape a life for themselves. These conditions will vary from person to person and might include the freedom to use public

---

[64] Dean Spade, *Normal Life: Administrative Violence, Critical Trans Politics, and the Limits of Law* (Durham: Duke University Press, 2015), chap. What's Wrong with Rights?
[65] Spade notes how legal equality approaches rely on a strategy of simile, which argues 'we are just like you; we do not deserve this different treatment because of this one characteristic', in Spade, 44.
[66] Elizabeth McDermott describes how a 'demography of homosexuality' foregrounds the sexual citizenship of white, gay, male, middle-class adults and marginalizes those who are 'queerer, female, black, younger and poorer', in Elizabeth McDermott, '"Counting" for Equality: Youth, Class and Sexual Citizenship', in *Sexualities Research: Critical Interjections, Diverse Methodologies, and Practical Applications*, ed. Andrew King, Ana Cristina Santos, and Isabel Crowhurst (London: Routledge, 2017), 44.

space without fear of violence, access to affirmative healthcare, confidence in the rule of law, recognition by the state and access to adequate housing and food. Conditions that make an individual's life liveable are not evenly distributed, whether in the UK or other parts of the world, and often require LGBTQ people to lead inauthentic lives, where they conceal their sexual orientation or trans identity as a prerequisite of access. As Butler has argued, the conditions that make life liveable also include those who 'understand themselves as requiring – and wanting – a clear gender category within a binary frame' and those 'who require a gender designation that is more or less unequivocal'.[67] Queer data is therefore not about erasing the categories of gender or sex. Nor is queer data about increasing the volume or diversity of data collected in an attempt to achieve total knowledge. Rather, LGBTQ people need to continually review the strategic value of participation in data collection exercises, evaluate where reform of data structures is achievable and, when the potential for harm outweighs the potential for good, withdraw consent and call for the abolition of data practices and systems.

Chapter outline

Part I explores the collection of gender, sex and sexuality data. With a particular focus on quantitative data and the emergence of contemporary LGBTQ identities in twentieth-century Britain, Chapter 1 examines the historical collection of data about people who transgressed normative ideas about gender, sex or sexuality, the methods used and the purposes of data collection exercises. As a productive and political practice, collection methods bring assumptions about the social world we inhabit, the possibilities as to what these methods can reveal and the participation of those from whom data is collected. Chapter 2 therefore reviews the use of surveys, one-to-one interviews and focus groups to collect data about LGBTQ people. I highlight how a queer approach to collection methods can encourage participants and researchers to evaluate their identities in new and unexpected ways, which simultaneously presents an account of the social world and changes what it seeks to describe. These issues surfaced during the design of questions for the UK's 2021 and 2022 censuses. Chapter 3 presents an in-depth account of the design process for the sex, sexual orientation and trans questions in

---

[67] Sara Ahmed, 'Interview with Judith Butler', *Sexualities* 19, no. 4 (1 June 2016): 491.

Scotland's census with particular focus on plans to introduce a non-binary response option to the sex question (in which respondents could answer 'male', 'female' or 'other'); the conceptualization of sexual orientation in question design; and efforts to avoid use of the term 'cis' in the census. Part I concludes with Chapter 4, which investigates the collection of gender, sex and sexuality data in nations and regions outside of the UK, with specific reference to national, transnational and international administrative practices, the capture of data about same-sex couples in the US census, data initiatives to address hate crime and violence in Latin America and the Caribbean, the provision of 'third gender' options in censuses in South Asia, the use of virtual censuses in several European countries, and the roll-out of a 'gender by default' approach to data in Canada and New Zealand. This review examines similarities and differences in approaches to gender, sex and sexuality data around the world to provide an exchange of lessons for researchers, practitioners and activists.

Part II investigates what happens after data is collected and how it is shaped through analysis. Chapter 5 argues that data analysis involves making decisions that can influence findings, and therefore the lives of LGBTQ people about whom the data relates. This occurs during the cleaning of data, where attempts to subvert the collection process are removed, as well as the aggregation or disaggregation of individual responses into categories such as LGBTQ. Data analysis is increasingly automated, where algorithms instruct computers of the steps to turn data into meaningful information, and invested in the promise of big data. Yet these developments can fail to recognize the impacts of homophobia, biphobia and transphobia on historical and contemporary practices of amassing data about LGBTQ people.[68] Chapter 6 focuses on how data is recognized as a valid representation of the social world and explores the role of self-identification (where an individual determines the validity of data about themselves), external-identification (where the power to decide lies with another individual or organization), biometric data (which reads physical markers in/on our bodies) and behavioural data (which makes decisions based on our encounters with everyday technologies, such as online browsing and mobile phones).

The third and final part explores the use of data for action. Chapter 7 explores who has a voice in discussions about queer data and whose voice

---

[68] Jen Jack Gieseking, 'Size Matters to Lesbians, Too: Queer Feminist Interventions into the Scale of Big Data', *The Professional Geographer* 70, no. 1 (January 2018): 150.

matters. With a particular focus on tactics deployed to shut down discussions about gender, sex and sexuality data in online spaces, I outline how enhanced queer data competence among decision-makers might foster opportunities for improved communication about data. Chapter 8 concludes with an account of how data can document the lives of LGBTQ people, challenge negative ideas of otherness and bring about material changes in people's lives (for example, the use of data to counter arguments that limit trans people's access to bathrooms).[69] The *queering* of data can both elevate the voices about whom data relates and ask new questions about how data is constructed, with implications for whose stories are positioned in the centre and on the margins. However, this might not be enough. Projects that examine the relationship between structural inequality, racism, patriarchy and data have highlighted the biased foundations of data and challenged the assumption that the collection of data is a source for good. Critical interventions from the United States, often led by people of colour, call attention to the need for LGBTQ groups in the UK to re-evaluate their relationship with data, assess whether existing structures are capable of reform and, if not, how might an abolitionist approach put data in the hands of those most in need.

* * *

We stand at a key moment in history. New technologies and approaches, from big data to data abolition, overlap with longer-term disagreements over how to recognize difference among identity groups, the representation of difference through data and its use as an evidence base for action. Failure to engage with agencies that collect, analyse and use data potentially locks out LGBTQ communities from recognition and access to vital funding and resources. Yet, participation in these practices requires submission to normative approaches to categorization that involve the inclusion and exclusion of particular lives and experiences.

This work cannot take place with LGBTQ people looking in from the outside. Data is more than numbers in a database – it also presents a method for individuals to join together and shout 'Look here, we exist!' However, at the heart of these developments lies a tension between 'being counted' and 'being beyond counting', which exposes the strained relationship between queer theory's disavowal of categories and the requirements of data

---

[69] Petra L. Doan, 'To Count or Not to Count: Queering Measurement and the Transgender Community', *Women's Studies Quarterly* 44, no. 3/4 (2016): 105.

to classify, arrange and make judgements based on these results. There is no simple solution to the push and pull that exists between understanding identity characteristics as something disparate and fluid versus something that you can tick on a diversity monitoring form. *Queer Data* navigates a path through this challenge that uplifts LGBTQ stories but also destabilizes the normalcy of data about cis, heterosexual people. How we think about data, a product of historical and cultural traditions, has blinkered us to how gender, sex and sexuality data can and should impact LGBTQ lives in positive ways. For those already engaged in data practices, *Queer Data* showcases ways to embed critical approaches in your work. For those new to these themes, I hope the following chapters demonstrate the diversity of initiatives underway, offer entry points to expand your queer data competence and embolden you to use data to challenge injustice. Queer data is a powerful weapon; in the right hands, it can reshape all of our futures.

PART I
COLLECTING QUEER DATA

CHAPTER 1
GAPS AND ABSENCES: A HISTORY OF QUEER DATA

I did not know where to start. I wanted to explore historical approaches to the collection of data about individuals considered 'gender and sexual outliers' in the societies where they lived but identifying a point in time or an event to anchor these stories seemed impossible to pin-down. Perhaps it was a result of my research background in history but I felt magnetically drawn to begin this journey in the archives. I sat down, open-text box on the screen, and typed in the keywords: 'homosexual', 'gay', 'lesbian', 'survey', 'prevalence' and 'data'. My limited enquiry focused on twentieth-century Britain and, although thousands of results were identified, only a handful related to research into the lives and experiences of homosexual men and lesbians. One particular entry that caught my attention was the *Social Needs Survey* conducted by an organization called The Albany Trust in 1970.[1] The Albany Trust was established in London in 1958 to support the psychological welfare of homosexuals, lesbians and sexual minorities in Britain. The survey was completed by 2,082 men and 588 women and asked participants to disclose their sexual orientation using a five-point scale from 'entirely homosexual' to 'entirely heterosexual'. It collected data about participants' age, marital status, education level, occupation, income and location, as well as questions about their same-sex experiences. The survey also asked if participants had sought advice concerning their homosexuality and the question 'Do you regard yourself as well adjusted to your homosexuality?', to which the majority of participants responded 'well adjusted'.

Although the social situation for many homosexual men and lesbians in Britain has improved in the past fifty years, several issues associated with the collection of survey data seemed familiar. The study overwhelmingly represented the views of men and, although the authors noted the low

---

[1] Albany Trust, 'Social Needs Survey: Results'. London, 1970 in The Hall-Carpenter Archives, London School of Economics and Political Science Library, Archives of Sexuality and Gender.

number of female participants, other markers of difference (such as race or disability) were overlooked. Furthermore, at the time of the survey, The Albany Trust and other organizations established in the 1950s faced opposition from a new wave of gay rights organizations, such as the Gay Liberation Front, which criticized the conservative tactics and upper-middle-class interests of their predecessors.[2] Although The Albany Trust succeeded in constructing new knowledge about the lives of homosexuals and lesbians, the results of the survey were never formally published. The research had intended to raise awareness of the social lives of sexual minorities and create an evidence base to initiate change but, as something kept hidden from the general public, it is unclear to what extent these ambitions were achieved.

My return to the archives reminded me of the historical specificities of homosexual and lesbian lives in Britain as well as similarities and differences in the use of research tools to demonstrate the prevalence of same-sex acts, desires and identities. The Albany Trust's *Social Needs Survey* sparked my interest as it was an example of data collection predominantly about homosexual men conducted by homosexual men to document the social needs of a minority community.[3] This differs from many of the historical sources discussed in this chapter, which are top-down 'expert' accounts of LGBTQ people that were not intended to improve the lives of those about whom the data related. However, while exploring the archive, I also questioned where we might look to find data sources from LGBTQ people intended exclusively for other LGBTQ individuals or audiences? What data might we find in love letters, poetry and art that – as a result of their qualitative and personal focus – were not preserved for the archive? With these limitations in mind, had gendered biases about what constituted 'data' disproportionately preserved sources that focus on cis, male and homosexual subjects?

* * *

[2] Ken Plummer, 'Introduction to the Albany Trust Archive', The Albany Trust and Hall-Carpenter Archives in Archives of Sexuality & Gender, Part I: LGBTQ History and Culture Since 1940, November 2001.
[3] Research about homosexual men by homosexual men has a long history. For example, Heike Bauer describes the work of leading nineteenth-century sexologists Havelock Ellis and Richard Krafft-Ebing who supported homosexual rights, engaged with (predominantly male) subcultures and were, themselves, homosexual, in Heike Bauer, 'Theorizing Female Inversion: Sexology, Discipline, and Gender at the Fin de Siècle', *Journal of the History of Sexuality* 18, no. 1 (2009): 87.

Any history of data about LGBTQ people in Britain is one of gaps and absences. What I present here is one history of queer data. Rather than a comprehensive account of the disparate and multilayered legacies of queer data, my focus is limited to a selective genealogy of data collection methods used to conceptualize and categorize LGBTQ people. It is not possible to trace a history of LGBTQ people using today's terms to look back into the past: the actions, desires and identities encapsulated by the LGBTQ acronym are relatively recent and have changed over time and across different cultures. For these reasons, this chapter references terms used by people to describe themselves at the time and/or assigned by others as labels, such as 'homosexual' and 'transsexual', even though the acceptability of these terms has since changed. When discussing history in general, I use the anachronistic term LGBTQ to describe people that transgressed normative expectations about gender, sex and sexuality.

When people we might now describe as LGBTQ were counted in datasets, it was often a result of observable actions understood as criminal (including male same-sex activities and cross-dressing), information bodies and minds were thought to provide about illness or disease, or as a means to confirm differences and cement the privileges of the majority group. My narrow focus foregrounds material about LGBTQ people (including actions, desires and identities) in England, Wales and Scotland. The data sources investigated mainly relate to legal, medical and scientific practices, which reflect the interests of those who had the power to survey, categorize and implement actions to control the behaviours of others. With these limitations in mind, there is little value in sharing a history of LGBTQ data collection in isolation. We already know the story. Although there are examples where data was collected to positively demonstrate the existence of gender, sex and sexuality minorities, data was most often collected to provide evidence of a 'problem' and used to justify further marginalization. The use of data to inflict violence *on* LGBTQ people was mirrored by violence directed towards archives and datasets that contained information *about* LGBTQ people.[4] As a result,

---

[4] Examples include the destruction of books, journals, objects, notes and questionnaires from Magnus Hirschfeld's Institute of Sexual Science by Nazi demonstrators in Berlin in 1933 and the removal, and assumed destruction, of pages from Constance Maynard's *Green Book*, a pioneer of women's education in London in the late nineteenth-century whose diaries documented her close relationships with women, discussed in Heike Bauer, *The Hirschfeld Archives: Violence, Death, and Modern Queer Culture* (Philadelphia: Temple University Press, 2017), 3; Elsa Richardson, 'New Queer Histories: Laura Doan's Disturbing Practices and the Constance Maynard Archive', *Women's History Review* 25, no. 1 (2 January 2016): 166.

data sources from the past that survived until today present a selective account of the potential richness of LGBTQ data and are skewed in favour of phenomena that reflect patriarchal ideas about law, medicine and science.

I instead want this chapter to tell a different story that blends a history of data *about* LGBTQ people with a history of the collection methods used to gather this information. When analysed together, this *queer data history* and *queer history of data* provide an account of what was known about people who transgressed societal expectations about gender, sex and sexuality, as well as the forces that shaped the research methods used to represent data 'outliers'.[5] My first line of enquiry considers data collected about people who did not fit expected ideas about gender, sex or sexuality, with a particular focus on the emergence of contemporary LGBTQ identities in twentieth-century Britain. Scholarship reveals the presence of people who transgressed normative expectations throughout history: from those in same-sex 'marriages' to those engaged in same-sex intercourse, from cross-dressers to people who underwent medical procedures to change their bodies from one sex to another.[6]

My second line of enquiry relates to the research methods used to collect this data. This history goes beyond the collection of data *about* gender, sex and sexuality to consider what researchers thought methods could reveal about the social world, the purpose of researching marginalized communities, and a growing awareness that methods bring with them biases that impact the data collected. Although I opened this chapter with the example of The Albany Trust's *Social Needs Survey*, which provided a window into how some homosexual men and lesbians made sense of themselves and their communities, most historical examples are top-down studies conducted by researchers and government officials that provide 'expert' accounts of the (predominantly male) homosexual subject. Both LGBTQ people and data collection methods, such as surveys and one-to-one interviews, possess particular histories. Tracing a history of data collection methods therefore

---

[5] As discussed in the Introduction chapter, my approach builds upon Doan's distinction of 'queerness-as-being' and 'queerness-as-method', in Doan, *Disturbing Practices*, viii–ix, 172, 179.
[6] My focus is therefore broader than contemporary definitions of LGBTQ and mindful of the historical overlap between ideas about sexuality and gender, and how people were understood through their actions (in many examples, society understood someone as different because their actions broke expectations about gender and sex). A more detailed account of these histories is presented in Brian Lewis, ed., *British Queer History: New Approaches and Perspectives* (Manchester: Manchester University Press, 2013); Christine Burns, *Trans Britain: Our Journey from the Shadows*, ed. Christine Burns (London: Unbound, 2018).

offers more than an account of how people were counted but also why these studies were conducted and how results were used to fix in time and place particular ideas about gender, sex and sexuality.

Counting a population

Identifying where to commence a history of data *about* LGBTQ people, the methods used to collect this data and what to include and exclude from this scope is difficult. Butler has noted how the material characteristics used by societies to mark differences between genders and sexes – such as genitals, body size, voice and hair – are historical and 'that the history of matter is in part determined by the negotiation of sexual difference'.[7] For example, Thomas Laqueur has documented that before the proliferation of a binary model of sexual difference, a one-sex model existed where male and female bodies were understood as different points on the same scale.[8] Rather than opposites, female bodies were an imperfect version of male bodies (for example, the ovaries were internal testes and the vagina an inside-out penis). Bodies could traverse the one-sex scale so that a person's gender, their social role, aligned with their physical sex (for example, there exist accounts of masculine women who develop a penis).[9] The history of people crossing these binaries or positioning themselves outside the poles of man/male and woman/female, as an individual or member of a community, has an equally long past that continues to inform contemporary ideas about gender, sex and sexuality.[10] Emma Donoghue notes how 'key early modern texts about same-sex possibilities are marked by convoluted structures, inconsistent theories, semantic confusion, coy disclaimers, denials, and jokes' and although 'we will never find a frame that will fit all the jigsaw pieces together. This is exactly what keeps bringing us back to take another look'.[11]

When looking back into the more distant past, what was understood as 'data' has implications for the historical presence or absence of LGBTQ figures,

---

[7] Butler, *Bodies That Matter*, 29.
[8] Thomas Laqueur, *Making Sex: Body and Gender from the Greeks to Freud* (Cambridge: Harvard University Press, 1990).
[9] See Eris Young, *They/Them/Their: A Guide to Nonbinary and Genderqueer Identities* (London: Jessica Kingsley Publishers, 2020), 67.
[10] Burns, *Trans Britain*, 12; Young, *They/Them/Their*, 63.
[11] Emma Donoghue, 'Doing Lesbian History, Then and Now', *Historical Reflections/Réflexions Historiques* 33, no. 1 (2007): 19.

particularly women who engaged in same-sex activities and relationships. For example, Anne Lister (1791–1840) was an entrepreneur and land owner from the North of England and is often described as 'the first modern lesbian'.[12] Lister kept extensive diaries, which run to over four million words, that detail her sexual relations with other women and a network of female relationships across upper-class society. Lillian Faderman's book *Surpassing the Love of Men* examines romantic friendships between women in the nineteenth-century and argues that because of how information about these encounters was recorded (if at all), figures such as Lister were unlikely to appear in what we might now understand as a 'dataset'.[13] More recently, and through the prism of the male 'expert', the sexological studies of Richard von Krafft-Ebing and Havelock Ellis attempted to describe and categorize the features of a lesbian identity using selective case studies (including Ellis's lesbian wife, Edith).[14] Although the motivations for the production of diaries, letters, poetry and case studies might differ, the exclusion of these sources from a historical review of 'data' means that lesbian, bisexual and queer women appear negligible or absent. As a result, the gendered history of data collection means that attempts to use existing and available sources to uncover LGBTQ figures cannot paint a comprehensive picture of the past. Although a broader investigation of qualitative sources is beyond the scope of this chapter, it is vital to underscore how the efforts of lawyers, medical professionals and scientists in the nineteenth-century to define, categorize and control sexuality were the product of patriarchal ideas about what was worthy of being counted.[15]

At a national or regional level, attempts by states to count phenomena – such as people, animals, crops and land – and make decisions based on these calculations date back to ancient civilizations, if not earlier. I therefore begin with the design and management of modern states in the seventeenth and eighteenth centuries, as this required new tools and techniques that evolved into many of the research methods that remain in use today. James C. Scott describes how maps, censuses and standard units of measurement presented ways for state officials to 'reduce an infinite array of detail to a set of categories that will facilitate summary descriptions, comparisons,

---

[12] Historic England, 'Anne Lister and Shibden Hall', Pride of Place: England's LGBTQ Heritage.

[13] Lillian Faderman, *Surpassing the Love of Men: Romantic Friendship and Love between Women from the Renaissance to the Present* (London: The Women's Press, 1997), 190–230.

[14] Martha Vicinus, '"They Wonder to Which Sex I Belong": The Historical Roots of the Modern Lesbian Identity', *Feminist Studies* 18, no. 3 (1992): 484.

[15] Ibid.

and aggregation'.[16] However, this process required data collectors to present a mediated account of the state that excluded phenomena that failed to fit their a priori expectations. Ian Hacking describes how mathematics became not only a tool for measurement but – through techniques such as standardization, categorization, aggregation and disaggregation – a means to construct a social reality.[17] As a result, these tools and techniques painted a picture of a society that was often at odds with the everyday lives and experiences of the population it claimed to describe.[18]

The management of modern states relied on the construction of an 'other', particularly in response to the social problems associated with urbanization in the eighteenth and nineteenth centuries. This involved the invention of 'scientific' methods to observe and document physical markers of difference such as skin colours, skull sizes and sex characteristics. In late-nineteenth- and early twentieth-century Britain, these methods underpinned the fields of statistics and eugenics and converged in the work of figures such as Francis Galton, Karl Pearson and Ronald Fisher, which marked the birth of modern social statistics and attempts to legitimate statistical racism.[19] Angela Saini describes how 'eugenics was more than a theory, it was a plan in search of policymakers' that engaged a diverse range of characters from birth control pioneer Marie Stopes to future Prime Minister Winston Churchill, who served as vice president at the first International Eugenics Congress held at the University of London in 1912.[20] An overlap between eugenics and statistics has continued into the present day. Tukufu Zuberi, for example, highlights how 'race continues to be seen as a biological and demographic variable by many scholars, even though it has been argued for years that race is, biologically and demographically speaking, an exceedingly complex matter and that subjective predispositions and biases, more than biology or demography, govern the way people think about it'.[21] Shaka McGlotten also notes the long history of technologies that reduced the lives of Black people to 'mere numbers' understood as 'commodities, revenue streams, statistical

---

[16] James C. Scott, *Seeing Like a State: How Certain Schemes to Improve the Human Condition Have Failed* (New Haven: Yale University Press, 1998), 76.
[17] Ian Hacking, 'Biopower and the Avalanche of Printed Numbers', *Humanities in Society* 5 (1982): 289.
[18] Scott, *Seeing Like a State*, 58.
[19] Tukufu Zuberi, *Thicker than Blood: How Racial Statistics Lie* (Minneapolis: University of Minnesota Press, 2001), 30.
[20] Angela Saini, *Superior: The Return of Race Science* (London: 4th Estate, 2019), 75.
[21] Zuberi, *Thicker than Blood*, 105.

deviations, or vectors of risk'.[22] For McGlotten, 'assigning numerical or financial value to black life' and then 'transforming experience into information or data, is nothing new'.[23] Saini, Zuberi and McGlotten offer more expansive accounts of race science than is possible to provide here. Rather, I intend to highlight parallels in the use of data to reify differences between the 'normative' and the 'other' through taxonomies and classifications that do not serve the interests of the people about whom the data relates.

By the late nineteenth-century, a new figure of concern appeared on the urban landscape for those invested in population management: the modern homosexual. Although there exists a long history of men having sexual and romantic relationships with other men, Jeffrey Weeks describes how urbanization in the late nineteenth and early twentieth centuries contributed to a change in family structures, positions of authority and the creation of new, anonymized spaces that constructed what we might now consider a modern homosexual identity.[24] This construction, of course, was only partial. Writing more broadly on 'the habit of naming the modern sexual subject', Doan highlights how 'historicizing inevitably occludes knowledge practices outside the logic of this framework'.[25] Although it is at this historical juncture where histories of data about (some) homosexual men and data collection methods began to converge, for Doan, historians looking for commonalities between the past and the present must also look beyond how the 'history of homosexuality' is produced to ask why this history is produced and for whom?[26] Doan's provocation applies not only to historical enquiries but, more broadly, calls on those engaged in the collection, analysis and use of LGBTQ data to reassess the intended outcomes of data projects and whose interests are served.

Counting the homosexual

The disruption and aftermath of the Second World War marked a turning point in the history of queer data. Faith in the promise of a planned society,

---

[22] Shaka McGlotten, 'Black Data', in *No Tea, No Shade: New Writings in Black Queer Studies*, ed. E. Patrick Johnson (Durham: Duke University Press, 2016), 3.
[23] Ibid.
[24] Jeffrey Weeks, *Coming Out: Homosexual Politics in Britain from the Nineteenth Century to the Present* (London: Quartet Books, 1977).
[25] Doan, *Disturbing Practices*, 139.
[26] Ibid., 22.

espoused by a new wave of technocratic experts, provided a bridge between the welfare programmes of Prime Minister Clement Atlee's post-war Labour governments and the emergent discipline of sociology.[27] Expanding on research methods used to diagnose 'social problems' associated with urbanization, a boom of studies were conducted after the Second World War into a range of topics such as the relationship between husbands and wives, encounters between fathers and children, privacy and the movement from urban to suburban areas.[28] This expert interest differed from previous studies as research not only investigated economic or social questions but also explored topics such as cultural taste, consumer behaviour and psychological well-being.[29] Mike Savage has documented how researchers in the 1940s and 1950s became more interested in 'sampling an ordinary, everyday social world, one no longer cast in overtly moral terms', a departure from studies that tended to use results to 'elicit, pathologize, and sometimes exoticize the morally deviant and disreputable, separating them out from the respectable and legitimate'.[30]

The popularization of data collection methods such as social surveys and one-to-one interviews shifted focus from external observations about households or environmental contexts to the hopes, fears, aspirations and feelings of individuals. A favoured method in the post-war researcher's toolbox was the social survey, which involved asking a large group of people a standardized list of questions. The survey departed from methods based on visual inspection (for example, ethnographic studies where researchers observed participants in real-world contexts) and instead invited participants to articulate their lives and experiences in their own words. Although participant selection and the design of survey questions continued to reflect researchers' paternalist and middle-class ideals, the popularization of the survey symbolized growing attention among experts

---

[27] Jordanna Bailkin, *The Afterlife of Empire* (Berkeley: University of California Press, 2017), 8.

[28] See Dennis Chapman, *The Home and Social Status* (London: Routledge & Kegan Paul, 1955); Michael Young and Peter Willmott, *Family and Kinship in East London* (London: Routledge and Kegan Paul, 1957); Ferdynand Zweig, *The Worker in an Affluent Society: Family Life and Industry* (London: Heinemann, 1961).

[29] Chris Waters, Frank Mort, and Becky Conekin, 'Introduction', in *Moments of Modernity: Reconstructing Britain, 1945–1964*, ed. Becky Conekin, Frank Mort, and Chris Waters (London: Rivers Oram Press, 1999), 14–15.

[30] Michael Savage, *Identities and Social Change in Britain since 1940: The Politics of Method* (Oxford: Oxford University Press, 2010), 7.

to participants' perceptions and feelings.[31] Social research in Britain in the 1940s and 1950s popularized an interest in everyday topics and it became common to see outputs that presented both the effects of policies and recommendations for action, such as suggestions on how to improve the design of poor quality social housing.[32]

Against this backdrop of developments in data collection methods, Emma Vickers describes how, before the war, there existed a greater plurality of sexual identities and a clearer distinction between acts and identities, which enabled people to experiment with same-sex activities without identifying themselves with a particular label.[33] Matt Houlbrook and Richard Hornsey also note how a diversity of fluid identities, present in urban communities before the outbreak of war, coalesced in the 1940s and 1950s to strengthen the idea of a heterosexual/homosexual binary.[34] As a response to the unrest of war, the government positioned the heterosexual family home as an integral component in the rebuilding of Britain.[35] This meant that by the 1950s homosexual men, in particular, appeared more incongruous than ever and, as Matt Cook notes, were 'depicted more determinedly outside and in opposition to supposed norms of the home and family'.[36] During this period, only a handful of social studies investigated the lives of homosexual men in Britain. The most notable research was conducted by the sociologist Michael Schofield (a pseudonym used by Gordon Westwood, a middle-class homosexual from the North of England). Schofield conducted hundreds of one-to-one interviews with homosexual men and presented findings in publications including *Society and the Homosexual* (1952), *A Minority*

---

[31] Jon Agar, *The Government Machine: A Revolutionary History of the Computer* (Cambridge: The MIT Press, 2003), 229; Claire Langhamer, 'Love and Courtship in Mid-Twentieth Century England', *The Historical Journal* 50, no. 1 (March 2007): 194.
[32] Angela Davis, 'A Critical Perspective on British Social Surveys and Community Studies and Their Accounts of Married Life c. 1945–70', *Cultural and Social History* 6, no. 1 (March 2009): 50.
[33] Emma Vickers, *Queen and Country: Same-Sex Desire in the British Armed Forces, 1939–45* (Manchester: Manchester University Press, 2012).
[34] Matt Houlbrook, *Queer London: Perils and Pleasures in the Sexual Metropolis, 1918–1957* (Chicago: University of Chicago Press, 2006), 6, 141, 147, 163; Richard Hornsey, *The Spiv and the Architect: Unruly Life in Postwar London* (Minneapolis: University of Minnesota Press, 2010), 10.
[35] Claire Langhamer, 'The Meanings of Home in Postwar Britain', *Journal of Contemporary History* 40, no. 2 (2005): 341.
[36] Matt Cook, *Queer Domesticities: Homosexuality and Home Life in Twentieth-Century London* (New York: Palgrave Macmillan, 2014), 144–6.

(1960) and *Sociological Aspects of Homosexuality* (1965).[37] Donald J. West, a psychiatrist based in London, also offered a tolerant yet detached account of anthropological, statistical and psychological evidence about homosexual men in *Homosexuality* (1955).[38] Schofield and West's landmark publications are some of the earliest attempts to present data about homosexual life in Britain, written by homosexual men, that constructed an evidence base to change legislation, improve the rights of LGBTQ people and build a more equal society.

In light of high-profile scandals, including the mathematician Alan Turing's 1952 conviction for gross indecency and subsequent suicide, the government felt obliged to respond to the 'homosexual problem'.[39] A government committee was convened in 1954, chaired by Lord John Wolfenden, to explore the issues of homosexuality and prostitution (the former focused on men, the latter on women). The committee published a report in 1957 that recommended the decriminalization of sex between men aged twenty-one and over. The Wolfenden Report offers a window into what was known, in terms of government-level expertize, about homosexual men in mid-1950s Britain. In a section of the report entitled 'The Extent of the Problem', the committee noted, 'So far as we have been able to discover, there is no precise information about the number of men in Great Britain who either have a homosexual disposition or engage in homosexual behaviour'.[40] The report discusses the work of American biologist and sexologist Alfred Kinsey, who used a seven-point scale to measure sexual orientation (where six equated someone exclusively engaged in homosexual activity and zero equated someone exclusively engaged in heterosexual activity). Kinsey reported that 4 per cent of white men in the United States were exclusively homosexual and 37 per cent of the total male population 'has at least some overt homosexual experience to the point of orgasm between adolescence

---

[37] Michael Schofield, *Society and the Homosexual* (London: Gollancz, 1952); Michael Schofield, *A Minority: A Report on the Life of the Male Homosexual in Great Britain* (London: Longmans, 1960); Michael Schofield, *Sociological Aspects of Homosexuality* (London: Prentice Hall Press, 1965).

[38] DJ West, *Homosexuality* (London: Gerald Duckworth and Company, 1955).

[39] Other scandals include the 1954 trial of journalist Peter Wildeblood for 'conspiracy to incite certain male persons to commit serious offences with male persons' and revelation of a Soviet spy ring of homosexual and bisexual men in 1951, which included Guy Burgess, Donald Maclean and Anthony Blunt, see Emily Bourne, 'Before the Passing of the 1967 Sexual Offences Act'. Parliamentary Archives, 8 June 2017.

[40] Secretary of the State for the Home Department and Secretary of State for Scotland, 'Report of the Committee on Homosexual Offences and Prostitution' (London: Her Majesty's Stationery Office, 1957), 17.

and old age'.[41] Medical witnesses reported to the Wolfenden Committee that if a comparable study was undertaken in Britain it was likely that research would report similar findings.[42]

Although the Wolfenden Report presents an account of the government's limited knowledge about homosexual men in 1950s Britain, the report's recommendation to decriminalize sex between men was not accepted by the government and was only brought into law as the Sexual Offences Act in England and Wales in 1967, followed by subsequent legislation in Scotland in 1980 and Northern Ireland in 1981. These legislative changes might have removed the risk of arrest for men aged twenty-one or over with access to private space of their own, but the surveillance and policing of male same-sex activities in public or semi-public spaces such as parks or toilets, or involving more than two men, continued. In the decade that followed decriminalization in England and Wales, the number of recorded acts of indecency between men doubled.[43] Houlbrook notes, 'the "victory" of 1957 and 1967 was achieved precisely because it deliberately excluded those unable to fulfil the requirements of respectability'.[44] Legislation to improve the lives of *some* homosexual men (white, middle or upper-class, with a home of their own) meant that those who failed to match this privileged criteria were cast as pariahs. The Wolfenden Report highlights an early example of how 'being counted' presented an ambivalent victory for homosexual liberation as it required the state to establish, and solidify in law, 'in' and 'out' groups. Although this improved the rights of those fortunate to find themselves counted as the 'in' group, the policing and persecution of those in the 'out' group continued at pace.

As the legal situation improved for some homosexual men in Britain, a high-profile court case invited public scrutiny of transsexual people and rolled back their ability to change the sex recorded on their birth certificate and marry people of a different sex. In 1966, a year before the decriminalization of sex between men in England and Wales, model and actress April Ashley requested that her estranged partner Arthur Corbett provide maintenance payments. Corbett disputed the claim on the grounds that their marriage was invalid because Ashley was born a man. The case went to court and, after hearing conflicting views from medical professionals as to whether

---

[41] Secretary of the State for the Home Department and Secretary of State for Scotland, 17.
[42] Ibid.
[43] Tim Newburn, *Permission and Regulation: Law and Morals in Post-War Britain* (London: Routledge, 1992), 62.
[44] Houlbrook, *Queer London*, 243.

Ashley was a woman or man, the judge decided that, based on psychological factors, Ashley was a man. This decision was a disaster for Ashley but also invalidated the marriages of all transsexual people in Britain, stopped the informal practice of changing the sex marker on birth certificates and invited critical attention to other areas of everyday life where sex was considered relevant (such as the age of retirement, recognition of rape as a criminal offence and the segregation of prisons).[45] Christine Burns explains, 'at a time when gay and lesbian people were beginning to make social progress, life for transsexual people was going downhill fast'.[46] As with the Wolfenden Report, the state's increased interest in gender, sex and sexuality initiated greater policing of these categories and led to a rollback of existing freedoms that negatively impacted the everyday lives of many trans people in Britain.

Queer academics and activists

Several charitable organizations were formed in the late 1980s and 1990s to improve the lives of LGBTQ people in Britain, including Stonewall (1989), Press for Change (1992), Mermaids (1995), the Equality Network (1997), GIRES (1997), LGBT Foundation (2000) and LGBT Youth Scotland (2003). Increasingly professional in their approach, the emergence of these organizations foreshadowed a period of unprecedented interest in the collection of data about LGBTQ people and its use to advocate for policy change and improved legal rights. Campaigns to advance equality for lesbians and gay men (and increasingly bisexual, trans and queer people) linked political demands to data about the experiences of particular identity groups, an approach that continues to drive the work of mainstream LGBTQ organizations in Britain and many parts of the world.

Identities as a basis for action contrasted the approach championed by an emergent group of scholars across the Atlantic. Queer theory and the related field of queer studies developed in North America in the late 1980s through the work of literary scholars and historians such as Eve Kosofsky Sedgwick and David Halperin.[47] Queer studies departed from the existing discipline

---

[45] Burns, *Trans Britain*, 125–6.
[46] Ibid.
[47] Ken Plummer, 'Critical Humanism and Queer Theory: Living with the Tensions', in *The SAGE Handbook of Qualitative Research*, ed. Norman K. Denzin and Yvonna S. Lincoln (Thousand Oaks: Sage Publications, 2005).

of lesbian and gay studies, exemplified in works such as John Boswell's *Christianity, Social Tolerance, and Homosexuality* (1980) that sought to locate gay identities in historical contexts, and directed greater attention to the presumptions, values and viewpoints that informed concepts such as 'homosexual' and 'heterosexual'.[48] Queer theorists examined how we construct knowledge about identity categories – such as gay, lesbian and heterosexual – and traced the process through which these categories came into being, for example through language and everyday practices. As a result, queer studies presented an anti-categorical view of LGBTQ identities, as the practice of categorization was understood as flawed and partly responsible for the creation of differences between identity groups that categories claimed to describe. For sociologists, this posed a particular challenge as many scholars understood the social sciences as a continuation of the natural sciences, with information about the social world revealed through scientific methods. Steven Seidman's edited collection *Queer Theory/Sociology* (1996) explored how queer theory might positively impact sociologists' use of quantitative and qualitative methods, such as surveys and interviews.[49] Although the edited collection presented a way forward, any appetite to *queer* the discipline took a long time to develop.[50] Throughout the 1990s and 2000s, there was a lack of critical engagement between sociological studies of lesbian and gay (and, less frequently, bisexual and trans) people and those who used quantitative methods, let alone those who questioned the biases of quantitative methods.[51]

[48] Patrick Dilley, 'Queer Theory: Under Construction', *International Journal of Qualitative Studies in Education* 12, no. 5 (1999): 461–2, 469.

[49] Steven Seidman, ed., *Queer Theory/Sociology* (Cambridge: Blackwell, 1996).

[50] Schilt et al. discuss the impact of Seidman's work, in Kristen Schilt, Tey Meadow, and D'Lane Compton, 'Introduction: Queer Work in a Straight Discipline', in *Other, Please Specify: Queer Methods in Sociology*, ed. Kristen Schilt, Tey Meadow, and D'Lane Compton (Berkeley: University of California Press, 2018), 3–4.

[51] Kath Browne, 'Queer Quantification or Queer(y)ing Quantification: Creating Lesbian, Gay, Bisexual or Heterosexual Citizens through Governmental Social Research', in *Queer Methods and Methodologies: Intersecting Queer Theories and Social Science Research*, ed. Kath Browne and Catherine J. Nash (Farnham: Ashgate, 2010), 231. However, Adam Isaiah Green has also described how queer theory has helped revitalize the discipline of sociology as 'sociologists have been challenged to sharpen their analytic lenses, to grow sensitized to the discursive production of sexual identities, and to be mindful of the insidious force of heteronormativity as a fundamental organizing principle throughout the social order', in Adam Isaiah Green, 'Gay but Not Queer: Toward a Post-Queer Study of Sexuality', *Theory and Society* 31, no. 4 (2002): 521.

Disagreement among LGBTQ people over the use of categories – to anchor political demands, tell histories or build communities – has a long track record. Throughout the second half of the twentieth-century LGBTQ groups debated how categories were determined, who had the power to include or exclude, for what purposes were categories constructed and deployed, and what might happen if categories were abolished altogether?[52] As queer theory challenged assumptions in the academy, a new wave of queer activism also developed on the streets. Elizabeth Freeman has documented links between the emergent field of queer studies and the grassroots activism of US groups such as ACT UP and Queer Nation.[53] LGBTQ activism of the 1980s and 1990s can provide contemporary lessons for queer data such as the use of goal-oriented direct action or zaps (public demonstrations intended to embarrass public figures or institutions and raise awareness of LGBTQ issues), coalition-building across racial and gender lines, and the in-your-face celebration of being out and proud. Queer activism acknowledged the fluidity of gender and sexual identities yet questioned a rights-based approach to equality, which prioritized access to existing structures of power for gays and lesbians. Instead, meaningful change could come from disrupting practices and systems that maintained the unjust hierarchy that positioned some gender and sexual identities above others. Activism therefore reflected how gender and sexual identities intersect with other markers of difference – such as race, disability and social class – and forged coalitions with other groups working to achieve the same goal.[54] Rather than suggest exclusive 'gay and lesbian' and 'queer' approaches to political organization, these examples show that a critique of identity categories does not necessarily neutralize the potential for radical social and political change. Doan, in her balanced appreciation of queer theory and histories of sexuality, has described how a queer evocation of history touches the past in ways that uncover emotional connections just as historians of sexuality similarly seek to reveal hidden histories.[55] The use of goal-oriented tactics to achieve desired outcomes, the formation of alliances

---

[52] For a detailed discussion of these debates in a US context, see Escoffier, *American Homo*.

[53] Elizabeth Freeman, *Time Binds: Queer Temporalities, Queer Histories* (Durham: Duke University Press, 2010), xv.

[54] In the UK, a notable example was the solidarity between the London Lesbians and Gays Support the Miners group and miners in South Wales during the strike of 1984–85, see Mike Jackson, 'Who We Are', London Lesbians and Gays Support the Miners, 2015.

[55] Doan, *Disturbing Practices*, 80–93.

with groups fighting against patriarchal, racist and capitalist structures, and the disruptive potential of LGBTQ visibility are possible without a fixed, stable, identity-based subject. Queer academics and activists show how data can positively impact the lives of LGBTQ people without reaffirming exclusionary categories or strengthening the power of practices and systems that cause harm to many LGBTQ people.

The internet, data compliance and legal equality

The internet reconfigured the collection of data about LGBTQ people in multiple ways. It created new spaces for LGBTQ individuals to meet others in online chat rooms, dating websites and apps; exchange information and organize action; and share stories about their lives and experiences, often to huge audiences, via blogs and social media. As payment for access to commercial spaces, companies collected behavioural data from users' online activities, which was exploited to develop targeted advertising and bespoke content.[56] This business model has proven extremely lucrative for companies such as Google and Facebook but has involved users being kept in the dark about the data collected or the full extent of its use.[57] The internet also changed how researchers collect data about LGBTQ people. Hosting surveys online, for example, introduced functions such as drop-down boxes and predictive-text technology that offered participants new ways to describe their identities to researchers. From the mid-1990s, online spaces, such as forums and message boards, offered previously unimaginable opportunities to locate and recruit research participants. Communication platforms, such as Skype and Zoom, made it possible to conduct one-to-one interviews with anyone in the world and feel as if you were engaged in conversation in the same room. The internet has reached into every element of many people's day-to-day lives. This has not only offered researchers new ways to collect data about LGBTQ people but also posed questions as to what *exactly* this data might reveal about the social world it claims to describe.

Utilizing technological developments in computing, the decades after the millennium also unleashed a rush of administrative practices related to EDI

---

[56] Jathan Sadowski, 'When Data Is Capital: Datafication, Accumulation, and Extraction', *Big Data & Society* 6, no. 1 (1 January 2019): 4–6.
[57] Benjamin Haber, 'The Queer Ontology of Digital Method', *Women's Studies Quarterly* 44, no. 3/4 (2016): 151–2.

in Britain's public, private and voluntary sectors. This revolution relied on a revised framework of equality legislation and compliance, underpinned by the collection, analysis and presentation of diversity monitoring data about individuals. In 2007, the UK Government consolidated the patchwork of agencies that oversaw compliance with equality legislation into a new organization called the Equality and Human Rights Commission.[58] As part of the overhaul, equalities groups received funding to undertake reviews of the current EDI landscape in Britain, this included an academic study into the inequalities that face trans people. Burns describes how the subsequent report from this research, *Engendered Penalties* (2007), was a landmark moment for the collection of data about trans lives as it presented 'the first proper study into trans marginalisation in Britain and also the largest ever study of trans people at the time', with almost 900 research participants.[59] To streamline the legal environment that underpinned the work of the EHRC, multiple pieces of legislation were brought together and expanded to become the 2010 Equality Act. The jurisdiction of the Equality Act covered England, Wales and Scotland, identified nine protected characteristics, required public sector organizations to regularly publish data on the composition of their workforce and report actions undertaken to address inequality.[60] UK Governments also introduced mandatory reporting on the average pay gap between men and women in organizations with more than 250 employees in 2017 and gender representation on public boards in 2018.[61]

To comply with these reporting requirements, organizations increasingly used a suite of administrative tools such as diversity monitoring forms (a short survey that asks individuals to disclose their identity characteristics, often using categories and language that aligned with the Equality Act) and equality impact assessments (an exercise conducted before the roll-out of a new policy to predict its effects on people of different identity

---

[58] The formation of the EHRC involved the merger of the Equal Opportunities Commission, Disability Rights Commission and Race Equality Commission.

[59] Burns, *Trans Britain*, 255–6. For the report, see Stephen Whittle, Lewis Turner, and Maryam Al-Alami, 'Engendered Penalties: Transgender and Transsexual People's Experiences of Inequality and Discrimination' (Press for Change, 2007).

[60] For further information on the Equality Act, see Equality and Human Rights Commission, 'What Is the Equality Act?', 19 June 2019.

[61] Gender pay gap reporting was introduced in 2017 following changes to the regulations of the Equality Act. In Scotland, the Gender Representation on Public Boards (Scotland) Act 2018 requires that 50 per cent of non-executive members on public boards are women by December 2022.

characteristics). There was, and is, much promise in the collection and analysis of diversity monitoring data to comply with reporting requirements. Data collected via diversity monitoring forms and the undertaking of an EIA can provide insights into how changes in policies might unfairly impact particular identity groups, expose gaps and absences within an organization, or highlight differences in outcomes. Data can establish the groundwork for radical action. However, the collection of diversity monitoring data, to comply with reporting requirements, can also create situations where those responsible for the collection and analysis of data fail to use findings to inform future activities. In their study of housing and homelessness services in Scotland, Peter Matthews and Chris Poyner document how the failure to meaningfully record diversity monitoring data about the gender, sex and sexuality of tenants and service users reinforced the heteronormative status quo.[62] For Matthews and Poyner, even though tenants and services users were invited to share *some* data about how they identify, the omission of questions on sexual orientation and trans/gender identity gave the impression that LGBT+ tenants and service users were either absent or had no problems to report. The implementation of an EDI initiative but its failure to meaningfully count LGBT+ people therefore had the effect of further masking experiences of discrimination and exclusion. Sara Ahmed has also interrogated the 'politics of documentation'; in particular, developments that followed the introduction of the 2000 Race Relations Amendment Act.[63] Later subsumed into the Equality Act, this legislation required public sector organizations to promote race equality and provide evidence to demonstrate the effects of activities undertaken. An understanding of EDI work as documentation has since proliferated. Interviewees in Ahmed's study noted how staff 'end up doing the document rather than doing the doing' and that 'too much time can be spent on actually writing policies and action plans'.[64] As Ahmed critically observes, 'the politics of diversity has become what we could call "image management"'.[65]

---

[62] Peter Matthews and Chris Poyner, 'Achieving Equality in Progressive Contexts: Queer(y)Ing Public Administration', *Public Administration Quarterly* 44, no. 4 (15 November 2020): 545–77.
[63] Sara Ahmed, '"You End up Doing the Document Rather than Doing the Doing": Diversity, Race Equality and the Politics of Documentation', *Ethnic and Racial Studies* 30, no. 4 (July 2007): 590.
[64] Ibid., 599.
[65] Ibid., 605.

Running parallel to the overhaul of EDI reporting and compliance, legislation was introduced across the UK to improve the legal rights of lesbian, gay, bisexual and trans people. Section 28 of the Local Government Act, which forbid local authorities from teaching 'the acceptability of homosexuality', was repealed in Scotland in 2000 and across the rest of the UK in 2003. This was followed by the introduction of civil partnerships for same-sex couples (from 2004) and the legalization of same-sex marriage (from 2014). Following a judgement of the European Court of Human Rights, which stated that the inability to change gender on a birth certificate breached the European Convention on Human Rights, the UK Government introduced the Gender Recognition Act (2004), which provided a legal route for trans people to apply for recognition as a sex different from the one assigned at birth. Critics of legal equality approaches have questioned the energy and resources spent on opening up historically conservative institutions, such as marriage and the nuclear family, to LGBTQ people.[66] Legal scholars, such as Reeva Siegel, have described legal equality approaches as 'preservation through transformation', where campaigns to radically redesign structures are sidelined in place of minor tweaks that disproportionately benefit the most 'deserving' among marginalized communities.[67] As a result, mainstream LGBTQ organizations are sometimes accused of emphasizing the demands of cis, white, middle-class gay men and lesbians, who already tend to hold positions of power within the LGBTQ community, at the expense of those most in need of support.[68] To an uncritical observer, this rush of legal equality victories might resemble the end point in a progressive, linear account of LGBTQ history in Britain. However, as with any apparent move forward, questions remain as to who was left behind?

* * *

---

[66] For a more extensive critique of legal equality approaches, see Spade, *Normal Life*; Cece McDonald, Miss Major Griffin-Gracy, and Toshio Meronek, 'Cautious Living: Black Trans Woman and the Politics of Documentation', in *Trap Door: Trans Cultural Production and the Politics of Visibility*, ed. Reina Gossett, Eric A. Stanley, and Johanna Burton (Cambridge: The MIT Press, 2017), 28.

[67] Reeva Siegel, 'Why Equal Protection No Longer Protects: The Evolving Forms of Status-Enforcing State Action', *Stanford Law Review* 49 (May 1997): 1113.

[68] Gwendolyn Leachman, 'Institutionalizing Essentialism: Mechanisms of Intersectional Subordination Within the LGBT Movement', *Legal Studies Research Paper Series*, 1383 (2016): 656–7.

The history of queer data presented in this chapter folds together developments in law, politics and academic disciplines such as sociology, history and queer studies. My focus on quantitative data, and the patriarchal biases of historic approaches to data, means that coverage is skewed in favour of male same-sex activities and the construction of the 'modern homosexual'. In an attempt to avoid perpetuating exclusions from the past, this chapter has presented a blended history of data *about* LGBTQ people and the methods used to gather this information. My discussion of Britain in the middle decades of the twentieth-century highlighted a solidification of ideas about heterosexual/homosexual and male/female binaries, strengthened by data collection methods that identified, categorized and (ultimately) policed those who did not conform with society's expectations about gender, sex or sexuality. The heterosexual family home became a key site of reconstruction after the Second World War, which further emphasized the incongruity of homosexual men. The decriminalization of sex between men reduced the risk of arrest, in particular circumstances, but did little to improve the scrutiny faced in other areas of public life. Likewise, from the 1970s, increased interest in the lives of transsexual people and the restriction of people's ability to self-identify made it impossible for many LGBTQ people to live an authentic life. The popularization of the social survey, expansion of research topics and interest in the everyday experiences of individuals meant that researchers increasingly understood the feelings of participants as valuable insights into the social world. How experts conceptualized data changed during this period, which has had a lasting effect on contemporary ideas about the collection, analysis and use of data about individuals' identity characteristics.

Some of the most crucial developments in the collection of data about LGBTQ people have occurred since the turn of the millennium. This remains a history in the making: queer data shapes how we conceptualize the differential impacts of the Covid-19 pandemic on identity groups, the sustainability of alliances forged through the Black Lives Matter and #MeToo movements, and the progress of legal changes in the Scottish and UK Parliaments to improve the lives of LGBTQ people, most notably reform of the GRA. Rather than being understood as administrative decisions, the historical evolution of data collection methods is an account of battles fought over who to include and who to exclude from official discourses. The absence of data about LGBTQ people is not accidental. A failure to ask inclusive questions about gender, sex and sexuality reflects the cis/heteronormative assumptions built into data collection methods and the attitudes of data collectors about marginalized groups. A *queer data history* and *queer history of data* invite us to consider how ideas about people we might now consider LGBTQ have shifted across different times and informed both how we conceptualize data and LGBTQ identities.

CHAPTER 2
MOVING TARGETS: QUEER
COLLECTION METHODS

I was sat in a police interview room. My call to 101 to report transphobic graffiti on the university campus had escalated quickly. 'To register the case we'll need you to come to the station', the telephone operator explained to me. By mid-afternoon, I was scrolling through photographs on my phone with a police officer explaining the hidden meanings of particular symbols and phrases like 'no gender self-id', 'natal women' and 'sex-based rights'. I signed a witness statement and left the police station feeling despondent about the visible animosity towards trans people on Edinburgh's streets. A few months later, I was registering an official complaint against a university for a breach of its EDI policies. Before submitting my complaint, I had spent hours reading and rereading official documents to pinpoint exactly where the university's actions had departed from their stated policies. My email was personal, pithy and evidence based but I knew the chance of the response being anything more than a cut-and-paste 'We acknowledge your concerns … ' was slim.

When we think of these practices as types of data collection, I was aware that they were unlikely to bring about meaningful change. My 101 call was not going to trigger a squad of officers to meticulously review CCTV footage to identify the person behind the graffiti nor was my complaint going to upturn the university's approach to EDI. However, I felt the need to register that something was wrong. By making a police report and lodging a complaint, I created data. My minor actions meant that somewhere – in a police file and on a university database – a box was created that transformed the frustration in my head into a problem that was tangible and real for other people who had more power to make the situation better. Without evidence, institutions such as police forces and universities can brush off the existence or extent of problems like transphobia, even when they are experienced by many people on a daily basis. In large and complex organizations, it is only when problems are noted, recorded and transformed into data that those in positions of power find themselves under pressure to take action.

* * *

This chapter explores queer approaches to data collection. I continue my focus on gender, sex and sexuality data but direct attention towards the knowledge foundations upon which identities are based and the methods used to capture this information. Collection methods typically used in the social sciences – such as surveys, interviews and focus groups – bring with them assumptions about the social world we live in, the possibilities as to what they can reveal and the participation of those from whom they seek to collect data. Paisley Currah and Susan Stryker have described the term 'enumeration', the practice of counting or ordering items within a group, as misleading. For Currah and Stryker, enumeration wrongly suggests that 'one is merely counting objects that already exist' whereas 'the enumerative process in fact has the capacity to create what it purports only to name, causing new kinds of people to appear on the social map'.[1] Similarly, Karin Schönpflug et al. have observed that 'data-collection processes cannot be interpreted as neutral processes of "revealing" or making "visible" but are productive and highly political practices through which (only) *certain* LGB(TI)Q populations are counted'.[2] This chapter's focus on 'queerness as method' therefore asks: in moments when data is captured, whose interests are prioritized? The interests of individuals or groups about whom the data relates (in other words LGBTQ people) or the interests of those who possess the power and resources to collect the data?

Data arrives with the researcher via a collection method. Its journey from participant to researcher can transform the meaning of the data collected, whether through the way questions were asked or assumptions made by participants about what the researcher expects to hear. Data collected might also present an account of how a participant relates to others in the study, with findings therefore relational and contingent on the composition of the group under investigation. Scholars in the field of science and technology studies have paid particular attention to how knowledge is constructed, a

---

[1] Paisley Currah and Susan Stryker, 'Introduction', *TSQ: Transgender Studies Quarterly* 2, no. 1 (1 January 2015): 2.
[2] Karin Schönpflug et al., 'If Queers Were Counted: An Inquiry into European Socioeconomic Data on LGB(TI)QS', *Feminist Economics* 24, no. 4 (October 2018): 22.

branch of philosophy called epistemology, and explored how phenomena (such as identity characteristics) are created through the methods used to describe them.[3] Although this does not make people's experiences of gender, sex and sexual identities any less 'real', I consider the impact of collection methods on project participants and the researchers that conduct studies. Sharing insights from my practice as an EDI researcher in higher education, I highlight how collection methods can encourage participants to evaluate their identities in new and unexpected ways. The collection of data related to identity characteristics can therefore operate as a form of consciousness-raising that provides participants with information and ideas about how they relate to others.[4] This back-and-forth between researcher and participant is not a one-way exchange of data. The *queering* of collection methods simultaneously presents an account of the social world while also changing the social world it claims to describe. In this account of the social world, identities – such as gay, trans, asexual or heterosexual – do not exist as something stable and fixed patiently waiting for researchers to discover them. Rather, they are partly constructed through data collection practices.

This chapter concludes by assessing the ethics of queer collection methods. I discuss how the collection of EDI data in large organizations, for initiatives such as diversity monitoring or gender pay gap reporting, can deploy methods that identify 'good data'. Subsequent initiatives are then focused on fixing the data rather than the problems the data represents. Furthermore, while the collection of data can present opportunities for consciousness-raising, problems emerge when researchers and participants disagree over the existence of problems. In these disputes, is it ever the responsibility of researchers to tell participants how they *should* feel about inequality in their organization? Surveys, interviews and focus groups can obscure important discussions about the data collected, the rationale for its collection and the role of researchers and participants. Queer data, as it relates to data *about* LGBTQ people and the collection methods used, provides a space for researchers to critically reflect on their influence on

---

[3] For discussion, see John Law, 'On Sociology and STS', *The Sociological Review* 56, no. 4 (1 November 2008): 633–4; John Law, 'Seeing Like a Survey', *Cultural Sociology* 3, no. 2 (July 2009): 239–56.

[4] Consciousness-raising, as associated with second-wave feminism and gay liberation movements of the 1970s, is a form of activism that involves increasing individuals' awareness of social and political issues in ways that encourage them to understand personal experiences as linked to societal injustices.

(and, in turn, how they are influenced by) data collection practices and what sort of social worlds these practices help bring into being.

Data collection methods

Scholarship has tended to focus on the findings of studies *about* LGBTQ people rather than how research methods – such as surveys, interviews and focus groups – were used and their potential to shape the data collected.[5] Other collection methods are available beyond those discussed in this chapter, including ethnographic and observational approaches, document analysis or self-reflective methods such as diary writing. I focus on surveys, interviews and focus groups as these collection methods are common in social research and present an entry point to a broader discussion about norms and data collection. As an example, the collection of gender pay gap data demonstrates how methods can influence what data tells us about a situation.[6] An organization's gender pay gap is the percentage difference between the average pay for male and female staff. To arrive at this figure, an organization needs to define who is counted as 'staff' (for example, whether to include or exclude atypical or agency staff) and the weight attached to each person (a headcount calculates every person as one but, in an organization, not everyone works full-time and some people work multiple roles). Data undergoes further transformation during analysis, which involves calculating a mean average or median average, and is then presented in ways that convey a convincing story. This is not to say that gender pay gap data is inaccurate or intentionally presents a false account of the numbers. Rather, this example demonstrates decisions made during data collection, and beyond, that are often viewed as neutral practices untouched by bias or the fingerprints of human choice.

---

[5] Examples of scholarship that has examined the effects of data collection methods on studies of LGBTQ people include Dilley, 'Queer Theory'; Browne and Nash, 'Queer Methods and Methodologies: An Introduction'; Patrick R. Grzanka, 'Queer Survey Research and the Ontological Dimensions of Heterosexism', *WSQ: Women's Studies Quarterly* 44, no. 3 (7 October 2016): 131–49.

[6] The United Nations Task Force on Communicating Gender Statistics has noted the lack of internationally recognized standards or language for the measurement of the gender pay gap, which means that a variety of approaches exist for how organizations collect, analyse and report data, in Task Force on Communicating Gender Statistics, 'Guidance on Communicating Gender Statistics' (United Nations Economic Commission for Europe Conference of European Statisticians, 2020), 4–5.

Researchers working with quantitative and qualitative data make decisions about categorization, the labels and weight they attach to categories, and the types of analysis undertaken. Decisions made affect the collection of gender, sex and sexuality data, with findings used as evidence about the lives of LGBTQ people. The norms that underpin data collection methods therefore contribute to how society conceptualizes different identity characteristics and partly informs how these identities are brought into being. Queer theory's problematization of what counts as knowledge, and in what locations knowledge is constructed, has expanded the pool of potential sources for researchers to investigate.[7] Queer theory's early flourishing in the disciplines of literary studies and history meant that sources were often textual and best-suited to qualitative methods. Although an association of queer approaches with qualitative studies continues, ignoring quantitative methods overlooks the sweeping critique that queer approaches pose for *all* data collection methods.[8] Browne and Nash note, 'while queer approaches might contest the possibilities of quantification of subjects, there is a danger in then asserting that queer epistemologies, methodologically, require the use of qualitative methods only'.[9] Kristen Schilt et al. reaffirm this position and argue that the *queering* of quantitative methods is critical to broader conversations about the future of queer methods.[10] For these reasons, my examination of collection methods looks beyond typically qualitative approaches (for example, interviews and focus groups) to also examine how typically quantitative approaches (for example, surveys and exercises such as the census) are reimagined when viewed through a queer lens.

Queer relations in time and space

In a 2006 article for the London Review of Books, Hacking described his research interest 'in classifications of people, in how they affect the people classified, and how the affects on the people in turn change the

---

[7] Under the umbrella of 'queer sociology', Schilt et al. explore 'a set of tenets that connect the disparate epistemological and methodological investments, areas of inquiry, and social locations of researchers and research' that constitute the field, in Schilt, Meadow, and Compton, 'Introduction', 17.

[8] See Dilley, 'Queer Theory', 457.

[9] Browne and Nash, 'Queer Methods and Methodologies: An Introduction', 11–12.

[10] Schilt, Meadow, and Compton, 'Introduction', 16.

classifications.[11] Hacking labelled the subjects of these studies 'moving targets' because researchers' investigatory efforts change them in ways so 'they are not quite the same kind of people as before'. For Currah and Stryker, in their account of trans enumeration, this 'frustrates the project of fixing embodied identities in time and space – a requisite operation for the potentially life enhancing project of counting trans populations'.[12] Ahmed has also explored how use of the word 'orientation', in terms such as sexual orientation, suggests that meaning is constructed through the relationships between two or more people.[13] If data is contingent on other data to establish its meaning, datasets become comparable to a planetary map: a three-dimensional domain that contains a diversity of objects moving at different speeds in haphazard directions. In place of documenting identity characteristics that are stable or reveal a 'reality', collection methods are instead understood to expose the relationship *between* research participants.

Data about an individual's identity characteristics is also historically situated, as discussed in the previous chapter. Information someone discloses about their gender, sex or sexuality might change over time; a temporal dimension of identity that surveys generally fail to consider and, in some examples, record as an error.[14] The fluidity of gender, sex and sexuality categories means that data collected about a sample can drastically change in a relatively short period of time. For example, Bonnie Ruberg and Spencer Ruelos surveyed 227 adults in the United States, born between 1980 and 1996, and asked if their 'sexual identities' had changed between when they were a teenager and the present day.[15] Over four-fifths of participants (83%) reported a change to their 'sexual identity'. For Ruberg and Ruelos this finding demonstrated that 'the sexual and gender identities of many LGBTQ people are in fact neither static nor singular'.[16] Ruberg and Ruelos's

[11] Ian Hacking, 'Making Up People', *London Review of Books*, 17 August 2006.
[12] Currah and Stryker, 'Introduction', 4.
[13] Sara Ahmed, *Queer Phenomenology: Orientations, Objects, Others* (Durham: Duke University Press, 2006), in Susan Stryker, Paisley Currah, and Lisa Jean Moore, 'Introduction: Trans-, Trans, or Transgender?', *Women's Studies Quarterly* 36, no. 3/4 (2008): 13.
[14] For example, Westbrook and Saperstein's study of four large, long-running and influential social surveys in the United States found that three of the surveys instructed researchers to record any change in participants' sex/gender categorization during the course of the study as an error, in Westbrook and Saperstein, 'New Categories Are Not Enough', 547.
[15] Bonnie Ruberg and Spencer Ruelos, 'Data for Queer Lives: How LGBTQ Gender and Sexuality Identities Challenge Norms of Demographics', *Big Data & Society* 7, no. 1 (January 2020): 2.
[16] Ibid.

conclusion is, of course, not unique to data about gender, sex and sexuality. Measurement tools must also account for how identities – such as religion, disability and ethnicity – are temporal and that repeated data collection and/or providing participants methods to 'update' their information is as important as the provision of new questions or addition of more response options.

Reimagining identity characteristics as 'moving targets' reconfigures traditional understandings of data collection methods and the information they provide about the lives of LGBTQ people. An example from my work in higher education helps demonstrate how the idea of 'moving targets' materializes in research projects. A few years ago I worked with a university that wished to introduce new initiatives, such as networking opportunities and a mentorship scheme, for its LGBTQ employees. To inform which initiatives to roll out, the university ran a survey to capture gender, sex and sexuality data about its staff. The design of the questions and response options were important because the exercise invited many employees to consider their sexual orientation and trans/gender identity for the first time. This was particularly true for cis, heterosexual staff, many of whom had no previous reason to critically consider these aspects of their identities. Rather than interpret this survey as an atomized account of individuals' identity characteristics, consider what it tells us about how participants identify their gender, sex and sexuality in relation to *other* staff at the university. For example, how might survey results differ in a climate where people were inclusive of gender, sex and sexual diversity compared to a climate where attitudes towards diversity were hostile? Writing about how people respond to questions in a census, Evelyn Ruppert describes this phenomenon as 'a reflexive practice of identifying oneself in relation to a whole'.[17] How staff respond to a diversity monitoring survey might therefore present an account of 'position statements' rather than document the presence (or absence) of innate identities. This is not to suggest that LGBTQ identities are any less 'real' than other identity characteristics; instead, this argument underscores how collection methods present a snapshot of a moment in time that is contingent on the relationship between participants in the research study.

The relational dimension of data is particularly pertinent among participants who identify with majority, normative identity categories – in

---

[17] Evelyn Ruppert, "'I Is; Therefore I Am": The Census as Practice of Double Identification', *Sociological Research Online* 13, no. 4 (July 2008): 2.

other words, those who are cis and/or heterosexual. Several scholars have noted a lack of familiarity or identification with terms such as 'heterosexual' and 'straight' among heterosexual/straight survey respondents.[18] As a possible solution, some suggest asking heterosexual/straight respondents whether they are 'gay (or lesbian)' or 'not gay (or lesbian)' to improve comprehension of the response options provided. Rebecca Geary et al., in their study of Britain's *National Survey of Sexual Attitudes and Lifestyles*, also describe how the presentation of response options as a continuum (for example, a seven-point scale where zero equals exclusively heterosexual and six equals exclusively homosexual) might improve respondents' ability to describe their sexual orientation.[19] Neither approach is ideal: the use of response options such as 'not gay' further solidifies the invisibility of 'heterosexual' as the normative default and the use of a numerical scale, in place of identity terms, makes it hard to establish whether respondents interpret points on the scale in the same way. Although imperfect, these approaches are already used in some major data collection exercises. For example, the *Census Barriers, Attitudes and Motivators Study* collected the views of 17,283 adults about reasons for engagement or disengagement with the US census.[20] Unlike the census, this study asked the question 'Which of the following best represents how you think of yourself?' and offered the response option 'Straight, that is not lesbian or gay'.[21] Although this frames straight participants as the default (the response option 'Lesbian or gay' did not include the clarification 'that is not straight'), it presents an approach to data collection that begins to acknowledge the relational dimension of data collected. In the fields of psychology and political science, several scholars have demonstrated how the use of a scale

---

[18] Heather Ridolfo, Kristen Miller, and Aaron Maitland, 'Measuring Sexual Identity Using Survey Questionnaires: How Valid Are Our Measures?', *Sexuality Research and Social Policy* 9, no. 2 (June 2012): 122; Stuart Michaels et al., 'Improving Measures of Sexual and Gender Identity in English and Spanish to Identify LGBT Older Adults in Surveys', *LGBT Health* 4, no. 6 (1 December 2017): 417; Daiki Hiramori and Saori Kamano, 'Asking about Sexual Orientation and Gender Identity in Social Surveys in Japan: Findings from the Osaka City Residents' Survey and Related Preparatory Studies', *Journal of Population Problems* 76, no. 4 (2020): 444, 446.

[19] Rebecca Geary et al., 'Sexual Identity, Attraction and Behaviour in Britain: The Implications of Using Different Dimensions of Sexual Orientation to Estimate the Size of Sexual Minority Populations and Inform Public Health Interventions', *PLOS ONE* 13, no. 1 (2 January 2018): 12.

[20] Nancy Bates, Yazmín A García Trejo, and Monica Vines, 'Are Sexual Minorities Hard-to-Survey? Insights from the 2020 Census Barriers, Attitudes, and Motivators Study (CBAMS) Survey', *Journal of Official Statistics* 35, no. 4 (1 December 2019): 712.

[21] Ibid., 713.

to measure gender can present more granular insights, expose hidden dimensions of inequality and unpack the broad categories of 'women' and 'men'.[22] For example, Amanda Bittner and Elizabeth Goodyear-Grant's research found that a traditional binary sex measure did not work for around 12–13 per cent of their sample and that use of a scale uncovered differences in political attitudes between those who described themselves as 'most masculine' and 'most feminine'.[23]

Abby Day's research into how people answered the question on religion in the 2001 English and Welsh census shines further light on the interplay between identity characteristics and the use of data collection methods. Day describes how interviewees in her study were initially ambivalent about their religious identities. However, when presented with a list of options, this crystallized their identity 'in a way that seemed to suggest not that they were, for example, Christian but – perhaps more importantly – that they were not one of the "others"'.[24] Day highlights how data collection methods not only inform how a participant self-identifies (in this case, as Christian after hearing other possible response options) but also present a 'position statement' of how a participant perceives themselves in relation to others. Day, writing with Lois Lee in 2014, argued that collection methods, such as the census or surveys, need 'to be seen as an instrument of relationality, not individuality, and the process of engaging with it as performative'.[25]

Day and Lee's account of how individuals position themselves in relation to population groups highlights the influences of time and space on data collected about identity characteristics. If we reimagine identity characteristics as 'moving targets', collection methods no longer reveal the existence of fully formed LGBTQ identities awaiting discovery but partly forge the identities they claim to locate. This bold claim has been explored by scholars working in the field of science and technology studies. Stephan Scheel explains how 'material-semiotic approaches conceive of methods not as mere tools for the extraction of knowledge from a reality "out there" but as performative devices that help to enact the realities they study and

---

[22] Devon Magliozzi, Aliya Saperstein, and Laurel Westbrook, 'Scaling Up: Representing Gender Diversity in Survey Research', *Socius* 2 (1 January 2016): 6.

[23] Bittner and Goodyear-Grant, 'Sex Isn't Gender', 1030, 1038.

[24] Abby Day and Lois Lee, 'Making Sense of Surveys and Censuses: Issues in Religious Self-Identification', *Religion* 44, no. 3 (3 July 2014): 346. For a more detailed discussion, see Abby Day, *Believing in Belonging: Belief and Social Identity in the Modern World* (Oxford: Oxford University Press, 2011), chap. Believing in Belonging: The Cultural Act of Claiming Identity.

[25] Ibid., 346.

describe'.[26] John Law has also described how methods can be understood as 'practices that do not simply describe realities but also tend to enact these into being'.[27] When framed as performative practices, the validity or objectivity of knowledge claims based on traditional social science methods is called into question. Spade has also documented how administrative practices, such as birth certificates and health records, do not simply manage the 'out there' but invent and produce meaning for the categories they administer.[28] Spade describes individuals' interactions with administrative practices as a type of 'subjection' as they inform 'the ways we understand our bodies, the things we believe about ourselves and our relationships with other people and with institutions'.[29] For those engaged in data practices *about* LGBTQ people, the work of Day, Lee, Scheel, Law and Spade reconfigure the relationship between data collection methods and the social worlds they claim to represent.

Collection methods, participants and researchers

A queer approach to data collection showcases the back-and-forth between participants and researchers. Feminist oral historians describe encounters between participants and researchers as intersubjectivity, as they require researchers to consider their role in data collection practices.[30] Amy Tooth Murphy observes that 'where intersubjective concerns have been discussed the focus has very often been on power: namely, the asymmetry between interviewer and interviewee'.[31] For Tooth Murphy, although it is vital to remain mindful of ethical considerations, focus on the power asymmetry between interviewer and interviewee (or in my case, researcher and participant) is oversimplified and fails to capture the nuanced relationship between the two actors.[32] As I also argue, the asymmetric exchange between

[26] Stephan Scheel, 'Biopolitical Bordering: Enacting Populations as Intelligible Objects of Government', *European Journal of Social Theory* 23, no. 4 (26 January 2020): 2.
[27] Law, 'Seeing Like a Survey', 239–40.
[28] Spade, *Normal Life*, 11.
[29] Ibid., 6.
[30] See Lynn Abrams, *Oral History Theory* (Abingdon: Routledge, 2010), 582; Sherna Berger Gluck and Daphne Patai, eds., *Women's Words: The Feminist Practice of Oral History* (New York: Routledge, 1991).
[31] Amy Tooth Murphy, 'Listening In, Listening Out: Intersubjectivity and the Impact of Insider and Outsider Status in Oral History Interviews', *Oral History* 48, no. 1 (2020): 3.
[32] Ibid., 4.

participants and researchers should encourage us to reconsider what each brings to data collection practices, what they leave behind and what leaves with them. I am particularly interested in how the collection of data *about* LGBTQ people operates at a micro level, and shapes how individuals make sense of their identities and their position in larger groups. For example, how does it feel for a trans person to complete a government survey that asks about their perceptions as someone who is trans? How does participation in a focus group on the experiences of lesbian Christians impact an individual's experience as a lesbian Christian? These examples show how data collection methods can encourage research participants to consider their identities in new ways.

My research in UK universities often involved studies where researchers collected data from participants in exchange for some type of incentive, such as a gift voucher. Although material incentives recognized the labour of participants and helped address barriers to participation, I was intrigued by the potential for research into EDI topics to function as a form of EDI work in itself. To better explain this idea, I want to return to the example of the gender, sex and sexuality staff survey, discussed earlier in the chapter, and introduce a participant called Nasir, a twenty-four-year-old closeted bisexual man.[33] Following the all-staff survey, the university supplemented data with additional one-to-one interviews to capture perceptions and experiences from a cross-section of staff. Nasir reluctantly volunteered to take part as he felt confident that the method of a semi-structured interview would present an opportunity to tell his story with no pressure to give right or wrong answers. Nasir used this encounter to speak from the heart and share feelings that he had never previously spoken out loud. In this private moment, the researcher was invited into Nasir's world. With this invitation came responsibility, as it became the researcher's role to tell Nasir's story accurately. By sharing his experiences, Nasir started to join the dots between emotions and events. A constellation of information coalesced in a way that clarified for Nasir his identity as bisexual. The researcher stuck to the interview script, they did not coax or elicit information. They simply presented a safe space for Nasir to voice his private feelings.

Although this example of Nasir is hypothetical, researchers investigating EDI topics will know many real-life Nasirs, where data collection methods

---

[33] Although based on previous experiences in research projects, the example of Nasir is fictional to ensure the anonymity of participants.

have presented participants with a reflexive opportunity to consider their identities in new ways. Catherine Connell asks, 'Can an interview change a life?' and reflects on her experience of conducting a one-to-one interview that emboldened a participant to come out as a lesbian to colleagues and their twelve-year-old daughter.[34] Connell described this turn of events as a 'reality of field and interview methods that we should do more to grapple with rather than simply ignore or wish away'.[35] When research is well-designed and does not involve leading questions or planting thoughts in the heads of participants, the collection of data about LGBTQ people can make participants feel recognized in ways that initiate monumental changes in their everyday lives.

Data collection methods can inform and shape how LGBTQ participants make sense of their own identities. They can also impact researchers undertaking these studies.[36] In Chapter 7, I explore the reflexive dimension of queer data, where researchers critically assess what biases and assumptions they bring to their studies. As with participants, a researcher's identity characteristics and how they relate to others are not fixed. For example, Alison Rooke describes how her research into a lesbian support group changed as, during the study, her identity as a lesbian became more fluid after she started a relationship with a transgender man.[37] The practice of conducting research, and engaging with participants, can also affect the views, attitudes and feelings of those leading the study. Tina Fetner and Melanie Heath report their experiences of researching anti-LGBT activism. They describe 'the emotional toll of repeated interactions with people who express anti-LGBT beliefs' and how 'the hurtful words we hear may cause discomfort or even pain'.[38] This back-and-forth has the potential to transform the lives of

---

[34] Catherine Connell, 'Thank You for Coming Out Today: The Queer Discomfort of In-Depth Interviewing', in Other, Please Specify: Queer Methods in Sociology, ed. D'Lane Compton, Tey Meadow, and Kristen Schilt (University of California Press, 2018), 133–4.

[35] Ibid., 135.

[36] For a more detailed discussion, the edited collection Out in the Field discusses the experiences of anthropologists undertaking research into sexualities and how this work can implicate researchers in the subject of their studies, in Ellen Lewin and William L. Leap, eds., Out in the Field: Reflections of Lesbian and Gay Anthropologists (Urbana: University of Illinois Press, 1996).

[37] Alison Rooke, 'Queer in the Field: On Emotions, Temporality and Performativity in Ethnography', in Queer Methods and Methodologies, ed. Kath Browne and Catherine J. Nash (Farnham: Ashgate, 2010), 25.

[38] Tina Fetner and Melanie Heath, 'Studying the "Right" Can Feel Wrong: Reflection on Anti-LGBT Movements', in Other, Please Specify: Queer Methods in Sociology, ed. D'Lane Compton, Tey Meadow, and Kristen Schilt (University of California Press, 2018), 149.

participants and researchers in both positive and negative ways. And, like the subjects of their studies, the collection of gender, sex and sexuality data can leave researchers forever changed.

Queer data ethics

This chapter has addressed two overlapping threads related to the collection of data: the 'reality' of what collection methods can uncover and the impact of these methods on the data collected, participants and researchers. Although a back-and-forth exists between participants and researchers, the relationship is not one of equals. Once collected, researchers can use (or fail to use) data in ways that do nothing to improve the lives and experiences of LGBTQ people. For example, Emilia Lombardi highlights the issue of researchers entering trans communities and extracting data about the people they meet, yet failing to use this data in ways that benefit those involved 'aside from providing academics with fodder for publications and promotions'.[39] As a result of this one-sided approach, Jennifer L. Glick et al. observe research fatigue among gender-minority communities as participation in studies often fails to result in any perceptible change for the community under investigation.[40]

A particular issue relates to the collection and presentation of 'good data', which documents positive change over time such as a reduction in the gender pay gap, as a celebration of success. In the majority of cases, the elevation of 'good data' – from a means to achieve an objective to an objective in its own right – is not a conscious attempt to obfuscate the existence of EDI challenges within an organization. Yet, this is a problem in UK universities where well-intentioned projects lose sight of their purpose and become obsessed with fixing the numbers. Rather than ask, 'How can we change the institution to make it more equitable?' the driving motivation becomes, 'What data will present the institution in a positive light?' There is clearly a role for the collection, analysis and presentation of data to help understand EDI challenges and identify where to target resources to fix problems.

[39] Emilia Lombardi, 'Trans Issues in Sociology: A Trans-Centred Perspective', in *Other, Please Specify: Queer Methods in Sociology*, ed. D'Lane Compton, Tey Meadow, and Kristen Schilt, (University of California Press, 2018), 73.
[40] Jennifer L. Glick et al., 'For Data's Sake: Dilemmas in the Measurement of Gender Minorities', *Culture, Health & Sexuality* 20, no. 12 (2 December 2018): 1371.

Quantifying a problem is often a prerequisite for action. There is also a place for good news stories. Writing about the collection of gender, sex and sexuality data in the United States, Kyle Velte reminds us, 'Stories matter. Stories mobilize movements. Stories attract allies.'[41] Problems emerge when numbers command the entire narrative and fail to bring to life the human stories behind the statistics. People are not numbers. Numbers only present a method for us to simplify and represent the social world. When the sole purpose of data collection becomes the location and presentation of 'good data' we find ourselves with data that is little more than a hollow shell. When cracked-open, these shells contain nothing but abstract numbers detached from people with real lives and experiences.

There is also an ethical dimension to the collection of data that does nothing to positively impact the lives of those about whom the data relates. Returning to the example of the research participant Nasir, he took a risk by participating in the survey and follow-up interview. Participants often share perceptions and experiences never previously discussed (in Nasir's situation, he came out as bisexual). When people participate in research related to EDI they give a piece of themselves to the work. They grant you access into their world. There is therefore an onus on the researcher to do something meaningful with the data collected. When data shared is not used for action, or even worse left unanalysed on a hard drive or cloud server, it benefits nobody and risks discouraging future participation in research projects.

A one-to-one interview can present a unique and personal experience for both participant and researcher. When conducted effectively, an interview can go beyond a call and response and offer an exchange of perceptions and experiences that links those involved to wider social contexts. This is the ideal. However, what happens in instances where the researcher (assessing available evidence) and participant (evoking their perceptions and experiences) disagree? For example, data from a staff survey might highlight a major issue with homophobia and transphobia among senior leaders in an organization but this is contradicted by qualitative data from LGBTQ staff who regularly engage with senior leaders and report no issues whatsoever. Gaps between perceptions and experiences often emerge when quantitative statistics clash with qualitative testimonies. They are also sometimes the product of environments where

---

[41] Kyle Velte, 'Straightwashing the Census', *Boston College Law Review* 61, no. 1 (29 January 2020): 108–10.

data is collected. Organizational contexts – whether in the public, private or voluntary sector – are not neutral and can foster cultures that police how participants engage in research, and therefore impact the data collected. This is particularly the case in research that involves the collection of data about bullying and harassment. Participants might feel unable to share their authentic experiences due to fears of repercussions or a sense that they are somehow to blame for the situation they wish to report. Individuals that wish to dissuade complaints being made against them might also use exploitative techniques. Gaslighting, for example, involves the manipulation of complainants so that they question the reality of their experiences and second-guess their memories. An accusation of homophobic bullying is a very serious claim and the suggestion that the accused said 'maggot' rather than 'faggot', in the heat of an expletive-filled outburst, might lodge a nugget of doubt in the complainant's head. This can fester, bring them to doubt themselves and dissuade them from pursuing the complaint.

I raise these points to further problematize the objectivity of data collected and show how, particularly in organizational contexts, we attach different weights and values to people's perceptions and experiences. Can research join the dots in situations where participants present positive perceptions (for example, 'I wholeheartedly believe my organisation operates gender-equal recruitment policies') that contradict quantitative data (for example, a disproportionate gap between the number of female applicants and the number of women appointed)? What happens when participants' perceptions and researchers' data disagree? It seems unethical for a researcher to tell participants how they *should* feel about issues in their organization that might negatively impact them. Yet, this ethical position sits uncomfortably with the notion of EDI research as a space for consciousness-raising where ideas not only flow from participant to researcher but also from researcher to participant.

Disputes are less likely to emerge when researchers select the right method(s) to answer their research questions. My research in higher education confirmed to me that quantitative methods, which only collect numerical data, can only tell one side of the story. Alongside numbers, those investigating topics related to EDI also had to understand how things felt for different staff and students. These insights emerged best from qualitative data on how people perceived situations and, in turn, how they were perceived by others. Framing quantitative and qualitative data as opposing sources of evidence therefore suggests a false account of how people experience racism, misogyny, ableism, homophobia and transphobia in their everyday lives.

Rather than construct a hierarchy of data collection methods, a project's research questions should determine the approach followed: for example, if you want to learn about homophobia in the workplace, use methods that will best provide information about homophobia in the workplace. Where possible, the triangulation of data from multiple methods is recommended. This involves using two or more collection methods and combining data during analysis. For example, an all-staff survey followed by a series of one-to-one interviews with a sample of survey respondents. By triangulating data collected from both quantitative and qualitative methods, this helps address the limitations of any one approach.

* * *

Researchers, practitioners and activists engage in the collection of data *about* LGBTQ people for a variety of reasons. This chapter has explored decisions made at the start of a research project about the selection of collection methods, what methods can tell us about the lives and experiences of LGBTQ people, and the role of methods in constructing the phenomena they claim to observe. My account of surveys, interviews and focus groups challenges the view that static LGBTQ communities exist waiting to be counted. Instead, identity characteristics are 'moving targets' where data is shaped during the collection process as it makes the journey from participant to researcher. Sharing examples from my work in higher education, I noted how intersubjective data collection practices can offer participants an opportunity to re-evaluate their identity, join the dots between emotions and events, and raise consciousness about issues such as homophobia and transphobia. For researchers, the collection of data can similarly highlight the fluidity of their identity characteristics and change their views, attitudes and feelings about the topic under investigation.

The collection of data *about* LGBTQ people involves an ethical obligation to ensure data collected is used to meaningfully impact the lives about whom the data relates. I have described how this ethical dimension is sometimes forgotten as those working with data lose sight of the actual topic under investigation. In organizations driven by metrics and key performance indicators, the collection of data can become focused on the collection of 'good data'. Over time, EDI work is transformed so that the purpose becomes to 'fix the data' rather than the problems the data was originally intended to represent.

Queer data upends assumptions about what data collected *about* LGBTQ people can tell us. Researchers rightly seek robust and reliable data that presents, as far as possible, an authentic account of the social world. Yet, the methods used to collect data are flawed and present an (inaccurate) representation of a social world that includes some people at the expense of others. Does this matter? I opened this chapter with a description of my role in the production of data about transphobia that, although unlikely to change the situation, recorded that something was wrong. An awareness of failure provides a basis for change. I therefore intend to continue to register my complaints, create data that documents injustice and inequality and share evidence so that those with the power to fix the situation feel pressured to take action.

CHAPTER 3
QUEER THE CENSUS: SEX, SEXUAL ORIENTATION AND TRANS QUESTIONS IN SCOTLAND'S CENSUS

What does a census do? We hear a huge amount from politicians, campaign groups and the media about the importance of completing the census but less frequently do we hear arguments about why they are conducted, what they *actually* tell us about a country and its residents, and their impact on the people they intend to count. In the UK, three separate censuses take place every ten years in England and Wales, Scotland and Northern Ireland. These censuses capture information on a range of topics including individuals' identity characteristics, their employment and daily commute, the types of housing where people stay and how their homes are heated.[1] Unlike data collection methods that capture information about a sample of the population (such as household surveys, which collect data from a small proportion of households and then extrapolate these results to establish a national picture), censuses aim to collect data about *everyone* within a population. Although this is never quite fully achieved, the collection of population-level data means that censuses initiate nationwide conversations about who to include and exclude from the count. However, as with other approaches to quantitative data collection, the appearance of neutrality associated with censuses also hides a catalogue of choices about the design of questions, who makes decisions and who is considered a legible data subject in the eyes of the state. These deliberations are particularly pertinent as 2021 and 2022 mark a milestone for LGBTQ inclusion in UK censuses. For the first time, the 2021 English and Welsh census included voluntary questions about an individual's sexual orientation and gender identity. The 2021 Northern Irish census also included a question about sexual orientation. The Scottish census, which was postponed until 2022 due to the Covid-19

---

[1] For questions asked in Scotland's 2022 census, see National Records of Scotland, 'Question Set', Scotland's Census, 20 July 2020.

pandemic, also asks questions about respondents' sexual orientation and trans status/history. Although this moment heralded a victory for LGBTQ campaign groups, who had long fought for representation in national data collection exercises, it also posed the question, 'Who do we *actually* count when we count LGBTQ people?'

This chapter explores issues related to the design of question stems, response options and supplementary guidance for the questions on sex, sexual orientation and trans status/history in Scotland's census. It considers the approach of the body responsible for the census, National Records of Scotland, as well as the arguments of campaign groups that supported and opposed the proposed changes. Adding or changing a census question is a detailed and lengthy process, which can involve multiple design iterations, rounds of research and testing, consultations with stakeholders and parliamentary scrutiny. In Scotland, this work was overseen by the Scottish Parliament's Culture, Tourism, Europe and External Affairs Committee, designated as the lead committee scrutinizing legislation related to the census. The passage of the Census (Amendment) (Scotland) Bill through the Scottish Parliament, and its scrutiny by the CTEEA Committee, left behind a trail of evidence that provides insights into decisions made and the uneasy relationship between state-organized data practices and LGBTQ identities.

I was not a neutral participant in these events. I used research to support the work of LGBTQ organizations fighting to ensure questions reflected how LGBTQ people wished to be counted.[2] I wrote policy briefs and disseminated them among Members of the Scottish Parliament, communicated with MSPs on the CTEEA Committee and blogged about developments related to the design of the census. Although it is too early to assess the impact of collecting sexual orientation and trans data, we should not overlook the magnitude of this development. For the first time in the UK, a nationally representative count of people who identify as LGBTQ will exist. Yet, as with the collection of data on identity characteristics in general, the publication of data is not an endpoint in itself. Data only becomes meaningful when it is used to take action that impacts the lives of real people. Furthermore, rather than focus on the battles won, we must equally consider what was lost along the way and ensure that the complexity, nuance and diversity of LGBTQ lives

---

[2] The main LGBTQ organizations involved in discussions related to the census in Scotland include the Equality Network, the Scottish Trans Alliance, LGBT Youth Scotland and Stonewall Scotland.

are not flattened through the addition of questions about sexual orientation and trans status/history to the census.

Assembling knowledge about Scotland's LGBTQ population

As a national data collection exercise, the undertaking of a census brings with it all the machinery of state power. Before the Covid-19 pandemic, the UK's censuses were estimated to cost more than £1 billion.[3] Research projects of this scale cannot take place in the shadows. As the accuracy of a census relies on widespread public participation, the more people engaged in the process, the easier it becomes for the state to present results as representative of the population. More so than other pieces of research, census data is framed by governments and policymakers as raw and objective information that reveals itself to society devoid of political biases.[4] A census therefore not only claims to present a reflection of reality but provides a method for the state to construct knowledge about its population.

This is not simply a case of knowledge for knowledge's sake. Greater knowledge of a population can enhance the disciplinary powers of the state, such as shaping data practices and approaches that govern norms and the borders of data possibilities. Expanding on this idea and building on the work of Foucault, Bruce Curtis has described the lack of examination of how Foucault's concept of governmentality applies in real-world contexts.[5] Ruppert has also noted how Foucault's work on the management, regulation and maximization of populations 'did not investigate the specific practices that make it possible to know and then act upon populations'.[6] Scheel, in an attempt to address this omission, discusses the application of these technologies and how they are contingent on bordered sites, a concept Scheel describes as 'biopolitical bordering'.[7] McDermott has also noted how statistics about LGB people can facilitate governance in multiple ways: most obviously by informing the design of state interventions but

[3] Larry Elliott, 'Household Census May Be Scrapped in Favour of Cheaper System', *The Guardian*, 11 February 2020.
[4] Browne, 'Queer Quantification or Queer(y)Ing Quantification', 32.
[5] Bruce Curtis, 'Foucault on Governmentality and Population: The Impossible Discovery', *The Canadian Journal of Sociology/Cahiers Canadiens de Sociologie* 27, no. 4 (2002): 505–33.
[6] Evelyn Ruppert, 'Population Objects: Interpassive Subjects', *Sociology* 45, no. 2 (April 2011): 219.
[7] Scheel, 'Biopolitical Bordering'.

also by shaping a 'neo-liberal sexual citizenship' through which 'sexually diverse people come to understand and regulate themselves'.[8] Considering the Scottish census through these theoretical lenses, where the census is not a neutral representation of reality but a tool to construct a governable population, raises questions as to whether the census is an exercise in knowledge construction or a tool to bolster the state's capacity to manage its population. These two objectives are not exclusive: improved knowledge likely facilitates the design of more efficient ways to coerce, control and discipline people who live within a state's jurisdiction. However, if the construction of knowledge is no longer the primary purpose of a census, this throws into doubt the need for a census to collect accurate information that authentically represents the lives and experiences of the people about whom the data relates.

When we challenge the primacy of the census as an exercise in knowledge construction, new considerations emerge as to the purpose of asking questions about individuals' sexual orientation and trans status/history. In Scotland, the census asks an increasing number of questions about sex, age, nationality, ethnicity, religion, health and impairments, sexual orientation and trans status/history. A critic might ask 'What business does the state have knowing these details about my life?' This question raises important issues about where we draw the border between public and private lives, and potential motives that lie behind the state's desire to collect data about identity characteristics.

Throughout most of the twentieth-century, discussions about LGBTQ lives and experiences in Scotland were perceived as 'personal affairs' or 'matters of the bedroom'.[9] Likewise, in their review of European surveys that captured data on sexual orientation, Schönpflug et al. found that 'data-generating and data-clearing procedures are influenced by heteronormative presumptions about families or parenthood' and 'also protective motives concerning the private sphere of LGB(TI)Qs'.[10] The cocooning of LGTBQ experiences in the private sphere dented their political capital and justified their omission from data collection exercises. In the rare instances where data about sexual orientation or gender diversity was discussed at all, it

---

[8] McDermott, '"Counting" for Equality: Youth, Class and Sexual Citizenship', 52.
[9] For an in-depth account of public discourse about male homosexuality in late-twentieth-century Scotland, see Jeffrey Meek, *Queer Voices in Post-War Scotland: Male Homosexuality, Religion and Society* (London: Palgrave Macmillan, 2015).
[10] Schönpflug et al., 'If Queers Were Counted', 22.

mainly concerned health inequalities and, from the 1980s onwards, focused on the HIV/AIDS epidemic.[11] The border between public and private knowledge has since shifted. In particular, social media has revolutionized the environments in which LGBTQ young people negotiate their public and private selves, and manage the disclosure of their identities.[12] LGBTQ people therefore find themselves at a crossroads: individuals appear more willing to share personal data about their gender, sex and sexuality, censuses now provide respondents with the opportunity to share this data, yet the motives that lie behind censuses might mean that LGBTQ participation facilitates a project that expands the powers of the state rather than illustrates an accurate account of the social world. With the addition of sexual orientation and trans questions to the census, it may seem like LGBTQ people are belatedly invited to a party from which they have historically been excluded. This historical moment, however, also presents a double-edged sword. Those in charge of the census can design collection methods to locate data that confirms identities they wish to bring into being. Improvements to the census tend to involve the addition of new questions or provision of more detailed response options rather than a fundamental overhaul of the knowledge that governs how identities are conceptualized in the census. At the same time, as this chapter will discuss, collection methods can ensure that particular identities, or ways of thinking about identity, are designed out of the process in ways that further compound the invisibility of the most marginalized among LGBTQ people.

Sex question

Having outlined some critical challenges to censuses and their potential incongruity with a queer approach to data, I now turn attention to consider the design of three questions in Scotland's census. My emphasis here moves from the general to the specific. Although my geographical focus is narrow, the themes presented stretch beyond Scotland and apply to the collection of gender, sex and sexuality data in other national contexts.

---

[11] Ibid., 9–10.
[12] Elizabeth McConnell et al., "'Everybody Puts Their Whole Life on Facebook': Identity Management and the Online Social Networks of LGBTQ Youth', *International Journal of Environmental Research and Public Health* 15, no. 6 (26 May 2018): 1078.

We cannot fully understand the addition of sexual orientation and trans questions without first discussing the census question on sex. The Scottish census has asked a question about sex since it was first conducted in 1801. It is the only compulsory identity question in the census that requires respondents to select one of two binary options and roughly splits the population in half (according to the 2011 census, 51.5 per cent of the population were female and 48.5 per cent were male).[13] The sex question has remained unchanged and is identical across all parts of the UK:

What is your sex?
Female
Male

As part of the preparation for the next census, NRS commissioned two research companies (Ipsos MORI and ScotCen Social Research) to test whether a non-binary sex question would affect how people complete the census and any potential impacts on response rates. Ipsos MORI and ScotCen concluded that the provision of non-binary response options was not more likely to invite inappropriate answers nor negatively affect people's likelihood to respond.[14] Although little research has been conducted internationally into the effects of providing or not providing a non-binary response option in survey questions, the findings of Ipsos MORI and ScotCen mirrored a 2020 study of general-population surveys in the United States, Canada and Sweden, which concluded that the use of non-binary response options did not evoke negative reactions from respondents.[15] In light of their findings, NRS proposed to change the sex question in Scotland's next census so that it presented three response options: male, female and other, with a write-in box. NRS argued that the introduction of a non-binary sex question would enable people who neither identify exclusively as male nor female to accurately record themselves in the national count.

Around the same time NRS published the results of their research, the Census (Amendment) (Scotland) Bill was introduced to the Scottish

---

[13] National Records of Scotland, 'Population and Households', Scotland's Census, 2018.
[14] National Records of Scotland, 'Sex and Gender Identity Topic Report', Scotland's Census 2021 (Edinburgh, 2018).
[15] Mike Medeiros, Benjamin Forest, and Patrik Öhberg, 'The Case for Non-Binary Gender Questions in Surveys', *PS: Political Science & Politics* 53, no. 1 (January 2020): 128.

Parliament to allow for the addition of two new questions on sexual orientation and trans status/history.[16] During the Bill's stage one reading, the Convener of the CTEEA Committee (Scottish National Party politician Joan McAlpine MSP) outlined her opposition to the inclusion of a non-binary sex question and noted that, following a vote on the proposal, the committee recommended maintaining a binary sex question in the next census. McAlpine described how the committee had voted 'by a majority, that the sex question should remain binary in order to maximise response rates'.[17] However, this explanation was at odds with findings from research commissioned by NRS.[18] When we consider the findings from Ipsos MORI and ScotCen's research alongside McAlpine's explanation for why the sex question should remain binary, a tension becomes apparent between the collection of census data as an exercise in knowledge construction versus the creation and/or protection of identity categories that align with pre-existing ideas that 'make sense' to those in positions of power.

Debate over whether the census should include non-binary response options was only the first flurry of activity related to the design of the sex question. Focus moved from the wording of the question and response options to consider the provision of supplementary guidance. This guidance, made available to census respondents on request, is intended to help people understand how they should answer the question. As with all other identity characteristics, the definition of sex is contested. Yet, the design of guidance for how respondents should answer the census question on sex attracted a disproportionate deal of scrutiny from women's organizations,

---

[16] The Census (Amendment) (Scotland) Bill was introduced to the Scottish Parliament on 2 October 2018, for further information on its passage through parliament, see Scottish Parliament, 'Census (Amendment) (Scotland) Bill', 18 July 2019.

[17] Scottish Parliament, 'Stage One Debate on the Census (Amendment) (Scotland) Bill' (Edinburgh, 28 February 2019).

[18] Ipsos MORI's research involved surveys with binary and non-binary sex questions being sent to 15,579 individuals at randomly selected residential addresses in Scotland. They found that 'the inclusion of the non-binary question does not significantly increase the level of item non-response in comparison to the binary sex question' and that 'regardless of the version of the sex/gender identity question received by respondents, there was no evidence of invalidating or tampering with these questions in Scotland', in National Records of Scotland, 'Sex and Gender Identity Topic Report', 45. Furthermore, ScotCen undertook quantitative testing to assess whether respondents understood and could answer a non-binary sex question. ScotCen's research found that less than 1 per cent of respondents stated that they had found the non-binary sex question difficult to answer, described in National Records of Scotland, 'Cognitive and Quantitative Testing', Scotland's Census 2021 (Edinburgh, 2017), 74.

LGBTQ groups, researchers and academics, politicians and the media.[19] In Scotland, the government ultimately agreed on guidance that, although vague, continued the practice of past censuses where respondents are advised to answer according to how they self-identify (as is the approach with all other census questions about identity characteristics). Although this decision angered campaign groups and researchers that sought to exclude trans women from data collected about women, self-identification guidance aligned with NRS's approach to other census questions and meant that the state, as far as possible, did not involve itself in the business of defining the borders of identity characteristics.[20]

In England and Wales, the issue of the census sex guidance ended up in the High Court. In February 2021, the ONS confirmed its guidance for the 2021 English and Welsh census, which explained: 'If you are considering how to answer, use the sex recorded on one of your legal documents such as a birth certificate, gender recognition certificate, or passport.'[21] To explain what informed the design of the guidance, the ONS shared their workings and noted that they had identified five concepts of sex that a census *could* collect data about: sex as registered at birth, sex as recorded on a birth certificate, sex as recorded on legal/official documents, sex as living/presenting and sex as self-identified.[22] Following an assessment of whether each concept would maximize census responses and ensure that any invasion of privacy was justified, the ONS ultimately concluded that 'sex as recorded on legal/official documents' was the best option for the 2021 census (although their study found that the concept 'sex as living/presenting' actually had a less negative impact on the census).[23] Outraged that the census intended to advise trans respondents to answer according to their sex on official documents (such

---

[19] See Martin Williams, 'Academics Urge MSPs Not to Change Census Sex Question', *The Herald*, 20 September 2019; Katie McQuater, 'Census Sex Question Guidance Could "Undermine Data Reliability"', Say Academics', *Research Live*, 16 December 2019.

[20] For example, see Lucy Hunter Blackburn, 'Sex Question Should Stick to Birth Certificate', *The Scotsman*, 15 September 2019; Sarah Ward, 'Academics Criticise Scotland's 2021 Census for Allowing Sex to Be Self-Identified', *The Scotsman*, 26 December 2019.

[21] Office for National Statistics, 'Final Guidance for the Question "What Is Your Sex?"', Census 2021, 12 February 2021.

[22] Helena Rosiecka, 'Methodology for Decision Making on the 2021 Census Sex Question Concept and Associated Guidance' (Office for National Statistics, 10 February 2021), 2.

[23] In the social sciences, scholars have noted that research is rarely interested in phenomena related to 'physiological or bodily aspects' of sex or legal concepts of gender but 'how individuals identify or express themselves from a social perspective', Lindqvist, Sendén, and Renström, 'What Is Gender, Anyway', 10.

as a passport, which may not align with the sex on an individual's birth certificate), campaign group Fair Play for Women took the ONS to court to demand that guidance was changed to remove the words 'such as' and 'or passport' so that respondents were advised to answer according to the sex recorded on their birth certificate or GRC.[24] The ONS chose not to defend their position and the guidance was revised on 9 March 2021, more than two weeks after the census had gone live.

The High Court case was never intended to alter how cis respondents (estimated to be around 99 per cent of the population) answer the sex question, as the provision of different guidance made no difference.[25] Rather, the intention of the case was to police how trans respondents without a GRC participate in the census. This example highlights a tension between (imperfect) evidence based decision-making, undertaken by statistical and research organizations, and crowdfunded legal challenges that can quickly undo months if not years of detailed research. Although unlikely to alter the tally of females and males in the 2021 English and Welsh census, confidence in organizations like the ONS to capture data about gender, sex and sexuality – in ways that are inclusive and representative of people's everyday lives – was likely damaged by the unfolding of events around the sex guidance.

Sexual orientation question

Unlike the sex question, the sexual orientation and trans questions are only completed by respondents aged sixteen and over. Respondents are unable to select multiple options and, although the question is voluntary, a 'Prefer not to say' response option is not provided.[26] There are many ways to collect data about sexual orientation. Scholars have noted how the concept of sexual orientation is an overarching descriptor for different, though related,

---

[24] Alexandra Topping, 'Guidance on Sex Question in Census Must Be Changed, High Court Rules', *The Guardian*, 9 March 2021.

[25] Government Equalities Office, 'National LGBT Survey', 14.

[26] Unlike skipping a question or leaving an answer blank, the provision of a 'Prefer not to say' option explicitly recognizes respondents' decision to refuse to disclose information, for whatever reason. I discuss the importance of recognizing those who refuse to disclose data in Chapter 8.

concepts including sexual identity, attraction and behaviour.[27] We can consider these dimensions, as follows:

- **Sexual identity:** how a person thinks of their sexuality and the identity terms with which they identify.

- **Sexual attraction:** sexual (and/or romantic) feelings towards one specific sex or gender, more than one sex or gender, or no-one.

- **Sexual behaviour:** whether someone has sexual partners of another sex or gender, the same sex or gender, or refrain from sexual behaviour.

Using survey data from the UK, Geary et al. show how the size of minority sexual orientations can vary depending on what dimension of sexual orientation is asked about. For example, while 6.5 per cent of men and 11.5 per cent of women reported some experience of same-sex attraction, only 2.5 per cent of men and 2.4 per cent of women identified as lesbian, gay or bisexual.[28] Geary et al.'s findings were similar to those reported in a 2019 study of sexual orientation data collected among Organisation for Economic Co-operation and Development member countries, which highlighted how use of 'sexual identity' as a measurement for sexual orientation was an inaccurate proxy for those with experience of same-sex attraction and/or behaviour. The OECD report noted, 'The size of the LGB population is 70 per cent larger when it is calculated based on individuals' sexual behaviour (instead of individuals' sexual self-identification), and more than twice as large when sexual attraction is taken as a criteria.'[29] McDermott has also argued that the use of fixed categories to capture data on sexual diversity is most effective as a measure for 'more privileged LGB people', with studies showing the limitations of this approach particularly among younger people and people of colour.[30]

The Scottish Parliament's CTEEA Committee did not review the dimensions of sexual orientation captured by the census question, though this topic had been investigated at length by the ONS in discussions about

---

[27] Rebecca Geary et al., 'Sexual Identity, Attraction and Behaviour in Britain', 2; Emma Mishel, 'Intersections between Sexual Identity, Sexual Attraction, and Sexual Behavior among a Nationally Representative Sample of American Men and Women', *Journal of Official Statistics* 35, no. 4 (1 December 2019): 859; Westbrook, Budnick, and Saperstein, 'Dangerous Data', 3.
[28] Rebecca Geary et al., 'Sexual Identity, Attraction and Behaviour in Britain', 5.
[29] Organisation for Economic Co-operation and Development, *Society at a Glance 2019: OECD Social Indicators* (Paris: OECD Publishing, 2019), 17.
[30] McDermott, '"Counting" for Equality: Youth, Class and Sexual Citizenship', 45, 49, 50.

whether to ask a sexual orientation question in the 2011 censuses.[31] Of sexual orientation's three dimensions, the question used in Scotland's census most closely aligns with the concept of 'sexual identity':

Which of the following best describes your sexual orientation?
Straight/Heterosexual
Gay or Lesbian
Bisexual
Other sexual orientation, please write in ...

As a data collection exercise that asks people to self-identify their identity characteristics and is chiefly interested in how people's experiences differ by sexual orientation, asking only about sexual identity seems like a logical decision. However, in narrowing the information captured about sexual identity, the census will not count people who do not identify as 'gay or lesbian' or 'bisexual' but have experience of same-sex attraction or engage in same-sex behaviours.

During discussions about the design of the sexual orientation question, the Convener of the CTEEA Committee stressed the need for response options to map to identity labels used in the UK's 2010 Equality Act.[32] For example, the Equality Act describes sexual orientation as 'a person's sexual orientation towards (a) persons of the same sex, (b) persons of the opposite sex, or (c) persons of either sex.'[33] This definition draws a link between concepts of sex and sexuality, though the Equality Act does not present a definition of 'sex' aside from noting it is in 'reference to a man or to a woman'.[34] However, the committee's interest in mapping sexual orientation response options was misdirected as there is no requirement for the design of the census to align with the wording or language used in the Equality Act. Most questions in Scotland's census do not relate to identity characteristics

---

[31] Lucy Haseldon and Theodore Joloza, 'Measuring Sexual Identity: A Guide for Researchers' (Newport: Office for National Statistics, 2009). Also see, Sally McManus, 'Sexual Orientation Research Phase 1: A Review of Methodological Approaches' (Scottish Executive Social Research, 2003).
[32] Culture, Tourism, Europe and External Affairs Committee, 'Session 5 - Official Report of Meeting' (Edinburgh: Scottish Parliament, 9 January 2020), 31–2; Culture, Tourism, Europe and External Affairs Committee, 'Session 5 - Official Report of Meeting' (Edinburgh: Scottish Parliament, 30 January 2020), 44.
[33] Equality Act (2010), sec. 12.
[34] Equality Act, sec. 11.

and, even when we consider questions about characteristics protected in the Equality Act such as disability and religion, the language used does not mirror the coverage of the Equality Act.[35] Ultimately, the final list of sexual orientations agreed upon included an 'Other sexual orientation, please write in … ' option. LGBTQ organizations welcomed the provision of this option as it reflected their research, which found that between 10 to 20 per cent of people who engaged with their services used the 'write-in' box in diversity-monitoring exercises to describe their sexual orientation.[36]

The census asks people to describe aspects of their identity in terms that they use and understand. With this in mind, asking a question about sexual orientation that only covers the dimension of sexual identity is understandable. However, this decision has implications for 'who counts' as lesbian, gay, bisexual or queer and how data practices can bring into being particular ideas about LGBTQ identities. The design process can obscure subjective deliberations and provide a glaze of impartiality to practices that circumscribe the borders of data possibilities. Browne has noted how data collection exercises can reveal who, within the LGBTQ community, the state does and does not recognize as legible subjects. For Browne, 'It is important to question the privilege, and differential realisation, of who can become lesbian, gay or bisexual citizens, and the nuanced positioning of those who become intelligible and unintelligible within such discourses and regimes'.[37] Following the lines of scrutiny pursued (and not pursued) by the CTEEA Committee, the focus on one dimension of sexual orientation highlights how the census can fail to capture the nuances of LGBTQ lives and experiences. My critical account of the process further calls into question LGBTQ participation in a data collection exercise that we know does not fully reflect the diversity of LGBTQ people. At a statistical level,

---

[35] The census asks whether respondents' day-to-day activities are 'limited a lot' or 'limited a little' because of a health problem or disability, 'limited a little' falls outside of the protected characteristic of disability covered in the Equality Act. Furthermore, the census question about religion is narrower than the coverage in the Equality Act, which protects both religion and philosophical belief, discussed in Equality Network and LGBT Youth Scotland, 'Letter to Culture, Tourism, Europe and External Affairs Committee', 1 October 2019.

[36] See Equality Network and LGBT Youth Scotland. In addition, multiple studies have demonstrated the existence of sexual identities beyond lesbian, gay, bisexual and heterosexual/straight, discussed in Sari M. Van Anders, 'Beyond Sexual Orientation: Integrating Gender/Sex and Diverse Sexualities via Sexual Configurations Theory', *Archives of Sexual Behavior* 44, no. 5 (2015): 1177–213; Anthony Lyons et al., 'Toward Making Sexual and Gender Diverse Populations Count in Australia', *Australian Population Studies* 4, no. 2 (16 November 2020): 16.

[37] Browne, 'Queer Quantification or Queer(y)Ing Quantification', 248.

the census risks undercounting Scotland's LGBTQ population as many people are unable to participate or forced to identify in a way that does not accurately reflect who they are. Rather than representing a step forward for LGBTQ people, there is a risk that asking about sexual orientation in the census fortifies the borders of what it means to be LGBTQ.

Trans question

Scotland's census also asks a voluntary question about whether respondents identify as trans or as someone with a trans history. The term 'trans history' can refer to people who no longer identify as trans but were assigned a different sex at birth (in other words, they have transitioned). As with the question on sexual orientation, the trans question is only to be answered by those aged sixteen and over:

Do you consider yourself to be trans, or have a trans history?
No
Yes, please describe your trans status …

Supporting guidance explains that the term 'trans' describes 'people whose gender is not the same as the sex they were registered at birth'. As with all identity questions in the census, respondents were instructed to answer in line with how they self-identify (in other words, there is no requirement to hold a GRC). The trans question in Scotland differs from the question asked in England and Wales. Census respondents in England and Wales were asked:

Is the gender you identify with the same as your sex registered at birth?
Yes
No, enter gender identity …

The ONS describes the question as a gender identity question, although it only collects data about the gender of people whose gender differs from their sex registered at birth. Cis people, whose gender identity is the same as their sex registered at birth, must select the response option 'Yes' and are therefore unable to input additional text in the write-in box (for example, 'man' or 'woman'). The decision of NRS and the ONS to depart from a shared question was based on research conducted by the two national statistical offices. Stakeholder engagement conducted by NRS identified a preference for asking a direct question about whether someone identified as trans or had a trans history, and testing of a trans question confirmed it 'produces good quality data'.[38] Whereas community testing conducted by the ONS found that the trans question format was not well understood, with a higher level of understanding for a question about gender identity.[39] The questions asked in both the Scottish and English and Welsh censuses can be described as a one-step approach as they capture data about the trans population in a single question. This differs from a two-step approach, which asks two questions (one about sex at birth and one about current gender identity) to deduce who might identify as trans or gender diverse (discussed in more detail in Chapter 4).

Although the designs of the trans and gender identity questions in the Scottish, English and Welsh censuses differ, they both attempt to navigate the same ambition: avoid use of the term 'cis'. Other census questions, related to identity characteristics, ask respondents to select the option with which they most closely identify. Questions require respondents to confirm an identity (for example, 'I am white Scottish') rather than negate an identity (for example, 'I am *not* Scottish Indian'). The design of the trans and gender identity questions depart from this approach as they require the majority of respondents (those who identify as cis, estimated to be around 99 per cent of the population) to answer in a way that negates an identity ('I am *not* trans'). Ashley has noted how, in English, 'currently, no word exists in our vocabulary for the broad category which includes being trans and being cis'.[40] This means that 'whereas the gay-straight binary, which renders invisible bisexual, pansexual, and other queer people, can be avoided through discussions couched in terms of sexual orientation, no analogous notion exists in relation to trans and cis people'.[41] Ashley's analogy is helpful as heterosexual/straight, gay, lesbian and bisexual are four examples of identity characteristics that sit under the category of sexual orientation. If the census question on sexual orientation adopted the same format as the trans question, it would ask: 'Do you consider yourself to be gay, lesbian or bisexual, or have a gay, lesbian or bisexual history?' This approach avoids mentioning heterosexual/straight

---

[38] National Records of Scotland, 'Sex and Gender Identity Topic Report', 3, 9.
[39] Office for National Statistics, 'Sex and Gender Identity Question Development for Census 2021', 26 June 2020.
[40] Ashley, '"Trans" Is My Gender Modality: A Modest Terminological Proposal', 1.
[41] Ibid.

and thus solidifies its presence as the hidden default. I recognize that the term 'cis' is new for many people, and there is a risk that asking about cis in the census might jeopardize the quality of data returned.[42] However, looking forward, a question to differentiate cis and trans populations needs to adopt the same format as other census questions on identity to challenge the normalcy of cis experiences and begin to recognize the diversity of communities that exist under the trans umbrella.[43]

Use of the term 'cis' in the census was discussed at a meeting of the CTEEA Committee in January 2020. Although questions proposed for Scotland's census never included the term 'cis', a research report produced by NRS and shared ahead of the committee meeting noted that question testing had analysed responses from cis and trans participants separately. In response to the use of the term 'cis' in the research report, committee member Kenneth Gibson MSP described cisgender as a 'contested and politicised term to which many people object and with which many people are completely unfamiliar'.[44] Gibson explained, 'until six months ago, I had not heard the term and I did not realise that I was apparently "cisgender"'.[45] He questioned why the NRS cannot 'just use the words "man" and "woman"' and accused the organization of having 'its own agenda on the issue, regardless of what other people think'.[46] Campaign groups opposed to the inclusion of trans people in the census have also attempted to frame the trans question as a question about gender identity.[47] This slippage of language is not accidental.

---

[42] The Gender Identity in US Surveillance Group has highlighted that questions used in population-level surveys to identify minorities need to be phrased in ways that people in the majority group understand. The risk that cis respondents answer questions incorrectly and skew the count of trans people is described as a false positive error and can jeopardize the quality of data collected, in Gender Identity in US Surveillance Group, 'Best Practices for Asking Questions to Identify Transgender and Other Gender Minority Respondents on Population-Based Surveys' (Los Angeles: The Williams Institute, 2014), xv.

[43] Leslie W. Suen et al. describe how the redesign of questions used to capture data on trans/gender identity could offer a more detailed account of diversity among trans people, in Leslie W. Suen et al., 'What Sexual and Gender Minority People Want Researchers to Know about Sexual Orientation and Gender Identity Questions: A Qualitative Study', *Archives of Sexual Behavior* 49, no. 7 (October 2020): 2303.

[44] Culture, Tourism, Europe and External Affairs Committee, 'Session 5', 9 January 2020, 21.

[45] Ibid., 22.

[46] Ibid.

[47] For example, Kath Murray, Lucy Hunter Blackburn, and Lisa Mackenzie, '2021 Census: Assessment of the Guidance Proposed by the UK Census Authorities to Accompany the Sex Question', 7 February 2020, 2.

Efforts to present the new question as a question about gender promotes the falsehood that the census now asks one question about sex and one question about gender. High-profile figures in these debates, including the Convener of the CTEEA Committee, proposed that the sex question in the census explicitly ask about an individual's 'biological sex'.[48] The introduction of a compulsory question on 'biological sex' would require some trans respondents to out themselves and identify in a way that failed to reflect how they identify or were perceived in everyday life.[49]

Attempts to use the census to drive a wedge between concepts of gender and sex, and obscure the existence of cis identities, highlight troubling lessons for the collection of gender, sex and sexuality data in Scotland. The use of different questions in Scotland, England and Wales represents efforts to avoid use of the term 'cis' in the census. As a result, the vast majority of census respondents are required to negate their identity as trans ('I am *not* trans') rather than confirm their identity as cis ('I am cis'). Cis is not a concept without problems. Toby Beauchamp has described the emergence of the term 'cisgender' in the early 1990s to describe individuals with a 'non-transgender identity', yet this framing relied on an understanding of gender associated with biological foundations and rooted in time and space (in other words, an individual required a fixed point from which to transcend).[50] Also critical of the term 'cis', Che Gossett explains: 'In American society, black people have always been figured as gender transgressive.'[51] Although used as a practical term to describe 'non-trans' people, any attempt to universalize gender or sex experiences under a cis umbrella will likely default to the experiences of those least disadvantaged by existing structures (in Gossett's example, white people). As I have argued in earlier chapters, there is a need for those with normative identity characteristics to reflect on what they bring to the room. However, at the same time, we must all equally question the histories and limits of the language used to construct data collection methods so they are best equipped to tackle inequality and injustice.

---

[48] The Scottish Parliament, 'Meeting of the Parliament' (Edinburgh: The Scottish Parliament, 12 June 2019), 67.
[49] Sharon Cowan et al., 'Sex and Gender Equality Law and Policy: A Response to Murray, Hunter Blackburn and Mackenzie', *Scottish Affairs* Online (22 October 2020): 15.
[50] Toby Beauchamp, *Going Stealth: Transgender Politics and US Surveillance Practices* (Durham: Duke University Press, 2019), 11–12.
[51] Christina Ferraz, 'Queerstions: What Does Cisgender Mean?', *Philadelphia Magazine*, 8 July 2014.

LGBTQ participation in the census

Although I have presented a critical account of the sex, sexual orientation and trans questions in Scotland's census, I want to conclude by considering these discussions in terms of their impact on individuals' lives. The proportion of Scotland's population who identify as lesbian, gay, bisexual or trans in the census is likely to be small. The 2019 Scottish Government household survey estimated that around 2.3 per cent of Scotland's adult population identified as lesbian, gay, bisexual or a sexual orientation 'other' than heterosexual/straight and, in a 2018 report published by the GEO, between 0.35 per cent and 1 per cent of the UK population were estimated to identify as trans.[52] This means that any minor mistakes in the design of the census will likely have a disproportionately large impact on findings. It is therefore vital that the biases, assumptions and political manoeuvres that informed the design process are exposed.

In the years preceding the 2022 census in Scotland there was an upsurge in scrutiny directed towards LGBTQ people who were forced to justify their lives and experiences to cis and heterosexual/straight representatives, for example in evidence sessions at parliament and multiple consultation exercises.[53] The demand to provide evidence exacerbated a hostile environment for LGBTQ people, many of whom already experienced mental health problems, bullying and harassment, and homophobic, biphobic and/or transphobic abuse.[54] The participation of LGBTQ people in the census is therefore not a clear-cut issue. For example, with knowledge that the census has designed out particular identities (such as non-binary people), can LGBTQ people engage in the census without being seen to condone this erasure? We also know that the sexual orientation question does not account for dimensions of sexuality such as sexual attraction and behaviour – should LGBTQ people participate when this risks simplifying LGBTQ

---

[52] Scottish Government, 'Scotland's People Annual Report 2019' (Edinburgh, September 2020), 7; Government Equalities Office, 'National LGBT Survey', 14.

[53] As an example, the lines on enquiry pursued by members of the CTEEA Committee at their evidence session on 6 December 2018, Culture, Tourism, Europe and External Affairs Committee, 'Session 5 - Official Report of Meeting' (Edinburgh: The Scottish Parliament, 6 December 2018).

[54] See LGBT Youth Scotland, 'Life in Scotland for LGBT Young People: Analysis of the 2017 Survey for Lesbian, Gay, Bisexual and Transgender Young People' (Edinburgh, 2018), 6; Stonewall Scotland, 'School Report Scotland: The Experiences of Lesbian, Gay, Bi and Trans Young People in Scotland's Schools in 2017', 2017, 6.

experiences and undercounting the total population? Divergent approaches to the capture of data in Scotland, England and Wales may also mean that trans populations across the UK differ because of how questions were asked. In response to these concerns, it is helpful to remind ourselves how LGBTQ people might benefit from being counted. Velte, writing on the absence or erasure of LGBT people in data collection exercises in the United States, describes how this 'perpetuates a set of stereotypes that are deeply harmful to addressing LGBT equality [including] the stereotype that LGBT people are wealthy, as well as the stereotype that LGBT people only live in urban environments'.[55] Velte describes how this has the effect of blunting the need for LGBT-inclusive anti-discrimination laws as 'LGBT people are presumed to be doing well'.[56] Rather than position a critique of state data practices and the construction of an authentic LGBT population as competing priorities that cannot be bridged, Velte instead calls for a pragmatic approach where LGBT people engage in data collection exercises but remain attuned to their limitations and inherent dangers. For Velte, 'if the government is in the business of creating identity through data collection, and distributing life chances through those categorical identities, LGBT people should be a part of that regime'.[57] McDermott has similarly described a way forward that navigates the balance of benefits and harms that might result from the addition of new questions on sexual orientation to national censuses. McDermott explains how 'the desire to be "known" by the state will bring with it, possibly, a new set of institutions, procedures, analyses, policies and guidelines creating a specific form of power that has as its target the LGB population. It is for this reason that we must critically engage with the new surveying of sexual subjects, keeping at the forefront of our analyses the potential power of state knowledge'.[58] Echoing this sentiment, and with specific reference to the need for improved data on trans lives and experiences, Petra L. Doan argues, 'the urgent need for transgender access to safe bathrooms and social services, including medical care, justifies the act of counting'.[59] With particular attention to civil rights activism in the United States, knowing the number of people affected by changes to (or failure to

---

[55] Velte, 'Straightwashing the Census', 104.
[56] Ibid.
[57] Ibid., 124.
[58] McDermott, '"Counting" for Equality: Youth, Class and Sexual Citizenship', 46.
[59] Doan, 'To Count or Not to Count', 89.

change) legislation strengthens the case of those taking claims to court.[60] The census is therefore a mirror for how some groups identify themselves, present to others and operationalize identity characteristics to advance civil rights in the courts. The inclusion of LGBTQ people in the census is also a form of registration and fight-back against campaign groups who call for the exclusion and erasure of LGBTQ communities. Increased confidence among LGBTQ people to engage in the process, and disclose information about their identity characteristics, means that datasets become richer and better able to present a meaningful (although not comprehensive) picture of society.

* * *

What is the point of the census? Is its primary purpose to present a representative account of the social world (in all its messiness) or to collect tidy data (even if this data fails to present an accurate picture)? The census is a political project intended to create a type of population knowledge that imbues individuals with identities that are knowable, in other words they 'make sense' to those in positions of power, and governable. The value of a census is not found in what it tells us about individual respondents. Instead, its power is located in what it says about how identity groups slot into wider structures of power that are gendered, racialized and in-built with cis/heteronormative assumptions about ability, class, nationality and other identity characteristics. These objectives are not exclusive and, through a critical account of the census as an exercise in knowledge construction, we can more clearly see what happens to data about LGBTQ people in data collection exercises conducted by the state.

This chapter has presented an in-depth account of discussions involving NRS, the Scottish Parliament's CTEEA Committee and campaign groups related to the design of the sex, sexual orientation and trans questions in Scotland's 2022 census. My engagement in the design process, as a researcher working with LGBTQ organizations, helped me see beyond the neutrality associated with censuses and critically examine decisions made about the design of questions, the lines of scrutiny pursued (and not pursued) by figures in positions of power, and the question of who do we *actually* count when we count LGBTQ people. It is too soon to assess the impact of

---

[60] Velte, 'Straightwashing the Census'.

collecting sexual orientation and trans data in Scotland or consider whether data collected was used in meaningful ways to improve the lives of LGBTQ people. However, we should not lose sight of this moment in history. The census is a translation of the social world rather than a carbon copy. It is possible to celebrate these developments, reflect upon what was lost along the way and continue the fight to ensure that when LGBTQ people are counted in national data collection exercises they are represented authentically and in ways that affirm their lives and experiences.

CHAPTER 4
BEYOND BORDERS: QUEER DATA
AROUND THE WORLD

Wherever you are in the world, from the northern tip of the Scottish Highlands to the deserts of Western Australia, people are counted and decisions made based on what these results reveal. Counting people involves categories that include and exclude, transforming data into meaningful insights. When counting is used to make sense of who we are, in terms of individual and group identities, it can position some people on the 'inside' and some on the 'outside'. Although the methods used to count differ, a relationship exists between counting, inclusion and exclusion that stretches beyond national borders. This chapter explores the collection of gender, sex and sexuality data in contexts outside of the UK. It examines similarities and differences in approaches to provide an exchange of lessons for researchers, practitioners and activists. The curated examples presented in this chapter primarily focus on the capture of quantitative, population-level data (for example, censuses) or nationally representative surveys (for example, where data is weighted to address issues of under- or over-representation in the sample), where information was available in English. As with Chapter 1's investigation of gender, sex and sexuality data throughout history, the availability of sources, and my assumptions as to what to investigate, mean that some examples are brought into view while others are overlooked or not considered at all. I therefore present this chapter as a showcase of queer data from around the world, rather than a complete survey of contemporary data practices. The first half of this chapter provides an overview of thematic issues related to gender, sex and sexuality such as language and cultural differences, administrative practices, the provision of more response options and the collection of less data. Several countries have recently expanded, or are in the process of expanding, their collection of data about sexual orientation and trans/gender identity at a national level.[1] Changes to collection practices have

---

[1] For example, both Canada and Argentina ask questions about trans/gender identity in their 2021 censuses. New Zealand has also confirmed that its 2023 census will ask questions about sexual orientation and trans/gender identity.

entailed a proliferation of associated research, policy, legislation and media interest, which have created a wealth of information about opportunities and barriers encountered during the roll-out of new or adapted questions on gender, sex and sexuality. The second half of the chapter adopts a narrower focus and investigates particular developments in a sample of countries, including the collection of data about same-sex couples, hate crime and violence, and 'third gender' categories; the use of virtual censuses; and the adoption of a 'gender by default' approach to data collection.

Language, administrative practices and the collection of data

Around the world, data about LGBTQ people is unevenly distributed and overwhelmingly sparse. In 2019 the OECD reported that just fifteen of their thirty-six member countries had conducted at least one nationally representative survey that asked respondents to self-identify their sexual orientation and only the United States, Chile and Denmark had collected nationally representative data about trans/gender identity.[2] When data was analysed across the fifteen member countries, at least 2.7 per cent of the adult population (or 17 million adults) identified as LGBT.[3] This was an undercount as many countries excluded trans people from their national totals. Furthermore, the limited availability of population-level data about sexual orientation and trans/gender identity makes the weighting of nationally representative surveys problematic as it is unclear how many LGBTQ people you would expect to find in an 'average' sample.

In many of these national contexts, the adoption of new ways to categorize and collect gender, sex and sexuality data mirrors values presented in the Yogyakarta Principles.[4] Established in 2006, following a meeting of international human rights experts, the Yogyakarta Principles highlight how existing international legal standards protect people based on sexual orientation and gender identity. In 2017, additional principles and

---

[2] The fifteen countries that collected nationally representative data on sexual orientation were Australia, Canada, Chile, Denmark, France, Germany, Iceland, Ireland, Italy, Mexico, New Zealand, Norway, Sweden, United Kingdom and the United States, in Organisation for Economic Co-operation and Development, *Society at a Glance*, 15–16.

[3] Organisation for Economic Co-operation and Development, 9.

[4] Drafting Committee, 'Yogyakarta Principles plus 10' (Geneva, 2017).

state obligations were added to the original list. Four of these principles and obligations specifically relate to the collection, analysis and use of data about LGBTQ people:

- **Principle 19: The right to freedom of opinion and expression** – States shall 'recognise that the needs, characteristics and human rights situations of populations of diverse sexual orientations, gender identities, gender expressions and sex characteristics are distinct from each other, and ensure that data on each population is collected and managed in a manner consistent with ethical, scientific and human rights standards and made available in a disaggregated form'.

- **Principle 31: The right to legal recognition** – States shall 'ensure that official identity documents only include personal information that is relevant, reasonable and necessary as required by the law for a legitimate purpose, and thereby end the registration of the sex and gender of the person in identity documents such as birth certificates, identification cards, passports and driver licences, and as part of their legal personality'.

- **Principle 34: The right to protection from poverty** – States shall 'ensure appropriate institutional arrangements and data collection with the view to reduce poverty and social exclusion related to sexual orientation, gender identity, gender expression and sex characteristics'.

- **Principle 36: The right to the enjoyment of human rights in relation to information and communication technologies** – States shall 'take measures to ensure that the processing of personal data for individual profiling is consistent with relevant human rights standards including personal data protection and does not lead to discrimination, including on the grounds of sexual orientation, gender identity, gender expression and sex characteristics'.

Although the Yogyakarta Principles present a framework for action and many countries are on track to meet some of these obligations, the collection of gender, sex and sexuality data faces major roadblocks in countries such as Poland, Hungary, Slovakia and Russia. Queer data challenges assumptions that gender, sex and sexuality data is fixed, immutable and grounded in biological phenomena – anathema to opponents for whom the social construction of gender is a threat to traditional, biological-based understandings of the heterosexual, nuclear family and its position in society.[5] Opposition to 'gender ideology' was apparent in Andrzej Duda's promise to 'defend children from LGBT ideology' in Poland's closely contested 2020 presidential election, the removal of accreditation and funding for gender studies programmes at Hungarian universities in 2018, and the prohibition of same-sex marriage in Slovakia in 2014 and Hungary in 2012.[6] Across these examples, gender is presented as a threat as it not only recognizes complexity and diversity in ways that improve the lives of LGBTQ people but, more worryingly for defenders of cis/heteronormative values, *queers* structures that make it possible to discriminate against people who break normative expectations about gender, sex and sexuality.

At its most extreme, data about LGBTQ people is a matter of life and death. The Chechen Republic in Russia is regarded as one of the most dangerous places in the world for LGBTQ people, with a growing body of evidence that documents police involvement in the imprisonment, torture and murder of people based on their sexual orientation and/or trans/gender identity.[7] The region's leader, Ramzan Kadyrov, told Interfax News Agency in 2017, 'Chechen society does not have this phenomenon called non-traditional sexual orientation.'[8] As Maria Brock and Emil Edenborg explain, Kadyrov's rhetoric cements queer erasure in at least two ways: it is stated there are no queer people in Chechyna but, even if they were to exist, 'there would be none, as they would be dead or would have fled the country'.[9] Statements that affirm the non-existence of queer people, within particular bounded spaces, have also been made in other contexts such as LGBT Free Zones in Poland.[10] Queer data can refute these claims and radically transform knowledge about LGBTQ people. Even small actions, such as the addition

---

[5] Alison Phipps highlights historical links between opposition to 'gender ideology' and the Catholic Church's obstruction of women's rights (most notably, abortion), defence of heterosexuality and resistance to use of the social/cultural term 'gender' in place of the biological term 'sex', in Alison Phipps, *Me, Not You: The Trouble with Mainstream Feminism* (Manchester: Manchester University Press, 2020), 21.

[6] Maya Oppenheim, 'Hungarian Prime Minister Viktor Orban Bans Gender Studies Programmes', *The Independent*, 24 October 2018; Organisation for Economic Co-operation and Development, *Society at a Glance*, 45; Shaun Walker, 'Polish President Issues Campaign Pledge to Fight "LGBT Ideology"', *The Guardian*, 12 June 2020.

[7] Andrew Roth, 'Chechnya: Two Dead and Dozens Held in LGBT Purge, Say Activists', *The Guardian*, 14 January 2019.

[8] Maya Oppenheim, 'Chechen Leader Ramzan Kadyrov Claims No Gay People Exist in Region Just Fake Chechens', *The Independent*, 7 May 2017.

[9] Maria Brock and Emil Edenborg, '"You Cannot Oppress Those Who Do Not Exist"', *GLQ: A Journal of Lesbian and Gay Studies* 26, no. 4 (1 October 2020): 674.

[10] Lucy Ash, 'Inside Poland's "LGBT-Free Zones"', *BBC News*, 20 September 2020.

of questions on sexual orientation and trans/gender identity to existing data collection exercises, can have huge impacts: the presentation of data unequivocally demonstrates the existence of LGBTQ people and destabilizes the precarious foundations that have historically privileged those who are cis and heterosexual.

These examples introduce some of the opportunities and challenges associated with the collection of gender, sex and sexuality data, particularly as it relates to LGBTQ people. However, when viewed through a western/Anglo-centric lens and reported in English, my account flattens the diversity of LGBTQ lives and risks identities being lost in translation. Established communities of people who sit outside normative ideas about gender, sex and sexuality exist in most, if not all, societies. However, not all of these communities identify in ways that sit under an LGBTQ umbrella, as conceptualized in the UK through legislation such as the Equality Act.[11] Language functions as a method to manage and police the categorization of gender, whether through the use of gendered nouns in Romance languages (such as in Spanish and French), the interchangeability of terms for gender and sex (such as in Danish, Norwegian and Swedish), gendered pronouns in English or the assignment of first and last names to individuals that present information about gender. In addition, the translation of concepts across languages can mean that people interpret identity terms in different ways according to the possibilities of each language and the cultural contexts in which terms are understood.[12] Language not only structures how we communicate with others but also provides the building blocks to conceptualize the world around us that informs how people think about, make sense of and experience LGBTQ identities.[13] As Butler has noted, 'Every time I try and write about the body, the writing ends up being about language.'[14] The collection of gender, sex and sexuality data requires

---

[11] This is particularly true when gender, sex and sexuality intersect with other ethnic, cultural, religious and/or spiritual identities, for example the experiences of Two-Spirit people in North America and the Hijra community in South Asia.

[12] Suen et al., 'What Sexual and Gender Minority People Want Researchers to Know about Sexual Orientation and Gender Identity Questions', 2313; Aliya Saperstein and Laurel Westbrook, 'Categorical and Gradational: Alternative Survey Measures of Sex and Gender', *European Journal of Politics and Gender* 4, no. 1 (February 2021): 14.

[13] Diane L. Zosky and Robert Alberts, 'What's in a Name? Exploring Use of the Word Queer as a Term of Identification within the College-Aged LGBT Community', *Journal of Human Behavior in the Social Environment* 26, no. 7–8 (16 November 2016): 597.

[14] Judith Butler, *Undoing Gender* (New York: Routledge, 2004), 198.

a language. Yet, what is collected – in terms of questions asked – depends on the language used. Like data, language can bring to life some identities and make the existence of others difficult if not impossible. For example, Anna Kłonkowska explains, 'in the Polish language, not only pronouns but also the noun, adjective, verb, and numeral forms express the gender of the person speaking and the person to whom the speech is addressed'.[15] For Kłonkowska, language is 'the bedrock of many social attitudes about gender', which exacerbates the incongruity of those who do not align with language's existing gender rules.[16] Łukasz Szulc also reports that, in interviews conducted with gender-diverse Polish migrants living in the UK, some found it difficult to speak about their gender and sexuality in Polish because they had learnt most of what they knew about their identity through English-language sources.[17] The limits of language, however, are not fixed. In Swedish, the non-gendered pronoun *hen* – as an alternative to *han* (he) and *hon* (she) – was popularized in 2012 after the publication of a children's book that used the non-gendered pronoun to describe its characters.[18] A study published in 2019 by Margit Tavits and Efrén O. Pérez found evidence to suggest that, since 2012, native-speaking Swedes used the pronoun *hen* to describe things where the gender was unclear or non-existent (for example, an androgynous cartoon character) and the popularization of *hen* may have improved attitudes towards women and LGBT individuals in public life.[19]

As with language, the social world regularly accommodates difference among individuals without losing sight of what holds communities together. As an example, Stryker, Currah and Lisa Jean Moore describe how the category of 'woman' can 'function as social space that can be populated, without loss of definitional coherence' by a diversity of people who engage with ideas of 'woman' in different ways.[20] Although 'porous and permeable', categories

---

[15] Anna Kłonkowska, 'Making Transgender Count in Poland: Disciplined Individuals and Circumscribed Populations', *TSQ: Transgender Studies Quarterly* 2, no. 1 (1 January 2015): 130–1.

[16] Ibid.

[17] Łukasz Szulc, 'Digital Gender Disidentifications: Beyond the Subversion Versus Hegemony Dichotomy and toward Everyday Gender Practices', *International Journal of Communication* 14 (13 October 2020): 5445.

[18] Adam Rogers, 'Actually, Gender-Neutral Pronouns Can Change a Culture', *Wired*, 15 August 2019.

[19] Margit Tavits and Efrén O. Pérez, 'Language Influences Mass Opinion toward Gender and LGBT Equality', *Proceedings of the National Academy of Sciences* 116, no. 34 (20 August 2019): 16781–86.

[20] Stryker, Currah, and Moore, 'Introduction', 12–13.

most often encounter difficulties when translated into administrative, documentary state practices.[21] This tension is apparent in two, interrelated areas: the provision of official identification and the legal recognition of categories such as gender and sex. Official identity documents, such as a birth certificate, represent a state's attempt to transform complex, social information into a legible and administratively convenient format. As with censuses, efforts to shore up what is 'known' by a state about a population have the effect of solidifying borders between in-groups and out-groups, pushing those who fail to match normative rules further outside the scope of what is possible or permitted.[22] Birth certificates involve the registration of details about a baby after a live birth and usually include the name of the baby and its mother, father (if relevant/known), the location of the birth and the baby's gender or sex (the term used will depend on how gender and sex are understood in different national contexts). Currah and Moore note that birth certificates are held in high esteem among administrators as they are understood 'as a documentary record of a static historical fact and as a primary document' authenticating the identity of a person'.[23] For J. Michael Ryan, the birth certificate is the 'most important official identity document' as it is not only 'the first piece of documentation marking one as a recognizable and accountable citizen of the world, but it is also the document upon which obtaining other documents will later be founded'.[24]

Although exercises such as the census might collect additional data about identity characteristics (for example, sexual orientation, ethnicity or religion), this is used for population-level analysis rather than decision-making about individuals. Administrative systems that exist for gender and sex are therefore not commonly replicated for other identity characteristics. For the majority of the population, the information registered on their birth certificate is unremarkable. However, for babies born with differences

---

[21] Ibid., 12.
[22] For example, Beauchamp describes how identification documents strengthen 'nationalist policing of deviance and illegitimacy' through the production of 'categories of legitimacy', in Beauchamp, *Going Stealth*, 49.
[23] Currah and Moore explain how officials in New York City's Department of Health and Mental Hygiene have described birth certificates as 'breeder documents' as they are used as evidence to apply for other sources of identification, in Paisley Currah and Lisa Jean Moore, '"We Won't Know Who You Are": Contesting Sex Designations in New York City Birth Certificates', *Hypatia* 24, no. 3 (2009): 126.
[24] J. Michael Ryan, 'Born Again?: (Non-) Motivations to Alter Sex/Gender Identity Markers on Birth Certificates', *Journal of Gender Studies* 29, no. 3 (2 April 2020): 271.

of sex development, sometimes described as intersex, and/or those who grow up to realize their gender or sex assigned at birth does not align with how they identify, the information recorded on a birth certificate can create administrative challenges. In many countries, the legal process for changing gender or sex information on a birth certificate is difficult, if not impossible. Butler has described how the naming of a child, and the associated assumptions made about a child's gender, mean that 'we are affected by gender terms before we have any sense of what they mean or any understanding of what kind of effects they have.'[25] For some LGBTQ and/or intersex people, miscategorization at birth can inaugurate what Butler describes as, 'a chain of injury.'[26]

It is at this juncture – where everyday lives clash with administrative practices – that trans people present a thorn in the side for the state.[27] In response, a burst of legislative activity has taken place since 2010 to address how states conceptualize and categorize legal concepts of gender and sex. In 2015, Malta became the first country in the world to make it voluntary for parents to register a gender on their child's birth certificate (although there is a requirement that a binary gender is added to the birth certificate before the child's eighteenth birthday).[28] In 2019, the Australian state of Tasmania introduced an 'opt-in' approach to the recording of sex on birth certificates.[29] Among adults, the Netherlands, Germany and several Canadian provinces have changed legislation so that people can request that the gender or sex marker is removed from their birth certificate or changed to a third category (for example, in Germany the category of *divers*, meaning miscellaneous or other).[30] Several countries and regions have also introduced a legal category of non-binary gender, including Australia, Bangladesh, Pakistan,

---

[25] Ahmed, 'Interview with Judith Butler', 484–5.
[26] Ibid.
[27] Currah and Moore, '"We Won't Know Who You Are"', 113; J. Michael Ryan, 'Expressing Identity: Toward an Understanding of How Trans Individuals Navigate the Barriers and Opportunities of Official Identity', *Journal of Gender Studies* 29, no. 3 (2 April 2020): 351.
[28] Lena Holzer, 'Non-Binary Gender Registration Models in Europe' (Brussels: ILGA-Europe, 2018), 52.
[29] BBC News, 'Tasmania Makes It Optional to List Gender on Birth Certificates', *BBC News*, 10 April 2019.
[30] Leyland Cecco, 'Transgender Rights: Ontario Issues First Non-Binary Birth Certificate', *The Guardian*, 8 May 2018; Maya Oppenheim, 'Germany Introduces Third Gender for People Who Identify as Intersex', *The Independent*, 1 January 2019; Anne Louise Schotel and Liza M. Mügge, 'Towards Categorical Visibility? The Political Making of a Third Sex in Germany and the Netherlands', *JCMS: Journal of Common Market Studies* Online (28 January 2021): 1.

India, Nepal, Ontario in Canada and California and New York in the United States.[31] This is in addition to countries that have introduced or simplified the processes for people who wish to change their legal status from male to female or vice versa, which might include changing the gender or sex on a person's birth certificate. Related to these developments, countries including Iceland, Australia, Malta and Denmark have introduced X markers on official identification as an alternative to male or female.[32] Legal concepts of gender and sex are rapidly evolving and by the time you read this it is likely more countries and regions will have changed their practices.[33]

Although states have a high degree of autonomy as to what data they collect about individuals' gender or sex, some regulations exist related to international travel. The International Civil Aviation Organisation, a United Nations agency that regulates aviation across the world, determines what information is required on an individual's passport. As of 2022, passports for international travel are required to include a 'gender marker', which is either F (female), M (male) or X (other). Although an X marker should be accepted in all ICAO member states, Lena Holzer has highlighted that countries that issue passports with an X, such as Australia, have warned passport holders that they may encounter difficulties during cross-border travel.[34] When pressed as to why a gender marker is required on a passport, ICAO has argued that the information can help officials identify passengers.[35] However, ICAO's rationale assumes that the gender marker in a person's passport aligns with their gender expression and depends on the biases of the official evaluating the travel documents. These assumptions and biases create problems for cis and trans travellers whose gender presentation does not conform to the expectations of the country they wish to enter. Describing Spade's work on administrative violence, Os Keyes argues that the people most harmed by categorization practices are 'disproportionately

---

[31] Holzer, 'Non-Binary Gender Registration Models in Europe', 23.

[32] Ibid., 16.

[33] For a detailed discussion of contemporary issues related to legal concepts of gender and sex in the UK, see Davina Cooper, Emily Grabham, and Flora Renz, 'Introduction to the Special Issue on the Future of Legal Gender: Exploring the Feminist Politics of Decertification', *Feminists@ law* 10, no. 2 (8 November 2020).

[34] Holzer notes the website of Australia's Department of Foreign Affairs and Trade, which states that those travelling on a passport with an 'X' in the sex field might encounter difficulties crossing international borders, in Holzer, 'Non-Binary Gender Registration Models in Europe', 20.

[35] International Civil Aviation Organisation, 'A Review of the Requirement to Display the Holder's Gender on Travel Documents' (Montreal, 2012), 2.

likely to be already marginalized, already marked – the poor, immigrants, people of color'.[36] Although my focus is primarily on data about gender, sex and sexuality, a queer approach recognizes how the interface between bodies and administrative practices expands beyond this narrow lens to inflict different levels of harm, depending on who has the power and resources to negate the worst effects of administrative violence.

Efforts to make the collection of data about LGBTQ people more inclusive can follow different approaches. In some countries and regions, data collectors have added categories beyond the man/woman binary to better capture the diversity of how people identify. As an alternative to the provision of 'more options', some countries and regions have adopted a 'less data' approach that re-evaluates exactly when and where data is required about a person's gender or sex. Although 'more options' and 'less data' are not always opposing positions, Principle 31 of the Yogyakarta Principles obliges states to 'end the registration of the sex and gender of the person in identity documents' and ensure official identity documents only include personal information that is 'relevant, reasonable and necessary'.[37] The Netherlands has particularly embraced this ideal. Holzer explains that the Dutch Government has 'committed to limiting the registration of legal genders wherever possible', this includes the removal of gender markers from student records at some education institutions and omitting gender from the personal information embedded in public transportation cards.[38] The cities of Amsterdam, the Hague and Utrecht have removed questions about gender from government forms, where deemed unnecessary, and ensure all official communication with residents is gender-neutral.[39] In line with data protection regulations in the European Union, Principle 31 requires data collectors to only collect information that is adequate, limited and necessary for the task at hand.[40] Furthermore, excluding data about gender in administrative records does not necessarily mean that less is known about gendered differences in areas such as crime, health, transportation and

[36] Os Keyes, 'Counting the Countless', *Real Life*, 8 April 2019.
[37] Drafting Committee, 'YP+10', 9.
[38] Holzer, 'Non-Binary Gender Registration Models in Europe', 6–7.
[39] Janene Pieters, 'Amsterdam Municipality Goes Gender-Neutral in Speeches, Letters', *NL Times*, 26 July 2017.
[40] Article 5 of the General Data Protection Regulation states, 'Personal data shall be adequate, relevant and limited to what is necessary in relation to the purposes for which they are processed ("data minimisation")', in European Parliament and Council of European Union, 'Regulation (EU) 2016/679' (2016).

education. For example, even when gender is not recorded on a student's education record, researchers can still conduct studies into educational experiences by gender but would need to collect this data as part of the research rather than rely on administrative sources.

My concern here is who decides if gender is relevant to the issue being discussed. An activity that might appear gender-neutral, such as the local government's collection of household waste, actually has many gendered dimensions related to the division of domestic labour and older people, who might find this activity physically difficult, are more likely women. There is also a risk that collecting data about gender, only when considered absolutely necessary, might evolve into an approach where data about gender is not collected at all. A 'gender blind' approach to data collection is particularly alarming when presented as something progressive that addresses inequalities between women and men. Data collection activities in France and Germany provide a window into potential problems, as it is uncommon (and in many situations illegal) to capture data about a person's race or ethnicity. These restrictions partly relate to historical legacies of the Second World War, including the use of identity documents and categorization of people during the Holocaust.[41] Critics of this approach argue that the notion of a 'universal citizen' obscures the marginalized experiences of racial and ethnic minorities.[42] In a letter to *Le Monde* newspaper, Sibeth Ndiaye (a spokesperson for the French Government who moved from Senegal to France aged sixteen), argued that the absence of statistics on race and ethnicity makes it easier for those opposed to anti-racist initiatives to claim that problems do not exist.[43] In Germany, initiatives such as the #AFROZENSUS are attempting to fill these data gaps through an online survey that collects the lived realities, discrimination experiences and perspectives of Black, African and Afro-diasporic people for the first time.[44]

---

[41] Prior to Nazi occupation in 1940, the Netherlands operated a population registration system that was adapted to record the Jewish population. Of the country's estimated 140,000 Jews, more than 107,000 were deported and 102,000 were murdered. This process was partly facilitated by information collected via the population registration system. Discussed in Jack Beatty, 'Hitler's Willing Business Partners', *The Atlantic*, April 2001.

[42] The idea of the 'universal citizen' relates to French republicanism and is often associated with efforts of the French state to limit the public practice of Islamic traditions, see Mayanthi L. Fernando, 'State Sovereignty and the Politics of Indifference', *Public Culture* 31, no. 2 (1 May 2019): 265.

[43] Philip Oltermann and Jon Henley, 'France and Germany Urged to Rethink Reluctance to Gather Ethnicity Data', *The Guardian*, 16 June 2020.

[44] See Each One Teach One, 'Welcome to #AfroZensus!', Afrozensus, 2020.

Data from the #AFROZENSUS will provide an evidence base that highlights ethnic and racial differences and, as a result, informs initiatives to address discrimination in Germany.

What is missing in debates as to whether organizations should collect more or less data about gender, sex and sexuality are the views of LGBTQ people, who are often disproportionately impacted by these decisions. A UK survey of 895 non-binary people, conducted by the Scottish Trans Alliance in 2015, found that just over two-fifths of respondents (41 per cent) supported the elimination of public gender registration altogether.[45] This would mean that states no longer record data about gender or sex on birth certificates, for example. Although the options were not exclusive, respondents could agree with multiple proposals, a far larger proportion of respondents (73 per cent) favoured the introduction of a 'third gender' category.[46] Findings from the STA's research are important to consider in discussions that often conflate the expansion of rights for trans and non-binary people with efforts to minimize the collection of data about gender and sex: it is not the case that those calling for improved rights for trans and non-binary people necessarily wish to minimize or erase categories of gender or sex.

Gender, sex and sexuality data – international case studies

Having showcased key themes related to the collection of gender, sex and sexuality data in countries outside of the UK, I now want to turn attention to consider specific examples from the United States, Latin America and the Caribbean, Nepal, India, Pakistan, Kenya, the Netherlands, Switzerland, Germany, New Zealand and Canada. The list of countries discussed and examples noted in this section are not exhaustive; rather, I intend to profile a variety of case studies that encourage readers to explore further.

United States of America: Same-sex couples

In 2011, Gary J. Gates calculated that around 3.8 per cent of adults in the United States self-identified as LGBT, with around half of this group

---

[45] Vic Valentine, 'Non-Binary People's Experiences in the UK' (Edinburgh: Scottish Trans Alliance, Equality Network, 2015), 73.
[46] Ibid.

identifying as lesbian or gay and half as bisexual.[47] His study also est that around 0.3 per cent of adults identified as transgender. Although the United States has run at least ten nationally representative surveys on sexual orientation and three on trans/gender identity, the addition of sexual orientation and trans/gender identity questions to national censuses, health and household surveys lags behind comparable countries such as Canada, New Zealand, Australia and the UK.[48] The situation was not helped by the election of Donald Trump as President in 2016: for example, one of the first actions of the Trump administration was to erase references to LGBT people from the White House website.[49] Some nationally representative surveys, such as The National Survey of Older Americans Act Participants, also stopped collecting data about sexual orientation, which means it is no longer possible to monitor differences between LGB and heterosexual/straight respondents.[50]

Against the backdrop of the Covid-19 pandemic, the United States commenced its twenty-fourth national census on 1 April 2020. Costing more than $15.6 billion (£11.7 billion), this was one of the largest data collection exercises in history.[51] The census asked only nine questions per respondent and collected information about individuals' sex, age and race. The census did not ask explicit questions about sexual orientation or trans/gender identity but captured data about same-sex spouses and partners. Census questions asked about the relationships between individuals within a household and provided options that included 'Same-sex husband/wife/spouse' and 'Same-sex unmarried partner'.[52] This meant that same-sex couples in the same household, whether married or unmarried, could register themselves in the national data collection exercise. The option of relating to another person in the household as an 'unmarried partner' was introduced in the 1990 census, to reflect a surge in cohabiting couples. Amanda Baumle explains, 'bureau officials were aware that same-sex couples might opt to use this category to identify their own relationships [but] the idea of deliberately measuring the LGB population through the census did not factor into the construction of

---

[47] Gary J. Gates, 'How Many People Are Lesbian, Gay, Bisexual, and Transgender?' (Los Angeles: The Williams Institute, April 2011).
[48] Organisation for Economic Co-operation and Development, *Society at a Glance*, 15–16, 56.
[49] Karen L. Loewy, 'Erasing LGBT People from Federal Data Collection: A Need for Vigilance', *American Journal of Public Health* 107, no. 8 (August 2017): 1217.
[50] Ibid.
[51] US Government Accountability Office, '2020 Decennial Census', 6 March 2019.
[52] US Census Bureau, 'Questions Asked on the Form', 2020Census.gov.

the survey'.[53] In the 1990 census, responses from people who identified as same-sex spouses were subsequently transformed during data analysis and counted as different-sex spouses (this involved changing the sex of one of the respondents).[54] In the 2000 and 2010 censuses, analysts transformed same-sex spouses to same-sex unmarried partners. Although this approach ended the practice of 'straightwashing' the census, discussed in more detail in the next chapter, it is estimated that 28 per cent of all same-sex couple households in the original 2010 census tabulations were in fact different-sex couple households (for example, where someone in a different-sex couple had erroneously ticked the wrong sex option they were incorrectly counted as a same-sex couple).[55] By transforming different-sex couples (where sex was miscoded) into same-sex unmarried partners, this meant that the 2000 and 2010 censuses overcounted the number of same-sex couples. With under 4 per cent of the US population estimated to identify as LGBT, this example highlights how false positive errors (where cis, heterosexual respondents are incorrectly counted as LGBT) can hugely impact the results presented.[56]

Although attempts to collect population-level data about same-sex couples in the United States were not without problem, census data has contributed to legal decisions that have reshaped the lives of many LGBTQ Americans. For example, the majority opinion of the Supreme Court's 2015 hearing of Obergefell v. Hodges (the case that legalized marriage equality at a federal level) cited a briefing from Gates, which noted that 646,464 same-sex couples were counted in the 2010 census and around one in five of these couples were raising children.[57] The briefing also describes

---

[53] Amanda K. Baumle, 'The Demography of Sexuality: Queering Demographic Methods', in *Other, Please Specify: Queer Methods in Sociology*, ed. D'Lane Compton, Tey Meadow, and Kristen Schilt, (University of California Press, 2018), 279–80.

[54] Michael Frisch, 'A Queer Reading of the United States Census', in *The Life and Afterlife of Gay Neighborhoods: Renaissance and Resurgence*, ed. Alex Bitterman and Daniel Baldwin Hess, The Urban Book Series (Cham: Springer International Publishing, 2021), 65.

[55] Martin O'Connell and Sarah Feliz, 'Same-Sex Couple Household Statistics from the 2010 Census' (US Census Bureau, September 2011).

[56] In their account of the demography of sexuality in Japan, Daiki Hiramori and Saori Kamano describe this as the 'heterosexual problem' as a lack of familiarity with different gender, sex and sexuality categories (among non-LGBTQ people) and asymmetric size of the two groups can return false positive errors that skew the overall findings, in Hiramori and Kamano, 'Asking about Sexual Orientation and Gender Identity in Social Surveys in Japan', 444, 446.

[57] Obergefell v. Hodges, 14 556 (US 2015); Gary J. Gates, 'Brief of Gary J. Gates as Amicus Curiae on the Merits in Support of Respondent Windsor', 2013, 15, 31.

how the census counted same-sex couples in all fifty states and 93 per cent of counties in the United States.[58] Even with imperfect methods, data illustrated the existence of same-sex couples across all dimensions of American life and provided evidence that positively impacted decision-making about LGBTQ people.

The count of same-sex couples in the US census was not intended as a proxy for sexual orientation. Most obviously, the count excludes bi, lesbian and gay respondents in different-sex couples. Beyond gender, sex and sexuality, a count of same-sex couples also differs along class and race lines: poor people and people of colour are less likely to be in a cohabiting relationship, which means that this measure over-represents affluent, white respondents.[59] With these caveats in mind, the collection of data about same-sex couples, and not sexual orientation, potentially strengthens an association between coupledom and 'deservingness' that grants *some* LGBTQ people the privilege of being counted.[60] While celebrating the benefits of collecting data about same-sex couples, a queer approach to data must also question the foundations upon which this count is based and the potential risk that the census further entrenches 'in' and 'out' groups among LGBTQ people.

Latin America and the Caribbean: Hate crime and violence

Being excluded can have very serious consequences. Some of the most courageous data collection practices are taking place in Latin American and Caribbean countries in projects that investigate LGBTQ hate crime and violence. Based on available data, the Regional Information Network on Violence Against Lesbian, Gay, Bisexual, Trans and Intersex People in Latin America and the Caribbean (*Sin Violencia*) reported that between 2014 and 2019 over 1,300 LGBTI people were murdered in the ten countries

---

[58] Gates, 'Brief of Gary J. Gates as Amicus Curiae on the Merits in Support of Respondent Windsor', 16.
[59] Centers for Disease Control and Prevention, 'Fertility, Family Planning, and Reproductive Health of US Women: Data from the 2002 National Survey of Family Growth', 23, 2005, fig. 46; Centers for Disease Control and Prevention, 'Fertility, Contraception, and Fatherhood: Data on Men and Women from Cycle 6 (2002) of the National Survey of Family Growth', 23, 2006, fig. 29.
[60] Spade argues that a focus on campaigns such as marriage equality mainly helps the 'least marginalized of the marginalized' and changes the lives of people for whom sexual orientation is the only characteristic that excludes them from equal treatment, in Spade, *Normal Life*, 44.

covered by their network.[61] *Sin Violencia's* mission is to 'apply quality control standards and the analytical framework of "prejudice-based violence" to produce robust, comparable, and publicly accessible data about homicides of LGBTI people'.[62] Alongside the capture of quantitative data, organizations such as *Visibles* in Guatemala and Human Rights Watch have undertaken qualitative studies to document the far-reaching impacts of violence against LGBTIQ+ people and provide evidence based recommendations on next steps. *Visibles'* report *Violence Against the LGBTIQ+ Population: Experiences and Dynamics That Sustain It* engaged seventy LGBTIQ+ people in in-depth interviews, life studies and focus groups; while the Human Rights Watch conducted interviews with 113 LGBT people from El Salvador, Guatemala and Honduras and ninety-three officials, representatives, journalists and stakeholders involved in work related to hate crime and violence.[63]

Many Latin American countries already have systems in place to collect data about the identity characteristics of LGBTI victims. Also, several countries have introduced hate crime legislation that explicitly protects people based on sexual orientation and trans/gender identity.[64] However, the consistency of data collection practices and willingness to act on existing legislation remains patchy. The Inter-American Commission on Human Rights has reported, 'Insufficient training of police agents, prosecutors, and forensics authorities might also lead to inaccurate reporting. For example, when trans victims are registered according to their sex assigned at birth, their gender identity is not reflected in the records'.[65] Even with these challenges, the collection, standardization and presentation of data are starting to change the discourse about LGBTI hate crime. In 2020, three

---

[61] The network includes Bolivia, Brazil, Colombia, Dominican Republic, El Salvador, Guatemala, Honduras, Mexico, Paraguay and Peru, in Sin Violencia LGBTI, 'Prejudice Knows No Bounds: Executive Summary' (Sin Violencia LGBTI, 2019).

[62] Sin Violencia LGBTI, 'Sin Violencia LGBTI'.

[63] G. Duarte et al., 'Violence against the LGBTIQ+ Population: Experiences and Dynamics That Sustain It' (Guatemala City: Visibles, 2020); Human Rights Watch, '"Every Day I Live in Fear": Violence and Discrimination against LGBT People in El Salvador, Guatemala, and Honduras, and Obstacles to Asylum in the United States', October 2020.

[64] Human Rights Watch notes that although hate crime legislation has covered sexual orientation and gender identity in Honduras (since 2012) and El Salvador (since 2015) no country has convicted anyone on these charges, in Human Rights Watch, '"Every Day I Live in Fear": Violence and Discrimination against LGBT People in El Salvador, Guatemala, and Honduras, and Obstacles to Asylum in the United States'.

[65] Inter-American Commission on Human Rights, 'Violence Against LGBTI Persons', 12 November 2015, 72.

police officers in El Salvador were found guilty and sentenced to twenty-year prison sentences for the murder of trans woman Camila Díaz Córdova – the first conviction for murder that involved a trans victim.[66] Although this ruling alone does not change the environment in El Salvador, the publication of data about the violence directed towards LGBTQ people across Latin America and the Caribbean is intended to shine a light on the issue, which is often ignored by law enforcement, and demonstrate to LGBTQ people that discrimination is inadmissible and their identities are not something to hide.

Nepal, India, Pakistan and Kenya: 'Third gender' categories

As of 2022, only censuses in the UK have asked a specific question about respondents' sexual orientation. However, censuses in several countries have collected or plan to collect data on respondents' gender identity, trans status/history or provided non-binary response options for questions about gender or sex. In 2011, Nepal became the first country to conduct a census that allowed respondents to identify as a 'third gender' (*tesro lingi*).[67] The category of 'third gender' is an umbrella term for a heterogeneous group of people that have in common the experience of identifying in ways that transgress a fixed woman/man or female/male binary. The term is flawed as it adds a tertiary category to the arrangement of woman/man and female/male, which might strengthen rather than challenge the normalcy of existing categories and entrench the view that gender identities are mutually exclusive.[68] In addition, when imprudently used by Western researchers to describe gender identities in other cultural contexts, Evan B. Towle and Lynn Marie Morgan note how the 'third gender' concept functions as a 'trendy signifier' that 'becomes a junk drawer into which a great non-Western gender miscellany is carelessly dumped'.[69] Although Nepal's approach had the potential to capture population-level data about the diversity of sexual and gender identities, in practice it faced several

---

[66] Oscar Lopez, 'El Salvador Police Sentenced in Nation's First Trans Murder Convictions', *Reuters*, 31 July 2020.

[67] Manesh Shrestha, 'Nepal Census Recognises "Third Gender"', *CNN*, 31 May 2011.

[68] Beauchamp, *Going Stealth*, 35; Lindqvist, Sendén, and Renström, 'What Is Gender, Anyway', 4.

[69] Evan B. Towle and Lynn Marie Morgan, 'Romancing the Transgender Native: Rethinking the Use of the "Third Gender" Concept', *GLQ: A Journal of Lesbian and Gay Studies* 8, no. 4 (2002): 473, 484.

major issues (which it attempted to remedy in its 2021 census).[70] Kyle Knight et al.'s investigation into the Nepali census found that enumerators employed to collect the data, which was conducted in person, were not presented with adequate guidance on how to categorize respondents who neither identified as female nor male.[71] There were also reports of enumerators denying respondents the opportunity to identify in ways other than female or male, by not providing the full list of response options or not accurately recording answers provided. In addition, the software used by the Nepali Government to analyse the data only recognized binary female/male responses. For respondents recorded in a way other than female or male, their data was therefore added to existing binary categories or removed from the analysis altogether. Similar issues were apparent in counts conducted in India and Pakistan. In India, three options were presented for the sex question in the 2011 census and 490,000 people were counted as a 'third gender' (0.04 per cent of a population of over 1.2 billion people).[72] Pakistan's 2017 census also counted trans people, although results reported a total of just 10,418 people in a country of 207 million people – a figure widely disputed by trans rights organizations.[73] Although promising in their intentions, the inclusion of a 'third gender' option in censuses highlights how these developments can only succeed when supported by adequate information and guidance, require the compliance of those tasked with collecting the data and technology that is capable of analysing all response options collected.

In 2019, Kenya undertook what is considered the first census in the world to collect data about its intersex population.[74] In this context, intersex referred to people born with physical characteristics that do not fit typical definitions of male or female and often face discrimination or difficulty in accessing rights, such as those related to education and employment. The census included intersex people as a 'third gender' even though Kenyan law

---

[70] Nasana Bajracharya, 'Still Labelled "Others", Nepal's LGBTQIA+ People Pin Hopes on Census', *OnlineKhabar*, 31 March 2021.

[71] Kyle G. Knight, Andrew Flores and Sheila J. Nezhad, 'Surveying Nepal's Third Gender: Development, Implementation, and Analysis', *TSQ: Transgender Studies Quarterly* 2, no. 1 (1 January 2015): 101, 105.

[72] Rema Nagarajan, 'First Count of Third Gender in Census: 4.9 Lakh', *Times of India*, 30 May 2014.

[73] Asad Hashim, 'Pakistan Passes Landmark Transgender Rights Law', *Aljazeera*, 9 May 2018.

[74] Boniface Ushie, 'Recognising Intersex People Opens Access to Fundamental Rights in Kenya', *The Conversation*, 28 August 2019.

does not recognize intersex as a distinct group (and many intersex people would not consider themselves a 'third gender').[75] However, this move was generally welcomed by intersex activists as it was understood as a means to increase public awareness about intersex people, boost recognition and serve as a wedge issue for improved rights related to gender, sex and sexuality.

The Netherlands, Switzerland and Germany: Virtual censuses

Undertaking a manual, nationwide survey every five or ten years is not the only method used to calculate demographic information about a country's population. A growing number of countries, particularly non-English speaking nations without colonial links to Britain, use alternative methods to calculate the size and composition of their population. In the Netherlands, for example, a traditional questionnaire-based census was last conducted in 1971. Since then, the Dutch Government has calculated its population using existing datasets, including data related to employment, taxation, housing and municipal records. This data is linked to create what the Dutch Government describes as a 'virtual census'.[76] Statistics Netherlands note that this method meant their 2011 census required just fifteen members of staff and a budget of €1.4 million – far more efficient than counts conducted in countries that follow questionnaire-based approaches.[77] Switzerland adopted a similar method in 2017 and Germany operates a hybrid system that mixes data from existing registers with traditional census questionnaires. In Switzerland, user feedback shows high levels of satisfaction with census outputs. Testing of the data's accuracy, which involves interviewing a small proportion of the population, also found that results were as reliable as when a manual count was undertaken.[78]

---

[75] Kenyans interviewed about the addition of a 'third gender' option to the census noted a preference for a broader, more inclusive descriptor (such as 'other'). However, James Karanja (Director of Intersex Persons Society of Kenya), noted how conversations about the census are a 'a gateway to a class of people who have historically been excluded from basic human rights', in Katie G. Nelson, '"Intersex" Is Counted in Kenya's Census — but Is This a Victory?', *Public Radio Exchange*, 10 September 2019.
[76] Statistics Netherlands, 'The Dutch Virtual Census' (Youtube, 22 November 2012).
[77] Statistics Netherlands.
[78] The Netherlands and Germany are also required to report accurate demographic data to the EU on a regular basis. The EU has not expressed concerns about the quality of data reported or its comparability to data collected via manual censuses by other EU members.

Although the linking of existing datasets to run a virtual census has obvious benefits, most notably the efficient use of resources, it does not resolve biases and assumptions associated with data collection methods. The quality and accuracy of a virtual census is reliant on data contained within existing datasets, with decisions about categorization or who to include and exclude made across different government departments or at a regional or local level. The spread of authority might increase the risk of 'black box data', where it is unclear to individuals what data is held about them, whether the data is correct and the processes in place to amend or remove data.[79] It is similarly unlikely that existing datasets contain information about individuals' sexual orientation or trans/gender identity, which means countries need to collect this data afresh to include it in the census.[80] There are also countries, such as the UK, that do not require people to register with the state as adults, which means that the only registration document that covers everyone is a birth certificate (and, as discussed earlier in the chapter, this invites other categorization issues). Virtual censuses offer a huge amount of potential.[81] However, if the data used to construct a virtual census is opaque or based on records that are out of date and difficult for individuals to update, it is hard to say whether the efficiencies outweigh the potential injury this approach might cause for LGBTQ people.

New Zealand and Canada: 'Gender by default' and a two-step approach

When the collection of new data about an individual's gender, sex and sexuality is required, several NSOs have attempted to standardize how this information is captured. For example, New Zealand's NSO, Stats NZ, has proposed a 'gender by default' approach to the government's collection of

---

[79] Frank Pasquale, *The Black Box Society: The Secret Algorithms That Control Money and Information* (Cambridge: Harvard University Press, 2015), chap. Introduction-The Need to Know.

[80] Bureau of the Conference of European Statisticians, 'In-Depth Review of Measuring Gender Identity' (Paris: United Nations Economic and Social Council, June 2019), 13.

[81] The ONS's Census and Data Collection Transformation Programme intends to make recommendations in 2023 about the future collection of population statistics in England and Wales based on 'research into administrative data, and increased use of alternative sources of data, along with the data collected in 2021, to make Census 2021 the last of its kind', in Office for National Statistics, 'About the Census and Data Collection Transformation Programme', 16 September 2020.

gender and sex data.[82] This approach 'defaults to the collection of gender data as opposed to sex at birth' with the 'collection of sex at birth information [viewed] as an exception where there is a specific need'.[83] Stats NZ stated, 'in most cases a person's gender—their social and personal identity—is most relevant for policy making and research rather than their sex at birth', with gender-based analysis 'used in a range of areas, from income equality to health and education'.[84]

A 'gender by default' approach to data collection follows three steps. Firstly, and in line with Principle 31 of the Yogyakarta Principles, data collectors ask whether they need to gather information about gender and/ or sex. Data collectors should not assume that 'more data' is always a good thing and instead need to ensure the potential benefits of data collection outweigh the potential negatives. Secondly, data collectors ask whether it is necessary to distinguish between trans and cis respondents. If not, Stats NZ recommends asking the following question about gender:

What is your gender?
Male
Female
Another gender (please specify):

In data-collection exercises where information about trans and cis populations is required, Stats NZ recommends a two-step approach where a question about sex at birth is followed by a question about gender. Thirdly, data collectors ask if they require information about the intersex population (an umbrella term that describes people with a wide range of variations in sex characteristics). If so, an additional question is necessary that specifically asks 'Were you born with a variation of sex characteristics (otherwise known as an intersex variation)?'

Although Stats NZ's approach is unambiguous in its foregrounding of gender, departs from use of the tautological term 'gender identity'

---

[82] Stats NZ ran a public consultation in 2020 on the principle of adopting a 'gender by default' approach to data collection activities, which received 1,424 submissions. Among those who responded to the consultation, just under 80 per cent strongly agreed or agreed with the adoption of a 'gender by default' approach, Stats NZ, in 'Sex and Gender Identity Statistical Standards: Findings from Public Consultation, July - August 2020', 2020, 8, 10.
[83] Stats NZ, 'Sex and Gender Identity Statistical Standards: Consultation', Stats NZ, 2 July 2020.
[84] Ibid.

and addresses the problematic use of 'other' as a response option (which can further marginalize people who identify with minority identity characteristics), it is not perfect.[85] Notably, in studies where researchers wish to explore differences between trans and cis respondents, such as experiences of employment or education, Stats NZ recommends the use of a two-step approach that asks about sex at birth followed by gender. Ruberg and Ruelos, for example, have described a two-step approach as 'inappropriate' as 'it requires trans and non-binary folks to report their sex assigned at birth' and 'positions transgender people as "not really" male or female'.[86] Rather than deduce whether someone is trans or cis from the combination of answers to two separate questions, asking respondents if they identify as trans or as someone with a trans history (to include those who transitioned in the past and no longer identify as trans) offers an alternative solution.[87] There also exists the potential to use a two-step approach only as a staging post to a single question about trans/gender identity. Canada's NSO has also adopted a 'gender by default' approach and noted that two-step questions can avoid making changes that might disrupt historical trends while studies transition to a single question about gender.[88] By bringing us back to the focus on gender-based analysis and working outwards from there, 'gender by default' cuts through the background noise and potentially provides an approach to data collection that, with further tweaks, might improve data collection practices across national contexts.

* * *

This chapter has interwoven the international landscape of data *about* LGBTQ people with wide-ranging questions about how identities are

---

[85] Several scholars have noted how describing an individual or group as 'other' is, in itself, a form of 'othering', discussed in Joy L. Johnson et al., 'Othering and Being Othered in the Context of Health Care Services', *Health Communication* 16, no. 2 (April 2004): 254–6.

[86] Ruberg and Ruelos, 'Data for Queer Lives', 6.

[87] The use of a two-step question can differentiate cis respondents from those who identify differently from their sex assigned at birth but do not identify as trans, discussed in Suen et al., 'What Sexual and Gender Minority People Want Researchers to Know about Sexual Orientation and Gender Identity Questions', 2315. In contrast, Scotland's 2022 census asks a one-step question on whether individuals identify as trans or as having a trans history (discussed in Chapter 3).

[88] Marc Lachance, Kaveri Mechanda, and Alice Born, 'Gender – Developing a Statistical Standard' (New York: United Nations Department of Economic and Social Affairs Statistics Division, 30 August 2017), 9.

conceptualized in different languages and validated by state administrative practices. Communities based on identity characteristics possess long histories of incorporating individual differences. However, the conversion of identities into data has highlighted particular tensions between the porousness of the social world and rules associated with data categorization. In response, many countries and regions have diversified their provision of gender options and simplified the process for changing official documentation related to gender and sex, such as birth certificates. Furthermore, in some contexts, states have introduced changes so that gender and sex data is only collected where relevant, reasonable and necessary. Greater consideration of when and where to collect gender and sex data is welcome. However, those passionate about the use of data for action must remain on guard that a 'gender blind' approach does not become misunderstood as a means to address inequality.

The collection of gender, sex and sexuality data across a range of national and regional contexts highlights benefits, opportunities and dangers. For example, data informed the Supreme Court's decision to implement marriage equality in the United States, has helped raise the profile of hate crime and violence against LGBTQ people in Latin America and the Caribbean, and presented a wedge issue for intersex activist groups in Kenya pushing for improved rights. Attempts to categorize individuals according to their gender, sex and sexuality can equally cause injury to individuals throughout their life. In the United States, and though not the intention of census officials, we see how the count of same-sex couples might entrench a division between 'deserving' and 'undeserving' LGBTQ people. I have also documented how proposed solutions to the counting of LGBTQ people, such as two-step questions or a virtual census, can create new problems that do not make data practices more inclusive nor improve the accuracy of data collected. However, in countries and regions where leaders doubt the existence of LGBTQ people and cite the lack or absence of data as evidence of their claims, data *about* LGBTQ people can transform existing knowledge. The projection of data about the total number of Russian LGBTQ people to the exterior of the Kremlin in Moscow and canvassing of politicians in the Hungarian Parliament with detailed data about the experiences of trans people are just two examples as to how data might play a role in activism that seeks to improve people's lives. Queer data – in what it tells us *about* LGBTQ people and the *queering* of methods used to capture data about all identity characteristics – provides an evidence base for radical action.

PART II
ANALYSING QUEER DATA

CHAPTER 5
STRAIGHTWASHING: THE CLEANING AND ANALYSIS OF QUEER DATA

I arrived late and was quickly ushered through the university museum and into the historic library – the grand location for a drinks reception to celebrate the conclusion of an international conference on gender equality. It was late August and unusually humid. Makeup was running, shirts were starting to show early signs of sweat and coiffed hair was slipping under the evening heat. Waiting staff dotted the room with trays of canapés. Glasses were quickly refilled with wine as soon as they showed signs of emptying. To address the heat, a row of air conditioning units pushed a stream of cold air from one end of the room to the other. Attendees had also taken matters into their own hands and refashioned conference programmes as make-shift fans, fluttering like butterflies in the grand setting. Glasses clinked and the principal of the university, hosting the conference, took to the floor. Flanked on either side by government ministers and local dignitaries, the principal's speech focused on the university's reduction of its gender pay gap (the percentage difference in average pay between male and female staff). The principal outlined the most recent data, the current mean and median gap, the previous mean and median gap, and the change in percentage points. The numbers were presented with passion and, for myself and others in the room, appeared to take on a life of their own as monuments of gender equality.

The speech concluded and the crowd broke into chatter. Attendees seemed impressed with the principal's account of gender pay gap data at the university. The numbers certainly sounded positive. But I felt something was missing and, as others returned to the food and drink, I was left with more questions than answers. I was unsure what the data *really* told me about gender equality at the university. What were the experiences of female staff and how did they compare to male and non-binary staff? How did this intersect with the experiences of Black staff, disabled staff and LGBTQ staff? I also wanted to know more about how the data was analysed. Who counted as staff? How were part-time staff or those with multiple roles counted? What were the differences between mean and median averages? Data analysis shapes the stories we tell about EDI. Analysis of data can provide a cover.

Statements that focus on what was uncovered, rather than how this was uncovered, provide data with a long leash that can depart from the original intentions as to why it was collected. The transformation of numbers into 'good data' can become an objective in its own right. As resources are always limited, there is the risk that the collection and analysis of data drain energy from other initiatives intended to address inequality. It is therefore vital that, as with the collection of data, a queer approach critically investigates what happens during the analysis of gender, sex and sexuality data.

* * *

The cleaning of data can remove its queerness: paper surveys where respondents score out the response options 'female' and 'male' and write their own answer, interview recordings where participants flip the focus and ask questions of the researcher, census returns where LGBTQ couples identify themselves as 'married' even when governments do not recognize same-sex marriage. These examples demonstrate how collection methods can fail to restrict how participants share data about their lives and experiences. Although the move from paper to online surveys has made it harder for participants to select multiple response options, write-in comments or answer questions not intended for them, data analysis offers an additional opportunity to ensure that results align with the expectations of those who designed the study and the social world they wish to bring into being. In this chapter, I examine the preparation, analysis and usability of gender, sex and sexuality data. This process begins with cleaning, which involves the removal of data that breaks established rules (for example, the deletion of respondents that started a survey but did not answer any questions). Tamraparni Dasu and Theodore Johnson have estimated that 80 per cent of data analysts' time is spent on the cleaning and preparation of data – yet this stage in data's journey often remains undiscussed.[1] Cleaning data also involves the use of available information, such as responses to other questions in a survey, to add missing values or change answers provided. After cleaning, analysts are then required to use their judgement to splice or split categories, a practice known as aggregation and disaggregation. The assumption, often misplaced, that the number of people in a population who identify as LGBTQ is small can halt research before it even begins and materializes as the 'I have no problem

[1] Tamraparni Dasu and Theodore Johnson, *Exploratory Data Mining and Data Cleaning*, Wiley Series in Probability and Statistics (New York: Wiley, 2003).

114

with LGBTQ people but they don't work here' argument. The aggregation of LGBTQ groups offers a response to when 'small numbers' is used as an excuse for inaction. However, if research is conducted into the experiences of LGBTQ people, and the number of cases is smaller than anticipated, organizations might also use data to halt initiatives or cut funding. Small numbers therefore present multiple dangers for the analysis of data about LGBTQ people.

Related to analysis is the topic of big data, where datasets are huge in volume, collected in or near real time and diverse in scope. The speed and scale of big data are ideal for algorithmic decision-making, in which machines execute complex instructions that shape people's everyday lives. However, big data's ambition for total knowledge often overlooks the effects of homophobia, biphobia and transphobia on historical and contemporary data practices and is ill-suited to qualitative methods, which tend to predominate studies of LGBTQ people. In response, I highlight the merits of small data and queer data's potential to uncover new insights when research is undertaken that cuts across both big and small approaches.

Part II is a bridge between the collection of queer data and its uses for action. Data collection can result in researchers facing a messy assortment of transcripts, datasets and documents that, on their own, are hard to fathom. Analysis is the process of making sense of what this data tells us. Yet, whether working with qualitative or quantitative data, decisions made about analysis are never value-neutral. Biases and assumptions that inform the meanings of gender, sex and sexuality data do not stop when the researcher closes the online survey or turns off their dictaphone. Decisions made during analysis equally shape the findings of a research project and ultimately determine data's potential to impact the lives and experiences of LGBTQ people. This chapter therefore concludes with a discussion of Browne's account of running a survey for Pride in Brighton and Hove and the challenge of conducting data analysis that authentically represents the lives of LGBTQ people yet also produces results that are useable for future action. I frame this example within a wider debate about Gayatri Chakravorty Spivak's concept of strategic essentialism and the use of analytical methods that misrepresent LGBTQ people as a means to advance social and political change.

Cleaning, disaggregation and aggregation

Cleaning implies there is something wrong with the data collected. However, for many LGBTQ people, providing the 'wrong' answer is not a mistake but an attempt to subvert cis/heteronormative assumptions that influenced the design of the collection instrument. For respondents who do not feel represented by the options offered, Ryan highlights 'a political obligation to alert the system of their presence by refusing to simply check one of the limited options with which they feel they are presented'.[2] Ryan tells the story of Jamie, who identifies as neither male nor female, who explains that 'for surveys where it's not going to be some big media frenzy thing I always write in my own thing and add things like intersex, other, transgender, and then circle transgender'.[3] Attempts to 'clean' LGBTQ transgressions during data analysis are evident in the recent history of the US census. In the 1990 census, for example, if two male respondents in the same household described their relationship as 'husband/wife' the census bureau would leave the relationship intact but change the sex of one of the male respondents to female.[4] As discussed in Chapter 4, Velte describes these practices as 'straightwashing' census data.[5] Although the option of 'unmarried partner' was added to the 1990 census, and several states provided legal recognition for same-sex couples during the period 2000 to 2010, the transformation of responses related to same-sex couples continued, to some extent, until the 2020 census. Michael Brown and Larry Knopp, commenting on the UK's 2001 censuses, have also noted that 'data-cleaning techniques and the lack of familiarity with same-sex couples' meant that 'census officials have had to closet some same-sex couples by recoding them, in order to maintain a consistent definition of household relation'.[6] These examples make clear the need for transparency about analytical approaches so that decisions, which reconfigure the meanings of data, are deliberated among the people about whom changes affect, rather than being presented as a natural part of data's journey from collection to use.

The idea of 'splitters' and 'lumpers' is another way to think about decisions made during data preparation.[7] Discussed by James Weinrich

---

[2] Ryan, 'Expressing Identity', 356.

[3] Ibid.

[4] Frisch, 'A Queer Reading of the United States Census', 65.

[5] Velte, 'Straightwashing the Census', 85.

[6] Michael Brown and Larry Knopp, 'Places or Polygons? Governmentality, Scale, and the Census in the Gay and Lesbian Atlas', *Population, Space and Place* 12, no. 4 (July 2006): 225.

[7] James D. Weinrich et al., 'A Factor Analysis of the Klein Sexual Orientation Grid in Two Disparate Samples', *Archives of Sexual Behavior* 22, no. 2 (1 April 1993): 157–68.

et al. in relation to the measurement of sexual identities, 'splitters' and 'lumpers' describe two opposing ways to bridge the gap between individual-level characteristics and population-level identity categories. For 'splitters', the grouping of identity characteristics should reflect individual nuances and complexities. The consideration of granular details means that it is likely that many categories will exist, some with very small numbers. 'Lumpers', on the other hand, favour an approach to classification that involves the smallest number of possible categories. As a result, bigger groups are created and there exists greater diversity within each group. There is no obligation to pick a side as both approaches are useful, depending on the research question under investigation. For example, imagine a survey of 100 people that provides twenty possible response options for sexual orientation. If respondents were equally spread across these twenty groups that would equate to only five people per sexual orientation category. The granular level of detail would make it hard for analysts to assess differences between sexual orientations and might ultimately mean that analysis by sexual orientation is abandoned altogether. Some aggregation is required. However, it is equally unnecessary to jump from twenty categories to two. Depending on the spread of responses, analysis can find a middle ground between the crude binary of heterosexual/homosexual and a potentially unwieldy list of twenty response options.

It is at this point in the analytical process where decisions can erase the experiences of bisexual people. Several scholars have commented on the dearth of studies that explore the topic of bisexuality within the wider field of queer studies, an omission that is often continued in practices related to gender, sex and sexuality data.[8] Efforts to respond to the 'straightwashing' of data can perpetuate the invisibility of bisexual respondents when they are aggregated into a wider LGB group and data is reported as representative of lesbian and gay respondents only (even when, as is often the case, bisexual

---

[8] April S. Callis, 'Playing with Butler and Foucault: Bisexuality and Queer Theory', *Journal of Bisexuality* 9, no. 3–4 (13 November 2009): 214; Surya Monro, Sally Hines, and Antony Osborne, 'Is Bisexuality Invisible? A Review of Sexualities Scholarship 1970–2015', *The Sociological Review* 65, no. 4 (1 November 2017): 663; Robin Rose Breetveld, 'Forms of Bisexual Injustice: Bi, Being, and Becoming a Knower', in *Bisexuality in Europe: Sexual Citizenship, Romantic Relationships, and Bi+ Identities*, ed. Emiel Maliepaard and Renate Baumgartner (Routledge, 2020), 156.

respondents constitute the largest proportion of those who identify as LGB).[9] Erasure of unique insights from bisexual respondents means that when data is published it seems as if bisexual people are missing.[10] The decision to 'split' or 'lump' must therefore consider whether this will minimize or maximize the future utility of the data. However, at the same time, excessive 'splitting' potentially dilutes the impact of data to change the social world and, in some cases, might give analysts a reason to abandon analysis of LGBTQ experiences altogether.

A similar challenge is common in research that aggregates minority racial and ethnic groups to form the acronym BAME. Particularly in light of the Black Lives Matter movement, researchers, practitioners and activists have critically examined whether the aggregation of racial and ethnic categories does more harm than good.[11] BAME is not a real-world reflection of an individual's identity but collates a mixture of histories, geographies, cultures, races and ethnicities. Foluke Ifejola Adebisi has argued, 'By putting everyone not white under the BAME umbrella, we describe no-one' and that 'BAME, like the porous idea of liberal "diversity" pretends all marginalized people are interchangeable'.[12] The BAME acronym also fails to underscore that, in the UK, those who identify as a mixed identity, which can cut across multiple categories including white, have a far younger age profile and are therefore likely to increase as a proportion of the population in the future.[13] Ọrẹ Ogunbiyi and Chelsea Kwakye, in their book *Taking up Space: The Black Girl's Manifesto to Change*, note how lazy uses of the BAME acronym silence frank conversations about the unique ways in which Black people, in particular, experience racism.[14] In addition, the acronym excuses those

---

[9] For example, in the 2018/19 academic year in UK higher education institutions that returned data to the Higher Education Statistics Agency, 3.1 per cent of students identified as bisexual whereas just 1.2 per cent of students identified as a gay man and 0.7 per cent identified as a gay woman/lesbian, in Advance HE, 'Equality in Higher Education', 309.

[10] Westbrook and Saperstein, 'New Categories Are Not Enough', 548.

[11] For discussion, see Cecilia Macaulay and Nora Fakim, '"Don't Call Me BAME": Why Some People Are Rejecting the Term', *BBC News*, 30 June 2020.

[12] Foluke Ifejola Adebisi, 'The Only Accurate Part of "BAME" Is the "and" … ', *Foluke's African Skies*, 8 July 2019.

[13] Data from the 2011 English and Welsh census shows that the average age of people who identified as a mixed ethnic group was eighteen whereas the average age of those who identified as a white ethnic group was forty-one, in Office for National Statistics, 'Age Groups', Ethnicity Facts and Figures, 22 August 2018.

[14] Chelsea Kwakye and Ọrẹ Ogunbiyi, *Taking up Space: The Black Girl's Manifesto for Change* (London: #Merky Books, 2019), sec. The B in B(A)ME.

in positions of power as they can claim they are helping 'BAME people' when overall data for the aggregated BAME group improves, even if they are doing nothing to improve the lives of people who experience anti-Black discrimination.

I have struggled with aggregation challenges in my research with university staff and students. In general staff or student surveys not focused on a particular identity group, the majority of respondents tend to identify as a white British ethnicity with other respondents spread across a diverse mix of ethnic groups. Even when data collection methods enable respondents to identify themselves as a specific ethnic group, the level of detail provided is often aggregated during analysis to form new groups that contain a larger number of respondents (such as Black, Asian or BAME). Gillborn et al. have described how the provision of *too few* ethnic categories produces meaningless results but that the provision of *too many* categories can be almost as bad.[15] They discuss a study of educational attainment in a school that used more than seventy separate ethnic categories to analyse the data. As so many categories were analysed, many with only one or two pupils, it was impossible to have any confidence in the results and the school reported no significant differences in attainment between ethnic groups. In this situation, analysts faced two options: aggregate ethnic groups into larger categories – using labels such as Asian, Black, mixed and white – or do not undertake any analysis due to the discrepancy in the size of the groups and the risk of over-analysing responses from a handful of participants. In my work, I have erred on the side that any disaggregated analysis, even at the very crude level of BAME versus white, is better than nothing at all.[16] I hope that in drawing attention to differences between high-level groups, the normalcy of whiteness is exposed and other researchers are encouraged to disaggregate their data, as much as possible, in future investigations.

When aggregating data related to race, ethnicity, sexual orientation and trans/gender identity, analysts also face the question of what to do with participants who select 'other' or 'prefer not to say'. Browne highlights an

---

[15] Gillborn, Warmington, and Demack, 'QuantCrit', 172.
[16] Critics of the term 'BAME', which intensified following the raised profile of the Black Lives Matter movement in the UK in 2020, highlight the need to disaggregate all data on race and ethnicity so that it describes the experiences of Black respondents. In particular, specific injustices related to anti-Black racism in areas such as education, health and policing are often lost when subsumed by the wider category of BAME.

assumption, among researchers, that participants who answer 'other' or 'prefer not to say' to a question about sexual orientation are most likely not heterosexual/straight.[17] Contrary to this assumption, Browne notes that if a participant wished to hide their sexual orientation they would assumedly select the response option least likely to invite attention (in other words, 'heterosexual/straight').[18] Heather Ridolfo et al. describe four types of participant that most frequently disclose as 'other' in a question about sexual identity: those who do not identify as LGBTQ but take issue with terms 'heterosexual' or 'straight'; those who reject traditional terms used to describe sexual identity; trans respondents; and those experimenting with or questioning their sexual identity.[19] The many reasons why someone might identify as 'other' highlights the error of assuming that responses should be aggregated into a broader category of LGBTQ rather than heterosexual/ straight. In their account of a sexual orientation and gender identity survey conducted in the Japanese city of Osaka, Daiki Hiramori and Saori Kamano describe the use of additional response options 'Don't want to decide, haven't decided' and 'I do not understand the question' to further assess what is lost under the umbrella options of 'Other' and 'Prefer not to say'. Their study found that a sizeable proportion (5.2 per cent) of respondents selected the option 'Don't want to decide, haven't decided'.[20] Decisions made about how to aggregate data, deliberated among analysts rather than the participants about whom the data relates, remind us of the many judgements made during data analysis that influence the results produced.

Small numbers

Decisions made during analysis are particularly impactful when data about LGBTQ groups involve working with small numbers. The Gender Identity in US Surveillance Group, convened by the Williams Institute (a research centre based at the University of California Los Angeles), has reported hesitancy among US national data collection agencies to gather data on groups that would likely comprise less than 0.5 per cent of the

---

[17] Browne, 'Queer Quantification or Queer(y)Ing Quantification', 242.
[18] See Peter Betts, Amanda Wilmot, and Tamara Taylor, 'Developing Survey Questions on Sexual Identity: Exploratory Focus Groups' (Office for National Statistics, August 2008).
[19] Ridolfo, Miller, and Maitland, 'Measuring Sexual Identity Using Survey Questionnaires', 122.
[20] Hiramori and Kamano, 'Asking about Sexual Orientation and Gender Identity in Social Surveys in Japan', 451, 455, 460.

total population.[21] With an estimate that around 0.3 per cent of the adult population in the United States identify as trans, this arbitrary benchmark would therefore rule out inclusion in national counts.[22] However, even when counted, the issue of small numbers can create several problems for LGBTQ people in how this data is analysed and subsequently used. Ridolfo et al. describe the asymmetrical size of minority and majority sexual and gender groups in nationally representative surveys, which means that 'the slightest degree of error can dramatically impact estimates'.[23] As described in the previous chapter's account of same-sex couple data in the 2000 and 2010 US censuses, errors can render *all* data collected about LGB people suspect whether the count seems too high or too low. When those responsible for data collection fail to meaningfully engage and instil confidence among communities covered by the count, design questions that are exclusionary and/or fail to fully acknowledge the diversity and complexity of gender, sex and sexual identities, small numbers can become even smaller than originally anticipated. Browne has warned that if, for whatever reason, counts fail to match assumptions about the size of LGB populations this might weaken arguments for LGB equality and justify further inaction.[24]

A partial solution to the challenge of small numbers is the quantification of qualitative data collected via open-text boxes in surveys. In their article 'What Sexual and Gender Minority People Want Researchers to Know About Sexual Orientation and Gender Identity Questions: A Qualitative Study', Leslie W. Suen et al. highlight a strong desire for write-in answer choices for questions on sexual orientation and gender identity among the seventy-four people who participated in their focus groups and cognitive interviews, particularly among participants of colour.[25] As data collected from open-text boxes do not usually map to items on an existing coding framework (for example, where female equals one and male equals two), analysis is potentially difficult and time-consuming, particularly in large-scale exercises

---

[21] Discussed in Currah and Stryker, 'Introduction', 6.

[22] Gary J. Gates and Jody L. Herman, 'Beyond Academia: Strategies for Using LGBT Research to Influence Public Policy', in *Other, Please Specify: Queer Methods in Sociology*, ed. D'Lane Compton, Tey Meadow, and Kristen Schilt, (Berkeley: University of California Press, 2018), 81–2.

[23] Ridolfo, Miller, and Maitland, 'Measuring Sexual Identity Using Survey Questionnaires', 114.

[24] Browne, 'Queer Quantification or Queer(y)Ing Quantification', 247.

[25] Suen et al., 'What Sexual and Gender Minority People Want Researchers to Know about Sexual Orientation and Gender Identity Questions', 2310.

such as a national census. The view that open-text data is hard to analyse has likely dissuaded researchers from including this type of question in surveys and diversity monitoring forms.[26] In defence of open-text questions, Gloria Fraser et al. have noted how this approach 'is rarely used as the sole measure of gender' and 'may represent a missed opportunity for quantitative researchers'.[27] Fraser highlights how an open-text question 'encourages participants to self-identify using as many terms as they wish' and points to studies that demonstrate efficient and accurate methods to analyse the data collected.[28] Approaches include the manual coding of a small sample of open-text data, for example 5 per cent of all responses received, followed by the use of analytical software to automatically code the remainder of the data (with a researcher required to address instances where the computer is unable to determine a match).[29] For example, Anna Lindqvist et al. tested the use of an open-text box for gender in a survey of 794 people and found that 98.99 per cent of responses were easy to code.[30]

The move to digital collection methods has also enabled researchers to utilize technology to assist with analysis. For example, NRS proposed using technology in the online version of Scotland's 2022 census that would predict and auto-populate a response option for people who started typing text in the write-in box for questions on sexual orientation, religion, nationality and ethnicity. NRS explained that the approach would improve the respondent experience (it would be easier to complete the census), data quality (auto-populated options would be matched to a coding list, reducing the risk of error from manually matching open-text data to a coding list) and efficiencies in the coding of the data (more of this work could be automated).[31] Respondents that provide an open-text answer would have the option of accepting the auto-populated response or writing-in something

[26] Guidance from the Gender Identity in US Surveillance Group noted that 'fill-in-the-blank questions do not work for surveys that include tens of thousands of people', in Gender Identity in US Surveillance Group, 'Best Practices for Asking Questions to Identify Transgender and Other Gender Minority Respondents on Population-Based Surveys', xv.
[27] Gloria Fraser et al., 'Coding Responses to an Open-Ended Gender Measure in a New Zealand National Sample', *The Journal of Sex Research* 57, no. 8 (November 2019): 980.
[28] Gloria Fraser, 'Evaluating Inclusive Gender Identity Measures for Use in Quantitative Psychological Research', *Psychology & Sexuality* 9, no. 4 (2 October 2018): 343–57.
[29] Lara M. Greaves et al., 'The Diversity and Prevalence of Sexual Orientation Self-Labels in a New Zealand National Sample', *Archives of Sexual Behavior* 46, no. 5 (2016): 1325–36.
[30] Lindqvist, Sendén, and Renström, 'What Is Gender, Anyway', 6.
[31] National Records of Scotland, 'Letter to Culture, Tourism, Europe and External Affairs Committee', 25 October 2019.

different. NRS noted that 'use of predictive text minimises errors such as spelling mistakes and abbreviations, which means clean codeable data is collected'.[32] As a result, the technology would maximize the usability of data collected on 'other' identity characteristics and potentially help address the issue of 'small numbers'.

Following news of NRS's plan to use predictive-text technology, media attention focused on the draft list of twenty-one response options that would appear in the open-text box for the sexual orientation question.[33] A list of sexual orientations was drafted with input from LGBTQ organizations and included options such as asexual, bicurious, pansexual and queer.[34] Organizations such as the Christian Institute and Catholic Church expressed opposition, while LGB Alliance (a UK trans-exclusionary campaign group) argued the proposal 'would suggest that other sexual orientations exist beyond attraction to the opposite sex, same sex or both sexes' and asked that the census not include the term 'Other sexual orientation' as a response option.[35] In April 2020, NRS wrote to the Scottish Parliament committee with oversight of the census to announce that it had decided not to use predictive-text technology for the sexual orientation question.[36] NRS's letter also explained that the decision did not apply to other census questions on identity characteristics and that NRS would continue to use predictive-text technology for questions on religion, national identity and ethnicity. Like the proposed list of sexual orientations, the work-in-progress options were based on previous censuses, other surveys, desk-based research and engagement with stakeholders, and included 116 religions, 274 national identities and 241 ethnic groups.[37]

Considering the complexity of categorizing religious, national and ethnic identities, what does this example from Scotland's census tell us about small

---

[32] National Records of Scotland, 'Letter to Culture, Tourism, Europe and External Affairs Committee', 18 December 2019.
[33] See Chris Musson and Ben Archibald, 'Scots Face List of 21 Sexualities to Choose from in 2021 Census Such as Gynephilic', *The Scottish Sun*, 29 October 2019; Gina Davidson, 'Scotland's 2021 Census to Have 21 Sexual Orientation Choices for Adults', *The Scotsman*, 31 October 2019.
[34] National Records of Scotland, 'Letter to Culture, Tourism, Europe and External Affairs Committee', 18 December 2019.
[35] LGB Alliance, 'Letter to Culture, Tourism, Europe and External Affairs Committee', 26 November 2019.
[36] National Records of Scotland, 'Letter to Culture, Tourism, Europe and External Affairs Committee', 2 April 2020.
[37] Ibid., 18 December 2019.

numbers and the use of technology to improve the accuracy and efficiency of data collected about sexual orientation? As discussed in Chapter 3, the census can bring into being a population that 'makes sense' to the cis/heteronormative majority and design-out LGBTQ lives and experiences that fail to match these ideals. In Scotland, the lack of concern about the use of predictive-text for questions on religion, nationality and ethnicity suggests that opposition expressed had less to do with the technology deployed and more to do with efforts to shore up a definition of sexual orientation linked to a fixed, binary and trans-exclusionary understanding of sex. There exists huge potential in the use of open-text data to expand opportunities for participants to self-identify and ensure that those who write in answers are meaningfully coded and counted. Furthermore, the automated coding of open-text data and use of technologies, such as predictive-text, means that the provision of 'more response options' does not exacerbate the problem of small numbers nor risk diluting the uses of LGBTQ data for action.

Big data

Kitchin describes big data as huge in volume (exceeding 1,000 gigabytes), high in velocity (collected in or near real-time) and diverse in variety (collected from multiple sources).[38] Big data can take many forms, from the information generated by the Large Hadron Collider to content shared on social media platforms, and differs from projects that make statistical inferences about a population based on a random or representative sample. For example, rather than infer how people use the London Underground from a sample of travellers, big data collects and analyses information from the travel cards of *all* five million passengers who use the system each day.[39] The volume, velocity and diversity of information involved in a big data project necessitates an approach to analysis that can operate at scale and is therefore associated with the use of automated computer algorithms. As a means to make sense of larger, more complex datasets (rather than a particular approach to analysis) an algorithm is a sequence of instructions designed to perform a specific task. Algorithms can run a range of analytical approaches, such as predictive analytics where machine-learning techniques

---

[38] Kitchin, *The Data Revolution*, 68.
[39] Ibid., 72.

are used to identify the likelihood of future outcomes based on historical data (for example, the use of past data to predict how people will travel on the London Underground next week).

In their description of critical data studies, Craig Dalton and Jim Thatcher observe that big data 'is never a neutral tool' but 'always shapes and is shaped by a contested cultural landscape in both creation and interpretation'.[40] Gillborn et al. also note how those enamoured by the powers of big data imagine an approach to analysis driven by machines where 'theories and human reasoning are rendered obsolete because the "numbers speak for themselves"'.[41] As Gillborn et al. highlight, in reference to data on race and education, the illusion that 'numbers speak for themselves' is harmful. Ideas and assumptions about big data therefore have implications for the analysis of gender, sex and sexuality data. Jen Jack Gieseking picks up this question in their examination of how big data relates to lesbians and queer women.[42] Gieseking describes the Lesbian Herstory Archive in New York, one of the largest collections of information about lesbian lives and activities in the world, and how the archive is too small and too qualitative to meet the demands of big data. For Gieseking, the Lesbian Herstory Archive exemplifies the mismatch between LGBTQ data projects and big data, as well as the risk that 'society's obsession with big data further oppresses the marginalized by creating a false norm to which they are never able to measure up'.[43] Failure to recognize the impacts of homophobia, biphobia and transphobia on the historical and contemporary practices of amassing data about LGBTQ people means that extant datasets are unlikely to match the size or complexity required of big data projects. As with the collection of data, the analysis and use of big data can present an impartial sheen that masks biases that disadvantage LGBTQ people. At a time where the attention of governments is increasingly focused on potential insights from big data and funding bodies channel limited resources to projects that foreground data on a grand scale, there is a risk that data projects about LGBTQ lives and experiences might lose out.[44]

In contrast, small data projects are best understood as the approach to data collection and analysis before the advent of big data. Small data studies

---

[40] Craig Dalton and Jim Thatcher, 'What Does a Critical Data Studies Look Like, and Why Do We Care?', Society & Space, 12 May 2014.

[41] Gillborn, Warmington, and Demack, 'QuantCrit', 167.

[42] Gieseking, 'Size Matters to Lesbians, Too', 150.

[43] Ibid.

[44] Kitchin, The Data Revolution, 28.

investigate a specific phenomenon, which might involve the collection of data about a sample to make inferences about a larger population. Kitchin notes, 'Small data studies seek to mine gold from working a narrow seam, whereas big data studies seek to extract nuggets through open-pit mining scooping up and sieving huge tracts of land.'[45] For example, a small data study of online dating among university students might invite a representative sample of 100 students to complete a survey where they describe their dating activities during the past month. In contrast, a big data project might capture data from dating apps on the smartphones of all students, in real-time, and cross-reference this information with data deduced about users' gender, sex and sexuality based on their online browsing habits. Giesking explains how big data's ambition for total knowledge (in this example, *all* dating activity data about *all* students) is antithetical to a queer feminist approach as it denies the situated nature of knowledge and the oppressive factors that shape data's collection and organization.[46] For these reasons, data about LGBTQ people and big data projects are not common bedfellows. D'Ignazio and Klein describe the framing of big data versus small data as a false binary and instead raise the question, 'How we can scale up data for co-liberation in ways that remain careful, community-based, and complex?'[47] There is no requirement to choose between big and small data, and future studies of LGBTQ people need to utilize the benefits of both approaches. An uncritical embrace of big data puts the collection and analysis of gender, sex and sexuality data at risk, with LGBTQ people engaged as participants in a game where the design of the rules means they are destined to lose. Yet, when done right, the use of big and small data creates opportunities to scale up small data studies, combine data from multiple projects and utilize techniques that automate practices and offer new analytical insights from gender, sex and sexuality data.

Useable findings

Analysis is the bridge between data collection and the use of data for action. How analysis is approached will depend on the research question under investigation and the intended use of results from the study. For example, if

---

[45] Ibid., 29.
[46] Gieseking, 'Size Matters to Lesbians, Too', 154.
[47] D'Ignazio and Klein, *Data Feminism*.

research into the experiences of LGBTQ young people in school is intended to change the public's attitudes to education then punchy, policy-focused findings will likely have a greater impact than a detailed and dense report. An outcome-oriented approach requires researchers to look into the future, imagine the results of their study and determine how analysis can maximize the impact of their project. Queer data projects need to identify an end goal, which positively impacts the lives of whom the data relates, and work towards it. This poses a troublesome question: are analytical decisions that smudge or even misrepresent the identities of participants justified if researchers are confident this will maximize a project's potential to positively impact lives and experiences? Browne provides an example of this dilemma in her account of undertaking a questionnaire of attendees at the 2004 Pride festival in Brighton and Hove, England. Browne developed the project with trustees for the Pride festival, who understood the research as a means to collect data that would ensure the festival's longevity. The survey was completed by 7,210 people and captured data about the multiple dimensions of respondents' sexual orientation, including identity, behaviour and relationships. The nuanced approach meant it was possible to analyse different dimensions of sexual orientation and how they related to the economic, social and cultural impacts of the Pride festival. However, this comprehensive analysis was not undertaken. Browne explains, 'The drive to generate usable findings meant that [...] there was pressure to re-establish the institutional discourses of sexualities which have validity when seeking support from sponsors, local authorities and grant awarding agencies'.[48] Even with the available data and a researcher conscious of not making decisions that flatten LGBTQ lives and experiences, the data's purpose (as a means to attract future funding and support) influenced the approach to analysis.

Browne's account of the Brighton and Hove Pride questionnaire highlights a tension of queer data: the push-and-pull between the analysis of data in ways that positively impact LGBTQ lives and the purity of methods used to achieve these outcomes. To conclude this chapter I want to position the queer tension between methods and outcomes within a wider body of scholarship, in particular Spivak's concept of strategic essentialism.[49] Spivak

---

[48] Kath Browne, 'Selling My Queer Soul or Queerying Quantitative Research?', *Sociological Research Online* 13, no. 1 (January 2008): 200–14.
[49] Gayatri Chakravorty Spivak, 'Subaltern Studies: Deconstructing Historiography [1985]', in *The Spivak Reader: Selected Works of Gayatri Chakravorty Spivak*, ed. Donna Landry and Gerald M. MacLean (New York: Routledge, 1996), 214.

describes how strategic essentialism involves the temporary presentation of an identity group as possessing fixed, intrinsic and innate qualities (or essences) as a means to advance political goals. Temporarily overlooking differences, and fixing in time and space the characteristics of an identity group, can provide a platform to mobilize action and make rights-based claims. Strategic essentialism has informed the contemporary field of identity politics, in which individuals forge political constituencies based on a diversity of shared characteristics. As an approach to the analysis of LGBTQ lives and experiences, strategic essentialism invites both benefits and dangers. The construction of constituencies based on identity relies on reductive stereotypes, an erasure of differences and inaccurate accounts of homogeneity that are sometimes hard to extinguish once unleashed (particularly as essentialist traits tend to benefit the least marginalized within groups).[50] As data makes the journey from collection to its use for action, any dilution of diversity and complexity likely favours individuals already within touching distance to the ideal of equality and where sexual orientation is the only characteristic that excludes them from full inclusion.[51] Moya Lloyd approaches the topic of strategic essentialism from an alternative direction and, while arguing that identities do not possess essential characteristics beyond what is constructed in the social world, challenges the view that essentialist and anti-essentialist positions are oppositional.[52] For Lloyd, essentialism and anti-essentialism are intertwined and a product of political systems based on the advocacy of political representatives and activists who speak on behalf of others, an arrangement that requires actors to couch demands in terms of defined and demarcated constituencies. If we adopt Lloyd's account, the use of gender, sex and sexuality categories to advance political goals cannot escape the pitfalls of strategic essentialism. Those working with queer data therefore need to tread carefully to ensure that analysis of gender, sex and sexuality data, which reduces and homogenizes difference, is reversible and ultimately improves the lives of LGBTQ people.

* * *

---

[50] Marie Moran, '(Un)Troubling Identity Politics: A Cultural Materialist Intervention', *European Journal of Social Theory* 23, no. 2 (May 2020): 265–6.
[51] Spade, *Normal Life*, 44.
[52] Moya Lloyd, *Beyond Identity Politics: Feminism, Power & Politics* (London: SAGE Publications, 2005).

The analysis of gender, sex and sexuality data marks another moment where the fingerprints of people, about whom the data does not directly relate, are evident. The cleaning of data suggests something is amiss with the accuracy of what was collected. In many cases, cleaning fixes unconscious errors on the part of participants – typing the wrong digit or answering a survey question not intended for them. However, among these errors, there also exist conscious attempts to subvert the rules and expectations of data collection practices. For LGBTQ people, *queering* data collection methods can offer a response to not being counted or being forced to identify in ways that fail to reflect an authentic account of an individual's life or experiences. The cleaning, disaggregation and aggregation of data therefore offer analysts a backstop and further opportunity to ensure data presents an account of the social world that those behind the project wished to bring into being. In projects that seek to use data to positively improve LGBTQ lives, aggregation and disaggregation techniques can maximize the usability of findings and boost the potential for impact. For example, the strategic aggregation of identity characteristics into groups, to refute the claim that some identities are 'too small' for meaningful analysis, or temporary overlooking of difference to form larger constituencies and strengthen a basis for political action. Analytical techniques are further supported by advances in qualitative approaches and technologies. For example, the development of new methods has made it more feasible to let respondents describe their identities, in their own words, in diversity-monitoring forms.

Debates about cleaning, aggregation and disaggregation take place against the expansive backdrop of big data and algorithms, which simultaneously analyse data and execute decisions based on the results. However, as Gieseking observes, big data does not generally accommodate information about LGBTQ people, which is often small in scope, qualitative and peppered with gaps and absences. The historical particularities of LGBTQ lives and experiences, and the methods used to collect data, means that a broad-brush approach to big data is ill-suited to many LGBTQ data projects. Data has a history. For big data to authentically represent LGBTQ lives and experiences it needs to accommodate these differences. The navigation of difference is equally core to discussions about the usability of data and the role of strategic essentialism to maximize gains in existing political systems. Again we return to an examination of who is included and excluded, and who makes these decisions. As with data collection, the analysis of gender, sex and sexuality data demonstrates how seemingly neutral data practices can actually entrench existing biases, assumptions and inequalities.

CHAPTER 6
QUEER VALIDATION: DATA PRACTICES AND THE RECOGNITION OF LGBTQ IDENTITY CLAIMS

Edinburgh's Charlotte Square was full of life. Tents for the city's International Book Festival filled the centre of the square as locals and visitors crowded the pavements, making their way between listings at that summer's Fringe festivals. My visit to Charlotte Square was not for cultural reasons but a meeting with NRS at their historic West Register House offices. After ringing the doorbell, I was escorted through a labyrinth of corridors in what felt like an abandoned government building before arriving in a small back room set up with monitors, papers and other meeting attendees. Myself and a handful of other representatives from LGBTQ and EDI organizations in Scotland had gathered for a consultation session on NRS's proposals for the census questions on sex, sexual orientation and trans status/history. Most of the issues discussed were not particularly new to anyone in the room but one announcement caught my attention. The design of the question on trans status/history appeared to depart from other census questions in the census about identity characteristics, as it asked:

Do you consider yourself to be trans, or have a trans history?

Respondents were then invited to answer 'No' or 'Yes', and provide further write-in information if they answered 'Yes' and wished to do so. The design differed from other questions in the census, which generally asked:[1]

What is your … ?

Followed by the characteristic under question, for example 'What is your sex?' with the response options 'female' and 'male'. Something seemed

---

[1] For example, the census asks 'What is your ethnic group?' and 'What religion, religious denomination or body do you belong to?', in National Records of Scotland, 'Question Set'.

peculiar about the wording of the trans question. When compared with the format of questions on sex and sexual orientation, which were also discussed during the meeting, the trans question seemed clunky. I could not quite put my finger on what was wrong. I talked through my confusion with others in the room – 'Is the question written in the passive voice? Is the word trans being used as a noun or a verb?' It was only after the stakeholder meeting that the reason for my discomfort became clear to me: unlike other census questions, the trans question underlined the self-identified nature of what was being asked. Whereas the format 'What is your … ?' suggests something uncontested about the identity characteristic under question, 'Do you consider yourself to be … ?' made clear that the answer was based on the opinion of the person answering the question.

In Scotland and across the UK, the concept of self-identification has emerged as a hot-button issue for some campaign groups, politicians, writers and media personalities, particularly in regard to the self-identification of trans women.[2] The limited discussion of how self-identification relates to other markers of identity (such as ethnicity, race, disability or religion) suggests that concerns voiced had less to do with self-identification and more to do with hostile attitudes towards trans inclusion.[3] My experience at West Register House highlighted how the addition of questions on sexual orientation and trans status/history, and provision of inclusive response options and guidance, did not guarantee that Scotland's census would count LGBTQ people in a meaningful way. The collection of data is not enough if people perceive the information gathered as little more than someone's personal views and detached from a wider reality. Census designers therefore also have to assess how data is understood as a valid representation of the social world, and who or what holds the power to determine data's validity.

* * *

[2] Most notably, in June 2020 author J. K. Rowling wrote a lengthy letter that detailed her alarm that the Scottish Government intends to proceed with reform of the GRA that, according to Rowling, 'will in effect mean that all man needs to "become a woman" is to say he's one', in J. K. Rowling, 'JK Rowling Writes about Her Reasons for Speaking Out on Sex and Gender Issues', *JK Rowling*, 10 June 2020.

[3] In regard to racial self-identification, there are high-profile examples of white women in the Unites States who self-identified as Black, including Jessica Krug (a professor of African American Heritage at George Washington University) and Rachel Dolezal (an activist and former President of the Spokane chapter of National Association for the Advancement of Colored People), in Poppy Noor, 'White US Professor Jessica Krug Admits She Has Pretended to Be Black for Years', *The Guardian*, 3 September 2020.

Data, on its own, does not tell us very much. Meaning comes from the relationship between data and the 'reality' it claims to represent. To achieve this ambition, data systems must permit only one representation to the exclusion of all others (for example, it is not practical for a census to collect data about an individual's biological, legal and lived sex when they are understood as measures of the same concept).[4] This chapter examines practices that determine the validity of data, which occur during and after the collection of data and are informed by biases and assumptions as to whether data is representative of the social world. I examine the concept of self-identification, in which the agency to identify is located with the individual about whom the data relates. I also explore alternative approaches where the validity of data is determined by others (external-identification) and/or based on biometric information or behavioural encounters with technologies such as social media and mobile phones.

Valid data is integral to the making of identity claims and the recognition of these claims by administrative systems that shape people's everyday lives. For example, someone who is non-binary and does not identify as a man or a woman is unable to register themselves as they wish in studies where the researcher uses visual cues to externally assign a binary gender or technologies that are pre-programmed with two, compulsory options. In this instance, a gap is established between an individual's self-identified identity (as someone non-binary) and the identity assigned to them through practices designed to collect and analyse data (man or woman). Data systems cannot register both responses as valid so what answer is ultimately recognized? For this reason, the validity of data about individuals' identities is often contested. In particular, many LGBTQ people find themselves entangled in contestations, where different validation practices arrive at different conclusions about gender, sex and sexuality. This is particularly pertinent in contexts where inequalities between genders, sexes and sexualities are baked into the law in areas such as marriage and adoption. As Ryan explains, 'official identity matters not just because it is how one is understood in the eyes of the law, but also because it is the means by which one can gain, or lose, access to certain civil rights and social resources'.[5] In this chapter, I highlight how researchers, practitioners and activists engaged

---

[4] Jeffrey Alan Johnson, 'Information Systems and the Translation of Transgender', *TSQ: Transgender Studies Quarterly* 2, no. 1 (1 January 2015).
[5] Ryan, 'Born Again?', 271.

in work with gender, sex and sexuality data need to look beyond collection and analysis practices to also consider methods that seek to demonstrate that data is a valid representation of the social world.

Self-identification practices

The view that people conceive of themselves as having an 'identity', and a say as to how this identity is understood by others, is a relatively recent and culturally specific phenomenon.[6] When someone self-identifies they assign a particular characteristic or categorization to themselves. For example, with sexual orientation, the agency to identify as gay is located with the individual who makes the statement 'I am gay'.[7] Self-identification differs from situations where a person assigns an identity to another person (for example, where a researcher might determine a person's gender based on perceptions about their name, clothes, hairstyle or voice).

Since the early 2000s, public attitudes towards same-sex relationships in Scotland have improved, as well as the proportion of the population who know someone who identifies as gay or lesbian.[8] Greater acceptability and awareness among the general population of LGBTQ issues have also raised interest in data about identity characteristics and introduced people to previously unfamiliar sexual orientations and gender identities. As discussed in Chapter 4, the challenge for many LGBTQ people is not making sense of their own identities but navigating cis/heteronormative administrative practices that recognize some identities, through concepts such as 'legal

---

[6] See Anthony Giddens, *Modernity and Self-Identity: Self and Society in the Late Modern Age* (Stanford: Stanford University Press, 1991); Tey Meadow, "'A Rose Is a Rose": On Producing Legal Gender Classifications', *Gender & Society* 24, no. 6 (December 2010): 816; Moran, '(Un) Troubling Identity Politics', 260.

[7] Butler described gender and sexual identities as performative as they are constructed through the repeated performance of the phenomena they claim to describe. Part of this practice involves speech acts, such as marriage declarations and coming-out statements, in Butler, *Bodies That Matter*, 2.

[8] Between 2000 and 2015, the percentage of people in Scotland who believed that sexual relations between two adults of the same sex was always or mostly wrong fell from 48 per cent to 18 per cent. Similarly, between 2010 and 2015 the proportion of respondents who had a family member who is gay or lesbian increased from 13 per cent to 21 per cent, in Scottish Government, 'Scottish Social Attitudes 2015: Attitudes to Discrimination and Positive Action', Social Research (Edinburgh: Scottish Government, 2016), 21, 78.

gender', but not others.[9] For example, Scotland's census asks respondents to self-identify for all questions related to identity characteristics. In other words, although there is a legal requirement to participate in the census and not provide false information, respondents are not invited to provide evidence nor does anyone check.[10] For many identities asked about in the census, the provision of evidence is not appropriate nor practical. For example, how would someone prove their sexual orientation, religion or ethnicity? Census officials assume that the person providing the information will know best. Importantly, an inability to provide proof does not mean that identities such as sexual orientation, religion and ethnicity are any less meaningful than those where the provision of documentation is possible (for example, someone who is married could show their marriage certificate or someone who has UK citizenship could show their UK passport).[11]

In many instances, the efforts of LGBTQ rights groups to raise awareness of trans, non-binary and queer people have been met by a backlash. National newspapers, for example, expressed outrage that school children were being informed of the existence of multiple and diverse gender identities.[12] What is particularly noteworthy in these reports is the hostility towards self-identification and scepticism as to whether individuals were *really* best placed to define their own identities. For example, media figures such as TV personality Piers Morgan (who self-identified as a 'two-spirit, gender-neutral, pan-neutral, gender fluid, femme penguin' in 2019) ridiculed the idea of multiple gender identities and self-identification at a time where LGBTQ people were invited to authentically identify themselves in the census for the first time and proposals to reform the GRA were underway in the Scottish and UK Parliaments.[13] Attacks on self-identification meant

[9] Meadow, "'A Rose Is a Rose'", 817.
[10] As noted in Chapter 3, the sex question in the 2021 English and Welsh census demonstrates a tension between self-identification and the requirement to identify in line with existing documentation. The final guidance advised respondents to answer according to the sex on their birth certificate or GRC but respondents were not required to consult the guidance nor was it possible for the ONS to verify how respondents answered this question. In effect, respondents could continue to self-identify for the question, contrary to the guidance presented.
[11] As I discuss in Chapter 4, administrative practices that determine who is awarded official documents (such as birth certificates) are also contested and potentially exclusionary.
[12] See Nicholas Hellen, 'BBC Films Teach Children of "100 Genders, or More"', *The Times*; Tariq Tahir, 'BBC Films Used in Schools Teach Children There Are "100 Genders or More" Despite GPs Only Recognising Six', *The Sun*, 8 September 2019.
[13] Kyle O'Sullivan, 'Piers Morgan Identifies as Penguin and Demands to Live in Aquarium in Furious Rant', *Daily Mirror*, 11 September 2019.

that LGBTQ lives became a topic of legitimate debate. The transformation of people's lives into a debate provided opportunities for cis, heterosexual people – who had no lived experience of the very thing they wished to 'debate' – to scrutinize the experiences of LGBTQ people and challenge the validity of LGBTQ identity claims.

External-identification practices

Whereas self-identification is the assigning of a particular characteristic or categorization to oneself, external-identification is where a person assigns a characteristic or categorization to someone else. While working on research projects that involved the collection of gender, sex and sexuality data about staff and students in higher education, I was intrigued as to what happens when the agency to self-identify was removed from the research participant and granted to someone or something else. Many research projects are, in fact, based on the collection of data about identity characteristics where participants are not allowed to self-identify. For example, surveys conducted by telephone often do not ask participants to state their gender or sex but infer this information from audio cues and the participant's name. Bittner, Goodyear-Grant and Lombardi, for example, have noted how major surveys continue to refuse opportunities for participants to self-identify their gender and/or sex and instead rely on the assumptions of interviewers to categorize each participant.[14] In other projects, such as studies that investigate the diversity of company boards, analysis of gender and sex is based on assumptions made about people's names, titles, biographies and photographs found on company websites and other relevant web pages.[15]

Outside of the UK, the roll-out of affirmative action policies to combat racial inequality in Brazil highlights potential dangers of external-identification practices. In the early 2000s, Brazil introduced several affirmative action policies intended to address race inequality in access to higher education and public sector employment. Initiatives included the introduction of quotas for Black, brown and Indigenous students at

---

[14] Bittner and Goodyear-Grant, 'Sex Isn't Gender', 1023; Lombardi, 'Trans Issues in Sociology', 71.
[15] For example, see Stephen Brammer, Andrew Millington, and Stephen Pavelin, 'Gender and Ethnic Diversity among UK Corporate Boards', *Corporate Governance: An International Review* 15 (1 February 2007): 396.

prestigious universities and the allocation of 20 per cent of public sector jobs to people who satisfied particular racial criteria. However, following the introduction of these policies, journalist Cleuci de Oliviera describes how 'a state of racial vigilance permeated campuses' as students and staff began to scrutinize individuals' racial identities and question who had benefited from affirmative action.[16] In response to increased suspicion of 'race fraud', some institutions installed race boards to evaluate applicants who wished to make use of affirmative action policies. Race boards were instructed to evaluate 'phenotypical characteristics' rather than 'arguments concerning the race of one's ancestors', which encouraged some board members to review applicants' hair, nose, lips and gums. Rogerio Reis, an anthropology professor who chaired a race board at one higher education institution, told de Oliviera, 'We saw the most incredible situations unfold [...]. People would shave their heads, wear beanies, get a tan. Just a series of strategies to turn themselves black'. Although affirmative action policies were intended to help address race inequality in Brazil, the execution of these policies unleashed crude, stereotypical ideas about racial physiology where 'experts' became the authority on the validity of data about applicants' race.

Although Brazilian race boards offer a nightmarish example of 'experts' overruling how individuals' self-identify, external identification methods are used to validate individuals' identity characteristics around the world. In Australia, for example, when Aboriginal and Torres Strait Islander People wish to access Indigenous-specific services and programmes, they might be asked to provide proof of their heritage through family history records or a letter of confirmation from someone in the community.[17] Closer to home, trans people in the UK that wish to change the sex marker on their birth certificate require a GRC, a process described as overly bureaucratic, invasive and humiliating for trans people as it requires an 'expert panel' to review medical and psychological information.[18] External-identification approaches encounter problems when there is a mismatch between how an

---

[16] Cleuci de Oliveira, 'Brazil's New Problem With Blackness', *Foreign Policy*, 5 April 2017. Also see Lulu Garcia-Navarro, 'For Affirmative Action, Brazil Sets Up Controversial Boards To Determine Race', *NPR*, 29 September 2016.
[17] Australian Institute of Aboriginal and Torres Strait Islander Studies, 'Proof of Aboriginality', 4 September 2020.
[18] As discussed in the Introduction chapter, the UK and Scottish Governments have expressed a willingness to reform the current system for legal gender recognition under the GRA, with support from most major LGBTQ organizations in the UK.

individual self-identifies and how they are perceived by an external 'expert'. Individuals are often mismatched when they do not 'pass', and are therefore perceived in ways that differ from how they identify, or do not wish to 'pass' but subvert normative assumptions about gender, sex or sexuality. In these examples, the classification of people's identity characteristics (by 'experts' who may never meet the person in question) denies individuals the opportunity to identify in ways that authentically reflect how they wish to live their lives.

Biometric practices

Identity management practices identify, authenticate and authorize someone to access services or systems. In 2020, the UK Government issued guidance for organizations on how to authenticate the identity of people who use their services to ensure only permitted users can gain access.[19] The guidance notes that authentication can involve something the user *knows* (a password or PIN), something the user *has* (a security key or digital certificate) and/or something the user *is* (a fingerprint or signature). This third strand of authentication involves the inspection of an individual's biometric or behavioural data, an area of growing relevance in identity management with particular implications for the validation of data about LGBTQ people.

Self-identification is based on a premise of trust and an expectation that you are truthful about how you identify. This reciprocal arrangement enables the operation of university scholarships for students of colour, literary prizes for LGBTQ writers, women-only exercise groups and mentorship programmes for working-class entrepreneurs without the need to 'check' people's identity claims. Initiatives instead function with the expectation that those who participate must identify as a member of the group the measure is intended to support. In situations where trust cannot be relied upon, such as immigration and law enforcement, other approaches to validating an individual's identity claims are required. For example, immigration and law enforcement officials use biometric data from an individual's fingerprints and eyes to cross-reference identity claims against information held in an

---

[19] Government Digital Services, 'Using Authenticators to Protect an Online Service', GOV.UK, 14 May 2020.

existing database, such as information submitted when a person applied for a passport. Beauchamp describes how the extracting of biometric data 'directly from the body' means that data is often characterized as 'more accurate and reliable than a corruptible trail of paper documents'.[20] Yet, as a means to verify an individual's identity, the linking of biometric and self-identified data still requires individuals to self-report data about themselves (for example, their name, age, sex and place of birth). What happens when an existing database of information about individuals' identity characteristics is unavailable or does not exist, and how might biometric data practices fill this gap?

Technologies that combine data, machine learning and algorithms to make judgements about an individual's identity characteristics have attempted to respond to this challenge. However, as discussed later in the chapter, the use of automated practices to validate data about individuals' gender, sex and sexuality invites the cis/heteronormative assumptions of those who designed the systems, which disproportionately disadvantages LGBTQ people who break from these rules. For example, automated gender-recognition technologies attempt to use information about a person's face, voice or body to infer information about their gender.[21] Joy Buolamwini and Timnit Gebru have documented how facial recognition tools used for this purpose are most effective at reading the faces of lighter-skinned men and least effective at reading the faces of darker-skinned women.[22] In the UK, research conducted by the BBC found that the Home Office's online passport application checker, which is intended to ensure applicants submit photos that meet Home Office regulations, struggled to read the faces of darker-skinned women.[23] Based on a sample of 1,000 photographs, images

---

[20] Beauchamp, *Going Stealth*, 94.
[21] Keyes' review of academic papers on automatic gender recognition technologies reports how these technologies operationalize gender in a trans-exclusionary way, in Os Keyes, 'The Misgendering Machines: Trans/HCI Implications of Automatic Gender Recognition', *Proceedings of the ACM on Human-Computer Interaction* 2, no. CSCW (November 2018): 1–22.
[22] Joy Buolamwini and Timnit Gebru, 'Gender Shades: Intersectional Accuracy Disparities in Commercial Gender Classification', ed. Sorelle A Friedler and Christo Wilson, *Proceedings of Machine Learning Research* 81 (2018): 12.
[23] Freedom of information requests uncovered that the Home Office were aware of issues with the technology when the service went live in June 2016 but decided to proceed with the roll-out, in Adam Vaughan, 'UK Launched Passport Photo Checker It Knew Would Fail with Dark Skin', *New Scientist*, 9 October 2019; Maryam Ahmed, 'UK Passport Photo Checker Shows Bias against Dark-Skinned Women', *BBC News*, 7 October 2020.

of dark-skinned women were deemed poor quality 22 per cent of the time whereas images of light-skinned men were deemed poor quality just 9 per cent of the time. One reason for this discrepancy is that to learn how to recognize characteristics, such as gender, facial recognition tools require a huge amount of existing labelled data (images of faces). It is not surprising to discover that datasets used to train facial recognition tools are skewed in favour of lighter-skinned men.[24] Controversial studies have also applied facial recognition tools to the question of sexual orientation to assess whether machines can determine a person's sexuality based on information about their face. One study, conducted by Michal Kosinski and Yilun Wang, claimed that AI could identify the sexual orientation of men 91 per cent of the time and women 83 per cent of the time after viewing just five images of an individual's face.[25] Subsequent investigations have, however, challenged these claims.[26] Whatever these studies tell us, the use of facial recognition tools to validate identity claims about gender, sex and sexuality poses questions about the data used to train technologies, the blurring of correlation and causation, and the perilous possibilities of technology that identifies someone's sexual orientation from data about their face.

We already see the negative effects of these developments in situations where gender recognition technologies are a component in a broader security and surveillance apparatus used to flag instances where bodies fail to match normative assumptions. Sasha Costanza-Chock has described their experiences of engaging with technologies used to enforce security at airports.[27] For example, full-length body scanners (where you are asked to stand in a pod and raise your arms) require security officials to externally assign a binary gender and input this information into the machine before you enter the pod, a practice that disproportionately identifies trans bodies

---

[24] Buolamwini and Gebru, 'Gender Shades: Intersectional Accuracy Disparities in Commercial Gender Classification', 1.

[25] Yilun Wang and Michal Kosinski, 'Deep Neural Networks Are More Accurate than Humans at Detecting Sexual Orientation from Facial Images', *Journal of Personality and Social Psychology* 114, no. 2 (February 2018): 246–57.

[26] BBC News, 'Row Over AI That "Identifies Gay Faces"', *BBC News*, 11 September 2017; Blaise Aguera Y. Arcas, Alexander Todorov, and Margaret Mitchell, 'Do Algorithms Reveal Sexual Orientation or Just Expose Our Stereotypes?', *Medium*, 11 January 2018; Andrew Gelman, Gregor Mattson, and Daniel Simpson, 'Gaydar and the Fallacy of Objective Measurement', *Unpublished*, 2018.

[27] Sasha Costanza-Chock, 'Design Justice, AI, and Escape from the Matrix of Domination', *Journal of Design and Science* Online (July 2018): 3.

as aberrations. For Costanza-Chock, the knowledge that their body is almost certainly going to be 'flagged as anomalous' creates a situation that is embarrassing, uncomfortable and humiliating.[28] Ashley has also described the use of voice recognition technologies by banks and how this security measure can lock trans people out of their account when their voice fails to match gendered expectations.[29] Cisnormative assumptions that underpin the design of airport body scanners or security measures used in telephone banking demonstrate how technologies intended to validate gender, sex and sexuality identity characteristics, in the name of enhancing security for *everyone*, cause particular harm to LGBTQ people that sit outside ideas of what constitutes a 'normal' body.

In some cases, the use of biometric data practices to validate (or invalidate) a person's identity characteristics has life or death consequences. Presented as a means to enhance the safety and security of the public, borders and the activities of immigration officers often serve as a testing ground for new technologies.[30] In 2009, the UK Border Agency trialled the Human Provenance Pilot Project as a method to establish the genetic ancestry of people, predominantly from East Africa, and vet asylum claims.[31] The method involved the analysis of samples of saliva, nails and hair from an applicant to confirm or deny their claim that they were Somalian, a country where people had fled persecution and were eligible for asylum in the UK. If an applicant refused to participate in the project or the results suggested they were from another country, their asylum claim was denied. The pilot was flawed for a variety of reasons, including the lack of reliability in the genetic testing and the belief that results (even if accurate) would align with contemporary African geography. Benjamin notes that the pilot project 'stands as a salutary warning about the ways in which supposedly objective technologies of identification are increasingly being used at international borders to disempower the already vulnerable still further.'[32] The use of identity management technologies to strengthen arguments that exclude people from the distribution of life chances, including those fleeing harm

---

[28] Costanza-Chock, 'Design Justice, AI, and Escape from the Matrix of Domination', 3.

[29] Florence Ashley, 'Recommendations for Institutional and Governmental Management of Gender Information', *NYU Review of Law & Social Change* 44, no. 4 (2021): 501.

[30] Pascal Emmer et al., 'Technologies for Liberation: Toward Abolitionist Futures' (Astraea Lesbian Foundation for Justice and Research Action Design, 2020), 20–1.

[31] BBC News, 'Experts Condemn Asylum DNA Tests', *BBC News*, 30 September 2009.

[32] Benjamin, *Race after Technology*, 132.

and seeking asylum, requires LGBTQ people to rethink their relationship to data.[33] Even though the use of biometric data to validate identity claims remains in its infancy, LGBTQ people must assess whether they wish to contribute gender, sex and sexuality data to systems that strengthen rather than dismantle the infrastructure that makes this future possible.

Behavioural practices

The final source of validation I wish to discuss is behavioural data practices. This is where data is collected about an individual through their engagement with technology, such as online browsing history, shopping behaviour tracked on a store card, library books borrowed, health information from a smartwatch or location tracking from a mobile phone. Behavioural data does not require someone to self-identify as LGBTQ nor is this identity assigned by an external other or from biometric data; instead, a person's gender, sex and sexuality are identified through data collected about their actions. The collection, analysis and use of behavioural data are most commonly associated with major tech companies including Google, Amazon and Facebook, where data 'about us' is used to develop targeted advertising and branded content.[34] For example, the disclosure of your gender and sexual orientation during the creation of a Facebook account is only one small segment of data held about your identity characteristics. Activity on the platform also offers a treasure chest of behavioural information based on your friends, shares, clicks and likes that – when pieced together – can provide detailed insights into your identity characteristics. In a 2009 study, Carter Jernigan and Behram Mistree demonstrated how it was possible to predict the sexual orientation of a Facebook user based on analysis of

---

[33] Tendayi Achiume (the UN's special rapporteur on racism, racial discrimination, xenophobia and related intolerance) submitted a report to the UN General Assembly in November 2020 that highlighted the prevalence of digital technologies used to advance xenophobic and racially discriminatory ideologies, in Tendayi Achiume, 'Report of the Special Rapporteur on Contemporary Forms of Racism, Racial Discrimination, Xenophobia and Related Intolerance' (New York: United Nations Office of the High Commissioner for Human Rights, 10 November 2020).

[34] Nick Couldry and Ulises A. Mejias describe the practices of these companies as 'data colonialism', in Nick Couldry and Ulises A. Mejias, 'Data Colonialism: Rethinking Big Data's Relation to the Contemporary Subject', *Television & New Media* 20, no. 4 (2019): 340.

their friends on the platform. The study noted, 'the percentage of a given user's friends who self–identify as gay male is strongly correlated with the sexual orientation of that user'.[35] Emma Mishel et al. have also investigated Google search data to see what we can learn about sexuality.[36] In their paper 'Google, Tell Me. Is He Gay?: Masculinity, Homophobia, and Gendered Anxieties in Google Search Queries about Sexuality', Mishel et al. compared the use of gendered search terms that asked about the sexuality of others, such as 'Is my son gay' and 'Is my daughter gay/lesbian/a lesbian?' Covering searches conducted in the United States between 2007 and 2018, they found 'consistent higher search interest asking about possible gay men and boys compared to possible gay women and girls across a range of gendered search options and phrases'.[37] Benjamin also notes that although streaming platforms such as Netflix thrive on tailored marketing, it is not necessary to ask viewers to explicitly disclose information (such as their race) as this data is discerned from prior viewing and search histories.[38] If asked to disclose information about their identity characteristics, a sizeable proportion of viewers might subvert the exercise – the clandestine collection of this data from how viewers engage with the platform therefore potentially offers a more robust account of viewers' identity characteristics.

Like other types of external-identified data, behavioural data requires instructions from human operators to make decisions. Although technologies are capable of learning, the data used to train them can introduce assumptions and biases that recreate existing inequalities.[39] Examination of whose interests are served through the extraction of data about users' identity characteristics highlights how commercial interests govern who is counted as LGBTQ in these technological spaces and in what ways these communities are understood and valued. For example, as a commercial enterprise, Noah Tsika and Rena Bivens have documented how Facebook's algorithms are primarily invested in using data to pre-empt

---

[35] Carter Jernigan and Behram Mistree, 'Gaydar: Facebook Friendships Expose Sexual Orientation', *First Monday* 14, no.10 (5 October 2009).
[36] Emma Mishel, Tristan Bridges, and Mònica L. Caudillo, 'Google, Tell Me. Is He Gay?: Masculinity, Homophobia, and Gendered Anxieties in Google Search Queries about Sexuality', *SocArXiv* Online (8 November 2018): 2.
[37] Mishel, Bridges, and Caudillo, 'Google, Tell Me. Is He Gay?', 2.
[38] Benjamin, *Race after Technology*, 18–19.
[39] See Frederik Zuiderveen Borgesius, 'Discrimination, Artificial Intelligence, and Algorithmic Decision-Making' (Strasbourg: Directorate General of Democracy, Council of Europe, 2018).

future behaviour, deliver targeted content and satisfy advertisers rather than provide conditions that authentically reflect LGBTQ lives. In 2014, the list of genders and sexualities for Facebook users in the UK was expanded to include over seventy possible options, including terms such as intersex man, asexual and hermaphrodite.[40] Facebook stated that this development was intended to reflect the diversity of the platform's users. Yet, as Tsika notes, behind-the-scenes Facebook lumped all users who selected options other than heterosexual/straight and cisgender into a unified LGBTQ category that targeted them with advertising content primarily designed for white, cis, gay men – a consumer group perceived as profitable by businesses and advertisers.[41] Bivens argues that despite the addition of more gender options, the gender binary in Facebook's software was not deprogrammed.[42] Even when technologies present a veneer of diversity and inclusivity, such as the provision of more ways to identify one's gender, the example of Facebook shows that this can mask underlying practices about how individuals are counted and data used about them.

It seems unlikely the uses of behavioural data will stop with targeted advertising on Facebook or the provision of bespoke content on Netflix. As we saw in the 2016 US Presidential elections and UK referendum to leave the EU, there is potential to use behavioural data to deliver other aims.[43] For example, a possible future exists where companies no longer ask their employees to disclose diversity monitoring data as a computer can determine this information from employee's online browsing habits. Although this approach addresses concerns people might have about reciprocal trust and self-identification, reliance on behavioural data removes an individual's agency to identify themselves and grants this power to a machine that often repeats existing biases and assumptions, serving the interests of its designer rather than the people about whom the data relates.

---

[40] James Vincent, 'Facebook Introduces More than 70 New Gender Options to the UK: "We Want to Reflect Society"', *The Independent*, 24 June 2014.
[41] Noah Tsika, 'CompuQueer: Protocological Constraints, Algorithmic Streamlining, and the Search for Queer Methods Online', *Women's Studies Quarterly* 44, no. 3/4 (2016): 117–18.
[42] Rena Bivens, 'The Gender Binary Will Not Be Deprogrammed: Ten Years of Coding Gender on Facebook', *New Media & Society* 19, no. 6 (1 June 2017): 894.
[43] For example, Cambridge Analytica's attempt to use data extracted from Facebook to influence the results of the 2016 US election and the Trump team's use of a dataset, with information on almost 200 million US voters, to deter around 3.5 million Black Americans from voting, in Alex Hern, 'Cambridge Analytica: How Did It Turn Clicks into Votes?', *The Guardian*, 6 May 2018; Channel 4 News Investigations Team, 'Revealed: Trump Campaign Strategy to Deter Millions of Black Americans from Voting in 2016', *Channel 4 News*, 28 September 2020.

Biases and assumptions

The four practices described in this chapter demonstrate how decisions about data validity are never neutral. As noted in previous chapters, quantitative and qualitative methods can create datasets that are biased in favour of the world view of the researcher who collected the data. Biases that influence data collection continue as data progresses through analysis. Automated practices, such as the use of algorithms to make decisions about data, are intended to discriminate – it is in their design to recognize difference between multiple pieces of information.[44] When applied to real people's lives, algorithmic decision-making reviews the available data and arrives at a judgement on issues as diverse as awarding a loan application to identifying someone as an 'error' when data about their gender and sex disagree. Several scholarly works have documented how gender and racial biases are built in to the operation of algorithmic decision-making and the devastating impacts of these biases on marginalized communities in areas such as health, finance and law enforcement.[45] Given their history, Nenad Tomasev et al. argue that 'algorithms have moral consequences for queer communities' and sketch emergent challenges in the areas of privacy, censorship, language, online abuse, health, mental health and employment.[46] As a response to data-based injustices, scholars have argued against methods that foreground biased individuals as the problem, as subsequent efforts to fix rogue individuals excuse wider systems that enabled their actions to flourish.[47] Benjamin describes how the 'bad apple' explanation means 'individuals are treated as glitches in an otherwise benign system'.[48] When the 'bad apple' is fixed (through unconscious bias training, for example) or removed from the

---

[44] Michael Veale and Reuben Binns, 'Fairer Machine Learning in the Real World: Mitigating Discrimination without Collecting Sensitive Data', *Big Data & Society* 4, no. 2 (2017): 2.

[45] See Cathy O'Neil, *Weapons of Math Destruction: How Big Data Increases Inequality and Threatens Democracy* (New York: Crown, 2016); Virginia Eubanks, *Automating Inequality: How High-Tech Tools Profile, Police, and Punish the Poor* (New York: St Martin's Press, 2017); Safiya Umoja Noble, *Algorithms of Oppression: How Search Engines Reinforce Racism* (New York: New York University Press, 2018).

[46] Nenad Tomasev et al., 'Fairness for Unobserved Characteristics: Insights from Technological Impacts on Queer Communities', *ArXiv:2102.04257* Online (2021).

[47] A focus on 'bad apples' means that rotten systems are preserved through minor tweaks, an idea described as 'preservation through transformation' in Siegel, 'Why Equal Protection No Longer Protects: The Evolving Forms of Status-Enforcing State Action', 1113, discussed in Chapter 1.

[48] Benjamin, *Race after Technology*, 87.

system (relocated to another organization where they negatively impact even more people), the system that facilitated biased behaviours can continue unchanged. Overattention to the individual biases of researchers and analysts engaged in gender, sex and sexuality data practices repeats the same mistake. Anna Lauren Hoffmann has described how 'the ideal of inclusion' has permeated efforts to mitigate problems of biases in data collection and analysis.[49] Going beyond calls to simply diversify, inclusion interventions bring more people into the room, add to the number of seats at the table where decisions are made and, most importantly, value the input of those included. Yet, for Hoffmann, 'inclusion represents an ethics of social change that does not upset the social order' as it positions existing data systems and practices as both the cause and solution to the problem of biases.[50] Keyes has also argued that 'reformist approaches to data science are insufficient' and that the energies of data activists need to focus on the development of a radical data science that is not controlling, eliminationist nor assimilatory and premised on 'enabling *plural ways of being*' that do '*not punish* those who do not participate in the system'.[51] The efforts of large tech companies such as Google, Amazon and Facebook to 'do better' has resulted in a shoring-up and expansion of power as the people who designed systems with in-built biases were tasked with fixing the mess they created.[52] Among those who believe data systems are capable of change, companies have designed and rolled out technologies to counteract existing biases in datasets and algorithms. For example, Accenture launched a service for companies to test the safety, reliability and transparency of the data and algorithms in their AI systems.[53] Computer scientists have also devised methods such as discrimination-aware data mining and fairness, accountability and transparency in machine learning to try and prevent the perpetuation of biases.[54] Although there is now a greater awareness of problems that exist, a queer response to these concerns needs to ensure that validation practices open up rather than

---

[49] Anna Lauren Hoffmann, 'Terms of Inclusion: Data, Discourse, Violence', *New Media & Society* Online (16 September 2020): 13.
[50] Hoffmann, 'Terms of Inclusion', 16, 20–1.
[51] Keyes, 'Counting the Countless'.
[52] Hoffman describes how tech companies 'readily admit that data technologies produce harmful or even violent outcomes but respond by positioning data science and technology as ultimately the solution to these violences', in Hoffmann, 'Terms of Inclusion', 16.
[53] Collett and Dillon, 'AI and Gender', 20.
[54] Veale and Binns, 'Fairer Machine Learning in the Real World', 3.

limit the distribution of life chances for LGBTQ people. Discussing the relationship between surveillance technologies and Black communities in the United States, Nabil Hassein has questioned whose interests are 'served by the deployment of automated systems capable of reliably identifying Black people' and stated that 'no technology under police control will be used to hold police accountable or to benefit Black folks or other oppressed people.'[55] As with the previous chapter's account of how seemingly neutral data practices can entrench existing biases and assumptions, we cannot fix problems by blaming 'bad apples' or relying on the promises of technology. Nor can we provide solutions to problems that only improve experiences for a subsection of LGBTQ people (likely to be those least disadvantaged by existing biases). As I discuss in the final part of *Queer Data*, answers might sit outside of existing practices or systems and require scholars, practitioners and activists to take control of queer data so that it is used as a productive force to reshape people's lives and experiences.

* * *

Self-identification, external-identification, biometric and behavioural data practices present four ways to validate gender, sex and sexuality identity claims and establish who counts as LGBTQ. Who or what determines whether data is valid, and recognized as an accurate representation of the social world, is an important stage in data journey's from its collection to its use for action. My focus in this chapter has looked beyond the diversion of individual biases to instead consider the design of systems and how they intersect with practices used to validate (or invalidate) people's identity claims. From self-identification in Scotland's census to the extraction of data about our online browsing habits, multiple methods are used to validate data about someone's identity as LGBTQ. Regardless of the methods adopted, the validation of identity claims entails problems: whether it is the controversial use of automated gender recognition technologies or algorithms in-built with cis/heteronormative assumptions. A thread running through external-identification practices is the removal of agency from LGBTQ people to decide how they wish to identify. At a time when opponents of queer data seek to police the borders of what it means to identify as LGBTQ, this chapter

---

[55] Nabil Hassein, 'Against Black Inclusion in Facial Recognition', *Digital Talking Drum*, 15 August 2017.

complicates assumptions that the collection of more data or provision of inclusive response options can solve historical inequalities. These actions alone are simply not enough. By tracing the influences on data throughout the process of analysis, further light is shone on who or what determines the validity of gender, sex and sexuality data. With enough evidence of the problem, it is now time to take action.

PART III
USING QUEER DATA

CHAPTER 7
LOUD VOICES: COMMUNICATING QUEER DATA IN ONLINE SPACES

My phone started to vibrate. Rather than one or two hums, it kept on going. This had never happened before. I glanced at my screen and saw several Twitter message notifications:

I didn't know you could get a doctorate in bigotry.
You're a fraud and a misogynist.
You're just another equal opportunity woman hater.

Like early tremors in an earthquake, this was a warning sign of what was to come. A stream of online abuse and harassment soon followed, amplified by thousands of likes and retweets. My Twitter account was accustomed to a handful of notifications per day; this experience sent it into overdrive. The comments were in response to a post I published on Twitter that criticized calls for Scotland's census to change how it asks about sex (from a self-identified question to one that asks about 'biological sex'), noting how this would force some trans people to answer the question in a way that did not accurately reflect their lives. I muted the conversation and tried to move on with my day. But the accusations stuck with me. As someone who does not identify as trans, was it my place to speak out about trans rights when the issues did not directly affect my life? And, by using my voice online, had I now centred myself in the story and potentially added fuel to the fire? Much online discourse related to gender, sex and sexuality data is unproductive for all parties involved (except for the platform, which benefits from increased traffic and ads revenue). My retelling of this relatively minor experience of online abuse and harassment is a lesson for those engaged in conversations about queer data to foreground the lives and experience of the people about whom the data relates and not let one's personal experiences become the headline. When we use our voice online we should 'speak up' when we can add something of value to the conversation and not 'speak over' others who wish to tell their story.

* * *

Who makes decisions about the collection, analysis and use of gender, sex and sexuality data? Who is listened to, who has a voice, and whose voice is recognized as an authority? In this third and final part, I turn attention to the uses of queer data for action, which involves an examination of the unequal distribution of power across genders, sexes and sexualities in different social contexts, between LGBTQ and cis/heterosexual communities, and among LGBTQ people with different experiences of marginalization. This chapter explores power relations between majorities and minorities, as well as within sexual minority groups, and explores the hazards of when people who lack queer data competence make decisions about data that disproportionately impacts the lives of LGBTQ people. Queer data that excludes LGBTQ individuals from its design, or only reflects the partial experiences of LGBTQ communities, is problematic. Moreover, recent political and legal advances for LGBTQ people, such as the addition of questions on sexual orientation and trans/gender identity to the census and the expansion of marriage to include same-sex couples, have required representatives from marginalized groups to justify their own lives and experiences, often in intimate detail, to figures in positions of power (who are overwhelmingly cis and heterosexual).[1] In national population-level studies, LGBTQ people will constitute a small proportion of the total. As a minority, their views are at risk of being overruled by the majority, particularly when methods are deployed that foreground numerical data, such as consultations, polls and referendums.[2] For example, responses from trans people to the UK Government's 2018 consultation on reform of the GRA were outnumbered by the volume of responses from a pre-filled online form circulated by an

---

[1] Examples include multiple consultations on the introduction of same-sex marriage in 2011 (Scotland) and 2012 (UK, Scotland), and reform of the GRA in 2017 (Scotland), 2018 (UK) and 2020 (Scotland).

[2] As a requirement of their constitution, the Irish Government held a referendum in 2015 to ask whether parliament should permit marriage between people of the same sex. Although 62 per cent of voters ultimately voted in support of the proposition, the different sizes of the LGB and heterosexual/straight populations meant that a decision that impacted the rights of LGB people relied on the votes of the majority heterosexual/straight population. In Scotland, the first government consultation on the topic of same-sex marriage was held in 2011 and gathered over 77,000 responses. Although most consultation respondents opposed the introduction of same-sex marriage, the government argued that a 'consultation is not a referendum on a particular proposal' and is instead 'a way of seeking views, on detailed points as well as on matters of principle'. The government ultimately made the decision to proceed with plans to introduce same-sex marriage, in Scottish Government, 'Marriage and Civil Partnership (Scotland) Bill - Policy Memorandum' (Edinburgh: Scottish Government, 2013), 25–6.

anti-trans campaign group.[3] Reliance on the decisions of a cis, heterosexual majority solidifies the power of the state to grant recognition to minority groups, determine when and where difference is permitted and confirm its position as the 'neutral' adjudicator in disagreements. As things stand, for LGBTQ people to change data practices that impact LGBTQ lives, they must appeal to cis, heterosexual gatekeepers.

In this chapter, I discuss past work on 'insider' and 'outsider' research, and ask the tricky question: must someone self-identify as LGBTQ to make decisions about queer data?[4] In adopting a reflexive approach to queer data, I also consider the baggage of identities and personal blind spots that I bring to my research and writing. I ask myself the question, 'Is it my place to speak?' A reflection that prompts further consideration of being complicit and my privilege as a beneficiary of unequal structures. Discussions about gender, sex and sexuality data, LGBTQ lives and experiences, self-identification and *queering* of research methods occur in online spaces such as social media platforms, blog posts, live video streams, message boards, newspaper and magazine articles. In the UK, online communication about gender, sex and sexuality data has tended to focus on the narrow question of how to count trans, gender non-conforming and non-binary people, talking points favoured by trans-exclusionary campaign groups rather than LGBTQ rights organizations (who would prefer to focus attention on the positive uses of data for action). I therefore explore how we can communicate ideas about queer data so it is used as a source of radical action, navigate the often toxic terrain of online spaces and avoid encounters that do nothing to positively impact the lives of LGBTQ people.

Who is in the room?

D'Ignazio and Klein, in their book *Data Feminism*, describe the problem of privilege hazards.[5] This occurs when people in privileged, decision-making positions lack knowledge, expertize or lived experience of the

---

[3] Vic Parsons, 'There Were More Responses to the Gender Recognition Act Consultation from an Anti-Trans Group than Actual Trans People', *Pink News*, 22 September 2020.
[4] Whether you need to identify as queer to do queer research is posed in Gareth Treharne and Chris Brickell, 'Editorial: Accessing Queer Data in a Multidisciplinary World: Where Do We Go from Queer?', *Gay and Lesbian Issues and Psychology Review* 7, no. 2 (2011): 84–6.
[5] D'Ignazio and Klein, *Data Feminism*.

issues they impact through their work. For D'Ignazio and Klein, 'lack of lived experience – this evidence of how things truly are – profoundly limits their ability to foresee and prevent harm, to identify existing problems in the world, and to imagine possible solutions'.[6] Although blind spots occur at the level of the individual, when teams lack diversity and consist only of like-minded people with shared life experiences these omissions are multiplied and become the dominant way of thinking. Privilege hazards are related to the idea of standpoint theory, a concept developed by feminist scholars including Harding, Haraway and Patricia Hill Collins that underscores how knowledge is socially situated and the value of knowledge that exists among marginalized groups (whose views are often ignored or excluded).[7] In current discussions about gender, sex and sexuality data – particularly as it relates to LGBTQ lives and experiences – many figures in positions of power do not acknowledge when the topic under consideration is beyond their expertize or experience. For example, Chapter 3 described Scottish politician Kenneth Gibson MSP's criticism of the use of the term 'cisgender' in a research report related to the census and his disclosure that he had only become aware of the term in recent months.[8] As a member of the parliamentary committee responsible for oversight of the census, including the design of the new census question on trans status/history, Gibson's admission encourages us to imagine an alternative future when those in the room where decisions are made possess knowledge and, ideally, experience of the matters under discussion. Rather than proceed regardless of how much or how little one knows about a subject, if those in positions of power disclosed blind spots and gave space to those with lived experiences (and about whom decisions were most likely to impact) we might begin to address biases and assumptions associated with gender, sex and sexuality data.

Engender, a Scottish feminist policy and advocacy organization, has drawn particular attention to the issue of privilege hazards, as they relate to the production of data about gender for policymaking, and the need for statisticians and analysts to 'move beyond simply counting women, and to fundamentally reconsider some of their assumptions about the world'.[9] For

---

[6] D'Ignazio and Klein, *Data Feminism*.
[7] See Sandra G. Harding, ed., *The Feminist Standpoint Theory Reader: Intellectual and Political Controversies* (New York: Routledge, 2004).
[8] Culture, Tourism, Europe and External Affairs Committee, 'Session 5', 9 January 2020, 22.
[9] Engender, 'Sex/Gender: Gathering and Using Data to Advance Women's Equality and Rights in Scotland', Engender Submission to the Office of the Chief Statistician, February 2020, 6.

example, data about men and women's experiences of higher education is less useful when collected in ways that fail to account for existing inequalities and differences (for example, in the wording of questions, provision of response options and methods used to collect the data). To address the problem of privilege hazards, Engender highlights the need to develop the gender competence of those responsible for the design of data collection instruments and recognition that gender analysis requires specific knowledge and skills.[10] Data does not speak for itself, others speak on behalf of data. By improving the gender competence of those working with data, we can help avoid flawed practices that are obvious to those about whom the data relates but slip by unnoticed because of the privileges of those behind the design.

Queer data competence

'Nothing about us without us', the powerful rally cry associated with disability rights activists has called into question whose voices are valued in decisions that particularly impact minoritized and marginalized groups.[11] Among those who make decisions about the collection, analysis and use of data that impacts the lives of LGBTQ people, we see instances where LGBTQ voices are absent, ignored or not recognized as an authority.[12] Nothing about data is too complicated nor esoteric for people without a qualification in statistics to understand, particularly when it relates to their own lives and experiences. Any failing in comprehension lies with how information is communicated, not the substance of the message. With this in mind, organizations responsible for the design of data practices have expanded efforts to meaningfully engage with stakeholders and consult communities likely to be impacted by any change in approach.[13] Although

---

[10] Engender, 'Sex/Gender', 19.

[11] The history of the expression 'Nothing about us, without us' is traced to disability rights activists in the early 1990s but has subsequently been embraced by other minority rights movements, in James I. Charlton, *Nothing about Us without Us: Disability Oppression and Empowerment* (Berkeley: University of California Press, 1998), chap. Nothing about Us without Us.

[12] For example, the design process of the sex, sexual orientation and trans questions in Scotland's 2022 census, discussed in Chapter 3.

[13] For example, ahead of the 2022 census, NRS ran several public consultations, events and workshops with the general public and specific community groups, in National Records of Scotland, 'Get Involved', Scotland's Census, 2020.

moving in the right direction, these initiatives are only partial and cannot fully encompass the diversity of people's intersectional experiences nor adequately value the labour of those expected to continually provide input to meetings and consultations. For example, reliance on a small number of people in a population – such as individuals who identify as Black and trans – to dedicate time and energy to data projects can hamper their capacity to focus on other areas of work (which are often traditionally associated with greater esteem).[14] Furthermore, and as noted in the Introduction chapter, an increased presence of LGBTQ people in decision-making roles (more gay, male faces in high places) might not necessarily lead to a *queerer* approach to data practices.

As custodians of data that neither belongs to them nor directly impacts them, how should cis, heterosexual decision-makers approach questions about gender, sex and sexuality data when it relates to LGBTQ lives and experiences? It is not practical to bring experiences of every identity characteristic into every room where decisions are made about data. But, building on Engender's concept of gender competence, queer data competence provides a bare minimum approach to follow for those who make decisions about data that impacts LGBTQ people. As with my account of queer data presented throughout this book, queer data competence consists of two interrelated strands. Firstly, queer data competence requires a basic knowledge of language and concepts associated with LGBTQ identities, an understanding that historical and social factors mean that equality of opportunity is a fiction, an awareness of power differences between and within LGBTQ communities, and attention to the intersection of LGBTQ identities with other identity characteristics. Secondly, queer data competence necessitates a willingness to assume a contrarian role in data discussions: present provocations, challenge categories and recognize different ways of knowing. Interventions might include ensuring deliberations start at the very beginning (as those making decisions often skip the question 'Do we need to collect data?') and asking how data practices will impact the most

---

[14] Examples of overburdening individuals in minoritized groups are found in the higher education sector, such as female senior leaders or Black academics. The desire to have diverse representation on working groups, recruitment panels and EDI initiatives means that staff in minoritized groups can have less time to conduct research, write or develop funding proposals, in Viviana Meschitti, 'Being an Early Career Academic: Is There Space for Gender Equality in the Neoliberal University?', in *Gender, Science and Innovation: New Perspectives*, ed. Helen Lawton Smith et al. (Northampton: Edward Elgar Publishing, 2020), 28.

vulnerable within minority groups (rather than minority groups in general, which tend to elevate the least vulnerable). There is also a responsibility for those who design decision-making practices, such as legislative or consultation exercises, to provide an escape chute for when discussions stretch the competence of those involved. Norms that govern how meetings are conducted in the UK present options for individuals who disclose a conflict of interest; in situations where someone acknowledges their lack of competence on an issue, how can we similarly enable an individual to recuse themselves? Going further, how might we develop ways of working so that when an individual recuses themselves this creates space for someone else with greater competence of the issue? The lenses through which we typically discuss and communicate ideas about data are historically, socially and culturally contextual. As a result, many of the queer considerations explored in this book are precluded from view. We cannot practically construct a future in which every decision-making room is perfectly representative of all constituencies under discussion, nor is this necessarily the best means to address blind spots. However, enhancing individuals' queer data competence, and encouraging a critical approach to data in general, can improve the quality of decision-making and prevent some of the most harmful decisions made at the intersection of data and identity.

Insiders and outsiders

I am also implicated in how power is distributed in decision-making about data practices. As a researcher and writer when, if ever, is it my place to speak? I am a white, Scottish, cis, gay man in my early thirties. I am married. I have no physical or mental impairments. I am not religious. I am middle-class and from a working-class background. I am therefore an 'insider' in research projects where I share identity characteristics with project participants (for example, a study of white, gay men's experiences of using public transport in Scotland).[15] This contrasts with being an 'outsider', where the identity characteristics of the researcher and participants differ. Although the insider/outsider description is a helpful way to explain relationships between researchers and participants, the binary framing does not fully convey how

---

[15] Susan Gair, 'Feeling Their Stories: Contemplating Empathy, Insider/Outsider Positionings, and Enriching Qualitative Research', *Qualitative Health Research* 22, no. 1 (2012).

people experience identities in the social world. Most often, researchers and participants bring a muddle of overlapping and intersecting identities to situations, which can make someone simultaneously feel both an 'insider' and an 'outsider'. When conducting studies with LGBTQ participants, is it the researcher's responsibility to disclose their sexual orientation and trans status or history? CJ Pascoe, in her description of a queer social science method rooted in feminist methodologies, underscores how the researcher's sexuality is a central part of the research process.[16] Although important, actively highlighting what the researcher perceives as shared characteristics might situate them as part of the research. Tooth Murphy has discussed challenges encountered in her oral history interviews where participants responded to an insider researcher by making assumptions about shared knowledge. In interviews with other lesbian women, Tooth Murphy noticed 'transcripts peppered with phrases such as, "Of course you would know all about that", or "Well, I don't need to explain that"'.[17] During interviews a shared sense of commonality, as lesbian women, helped foster a strong rapport but also meant that Tooth Murphy was asked to fill absences where participants did not feel it was necessary to explain experiences in their own words.

Being on the 'inside' also privileges researchers who are visibly 'out' about their sexual orientation and trans status or history. The ability to disclose information about your identity characteristics assumes a degree of control over the research environment that is not available to everyone and can vary according to the contexts where research is conducted. Furthermore, identities often associated with physical markers, such as race or disability, can complicate a researcher's agency to 'out' themselves to participants. When left undiscussed, participants might impress upon the researcher particular assumptions about their identity. Participants' preconceptions, however, may not match how the researcher self-identifies. In his study of whiteness and education in the United States, Nolan Cabrera explains that when participants were asked to guess his racial identity answers included 'mixed race', 'southern European' and 'Russian'.[18] Cabrera, in fact, identifies as Chicano. As someone who looks identifiably 'like a lesbian' and is recognizable to others in the LGBTQ community, Tooth Murphy has also

---

[16] Pascoe, 'What to Do with Actual People?', 295.
[17] Tooth Murphy, 'Listening In, Listening Out', 15.
[18] Nolan Cabrera, 'When Racism and Masculinity Collide: Some Methodological Considerations from a Man of Colour Studying Whiteness', *Whiteness and Education* 1, no. 1 (2 January 2016): 18.

asked how researchers interact with participants when they do not present in an immediately recognizable way.[19] To assert one's position as an insider researcher and strengthen rapport with participants, outing strategies might include mentioning a same-sex partner or reference to a personal experience of 'coming out'.[20] By considering how a researcher identifies and how they are perceived by participants further complicates the insider/outsider binary and the question of whose voice matters in discussions about the collection, analysis and use of queer data.

'Being complicit'

Although I am unaware how participants perceive my identity characteristics in research projects, I generally experience life as part of a majority group and have benefited as someone white, cis, male, non-disabled and middle-class. I have profited from biases that favour men and masculinity, the freedom to access public spaces without barriers that disable me because of my physical or mental abilities, the ease of using gender-segregated spaces without risk of being attacked because of how others perceive me, and an absence of fear as to how the police will treat me as someone white and middle-class. My reflections are particularly personal. They bring into the open an exploration of power and privilege, the limitations of being reflexive (in other words, *thinking* about the identities you bring to projects is not enough) and the benefits we all enjoy – at different times and in different contexts – because of the disadvantage of others. When we move the focus to consider 'being complicit', rather than 'being reflexive', this foregrounds the active practice of reaping the benefits that come with particular identity characteristics. 'Being complicit' entails the involvement with others in unlawful or morally wrong activity. 'Being complicit' is when your identity characteristics – such as gender, race, sexual orientation, language or social class – enable you to benefit, as an individual that is part of a wider group, from an unequal structure. Raewyn Connell has addressed this theme in her work on masculinities and the concept of the patriarchal dividend, which argues that all men (to varying degrees) benefit from their masculinity.[21] Living

---

[19] Tooth Murphy, 'Listening In, Listening Out', 9.
[20] Ibid.
[21] R. W. Connell, *Masculinities* (Berkeley: University of California Press, 1995), 79.

in a patriarchal society means that men accrue unearned social capital simply as a result of their masculinity. For example, a panel interviewing applicants for a senior leadership position might view a male applicant favourably because of biases that associate leadership and masculinity, rather than the skills or competencies of the applicants. Connell's concept of the patriarchal dividend has implications for the volume and value of voices in discussions about gender, sex and sexuality, where an individual's identity characteristics can accrue unearned capital that advances the opportunities of some at the expense of others. The situation is often more complex in everyday life. People do not exist as monolithic identities nor do they operate in spaces where they are always advantaged or always disadvantaged. Life is multilayered and messy. But this takes place within structures – whether they are social, cultural, economic or political – that were historically designed to make the lives of some people easier and the lives of some people harder.

What might these reflections mean for queer data and how can they transform into actions? Queer data departs from an 'everyone wins' approach to addressing inequality and invites critical reflection of our colleagues, family members, friends and ourselves to assess who has unfairly benefited from existing structures. Action must then follow reflection. Queer data can provide an evidence base to justify redistributive measures, such as positive action initiatives that change structures to foster equality of outcomes rather than equality of opportunities. To adopt the approach of Engender, redistributive measures will only impact the people most in need when those responsible for their design and implementation are competent and knowledgeable about the lives of the people the measure is intended to help. For those who have benefited from structures that were designed to strengthen their hand, this can throw into doubt the merit of what they have achieved. However, to move forward we must look outwards and inwards. Rather than attacking an abstract system or a nameless elite, the focus of critique becomes people close to us – including ourselves. Without difficult discussions we cannot meaningfully ask 'Is it my place to speak?' The reservation of ex-officio seats at the table for the same voices, who lack both lived experiences and technical expertize of the matter in hand, has perpetuated biases and assumptions about gender, sex and sexuality data. A queer approach to data provides an opportunity to upend traditions and introduce new ways of working that help get us out of this mess.

Illegitimate concerns

The UN Taskforce on Communicating Gender Statistics notes, 'Getting a message across to audiences with strong attitudes and prejudices about gender issues and strong views about gender roles presents additional challenges'.[22] In the UK, discussions about how to count trans, gender non-conforming and non-binary people have dominated online discourse about gender, sex and sexuality data. The relatively narrow coverage is often not the choosing of LGBTQ rights organizations, who would prefer to focus attention on how data can address inequalities that LGBTQ people experience, but instead reflect the talking points of trans-exclusionary campaign groups. As an example, proposals from public, private and voluntary sector organizations to update data collection practices – so that they better reflect the lives of the people about whom the data relates and the needs of data users – regularly invite a huge amount of scrutiny that requires those who support changes to (repeatedly) explain their rationale.[23] When a rationale for change is communicated online, and particularly when change pertains to data practices that are inclusive of trans people, those sharing information often face a barrage of hateful content. As documented in a study conducted by Amnesty International UK, gender and race play a role in who is targeted by online abuse.[24] The study reviewed a sample of tweets that mentioned female MPs in the UK active on Twitter during the period January to June 2017 and found that twenty female BAME MPs received almost half of all abusive tweets

---

[22] Task Force on Communicating Gender Statistics, 'Guidance on Communicating Gender Statistics', 15.

[23] For example, in November 2019, the Universities and Colleges Union (the main trade union for university and college staff in the UK), stated its commitment to 'ending all forms of discrimination, bigotry and stereotyping [and its] long history of enabling members to self-identify whether that is being black, disabled, LGBT+ or women'. Although nothing had changed about their position, this explanation attracted negative media attention, see Glen Owen, 'Anyone Should Be Allowed to "Identify" as Black Regardless of the Colour of Their Skin or Background, Says the University Lecturers' Union', *Mail Online*, 17 November 2019; Richard Hartley-Parkinson, 'Anyone "Should Be Allowed to Identify as Black, Regardless of Their Skin Colour"', *Metro*, 18 November 2019.

[24] Amnesty International UK, 'Black and Asian Women MPs Abused More Online', 2017. Francesa Sobande has also discussed experiences of anti-Black misogyny in online spaces, in Francesca Sobande, *The Digital Lives of Black Women in Britain*, Palgrave Studies in (Re) Presenting Gender (Cham: Springer International Publishing, 2020), 14, 17–18.

reviewed, despite there being almost eight times as many white MPs in the sample. Being sent hundreds, if not thousands, of abusive messages on Twitter within a concentrated period is called a pile-on. Hateful comments are further amplified through likes, retweets and quote tweets, often fuelled by social media profiles that lack a real name, meaningful biography or personal photograph. Outside of the UK, an investigation by DEMOS analysed the circulation of gendered disinformation on Twitter in Poland and the Philippines, and described the toxicity of online spaces where 'if women dare to enter, they are abused, undermined, threatened, gaslit, delegitimized, and insulted'.[25] The example of an online pile-on raises questions as to the tactics deployed to shut down discussions about gender, sex and sexuality data, the purposes they serve and how this might pre-emptively dissuade people, particularly those new to discussions, from speaking about queer data in online spaces.

My interest here is not in refuting specific claims of trans-exclusionary campaign groups in Scotland and the UK. I instead want to underscore how the voices of a small number of campaigners have shaped the contours for how those working on topics related to gender, sex and sexuality data communicate ideas in online spaces. Trans-exclusionary communication about data tends to highlight several recurring themes, such as the belief that advocates of a 'sex-denialist transgender ideology' have captured control of policy-making mechanisms and that women's right groups (who hold 'gender critical' views) are excluded from the decision-making process.[26] Using analysis of freedom of information requests and detailed desk-based research, claims are presented as a forensic account of the evidence and draw on the contributions from a small number of scholars to suggest a dissonance between experts and activists.[27] For example, Alice

---

[25] Ellen Judson et al., 'Engendering Hate: The Contours of State-Aligned Gendered Disinformation Online' (London: DEMOS, October 2020), 37.

[26] Jones and MacKenzie, 'Sex and the Census', 8. However, in the context of Scotland, this claim ignores the participation of several major women's rights organizations in the census design process (including Scottish Women's Aid, Close the Gap, Rape Crisis Scotland, Engender and Equate Scotland), in Scottish Women's Aid et al., 'Scottish Women's Sector Note - Census (Amendment) (Scotland) Bill', December 2018.

[27] However, commenting on Kath Murray and Lucy Hunter Blackburn, 'Losing Sight of Women's Rights: The Unregulated Introduction of Gender Self-Identification as a Case Study of Policy Capture in Scotland', Scottish Affairs 28, no. 3 (31 July 2019): 262–89, Cowan et al. note the article's 'lack of academic rigour' and how 'other than one brief reference to a chapter in an edited collection, it does not cite peer-reviewed references; instead references are made only to news articles, personal blogs and institutional reports', in Cowan et al., 'Sex and Gender Equality Law and Policy'.

Sullivan has warned that 'genderist' LGBTQ organizations are attempting to halt the collection of data about sex and stoked fears that 'postmodernists who used to denigrate all quantitative research are now coming for our questionnaires'.[28] Communication also tends to centre the individual speaking about the data, rather than the people about whom the data relates, and bring to the fore personal experiences of being cancelled or fears about expressing their views.[29] In the vortex of contemporary media coverage, details of an individual's traumatic experiences echo throughout other mediums and become detached from the original matter under discussion (in other words, the story becomes the experience of the researcher rather than their views on trans-inclusive data practices).[30]

There is much promise in dialogue about how identities and data intersect. However, this can only occur when those involved follow basic ground rules that recognize the existence of all parties. Ahmed explains, 'Transphobia and antitrans statements should not be treated as just another viewpoint that we should be free to express at the happy table of diversity. There cannot be a dialogue when some at the table are in effect (or intent on) arguing for the elimination of others at the table.'[31] For Ahmed, 'debate' that calls into question the existence of trans people is deleterious as it demands, through the form of a rebuttal, that trans people provide evidence of their existence.[32] Simply existing is not enough – those who wish to 'debate' the validity of trans lives also demand the forensic collection, analysis and presentation of data. Ahmed rightly identifies demands for evidence as a trap, as the information requested can shift and trans people find themselves in a never-ending struggle to accumulate data that proves their existence.[33] Ahmed's warning demonstrates how the current climate has made online spaces no-go zones for many people who wish to

---

[28] Sullivan, 'Sex and the Census', 5, 7.

[29] For example, Sullivan describes her experience of being invited to speak at a research methods seminar on sex and gender issues, which was subsequently cancelled after other speakers raised concerns about her views, in Sullivan, 6. Kath Murray and Lucy Hunter Blackburn also describe how 'some women have not felt able to articulate their concerns about gender self-identification for fear of repercussions', in Murray and Hunter Blackburn, 'Losing Sight of Women's Rights', 285.

[30] Sullivan's experience was subsequently covered in *The Times*, Sian Griffiths, 'Stonewall's New Boss Nancy Kelley Let Census Expert Be No-Platformed', *The Times*, 24 May 2020.

[31] Sara Ahmed, 'An Affinity of Hammers', *TSQ: Transgender Studies Quarterly* 3, no. 1–2 (May 2016): 31.

[32] Ibid., 29.

[33] Ibid., 30.

critically explore ideas related to gender, sex and sexuality data.[34] The narrow focus of discussion, instigated by trans-exclusionary campaign groups, also means that other fertile areas for investigation have received less attention, such as commonalities and differences between gender, sex and sexuality data and other identity characteristics such as race and disability. Yet, online spaces offer much potential as a formative location to bring together people from around the world to discuss gender, sex and sexuality data. We therefore need to know how to speak about queer approaches to data without falling into traps laid by those who wish to exclude trans people from the conversation. The experience of a pile-on, which is both gendered and racialized, can make people doubt whether it is their place to speak on issues that may not directly impact them. Rather than playing by the rules of those opposed to a queer approach to data, it is vital we pull back the curtain and expose these tactics for what they are: conservative techniques, sometimes dressed-up in radical clothing, bigotry refashioned for twenty-first century online consumption, designed to halt change and stifle communication about critical approaches to data.

* * *

Who has a voice in discussions about queer data and whose voice matters? To establish where power lies in discussions about queer data, this chapter has explored the limitations of insider/outsider approaches, the privilege of 'out' researchers and the potential gap between how researchers self-identify and how they are perceived by participants. Looking inwards, I examined the baggage of identities that I bring to my research on data and how, as a result of my identity characteristics, I have benefited at the expense of others. This critique of myself – as well as my colleagues, friends and family – throws into doubt when, if ever, is it my place to speak? The next and final chapter takes us one step further and explores practical ways to use queer data for action, ensuring this is done in a way that elevates the voices of LGBTQ people. I move my focus from the reflexive responsibilities of researchers to instead consider queer data as a productive force that challenges traditional approaches to data, unsettles the normalcy of cis/heteronormative practices, and improve the lives and experiences of LGBTQ people.

---

[34] In reference to their study of gendered disinformation in Poland and the Philippines, DEMOS warns 'Not only can this cause serious harm for individuals involved, but creates a public sphere in which women are not free to express themselves, or to participate in politics, or to speak up against injustice and oppression', in Judson et al., 'Engendering Hate', 37.

CHAPTER 8
FIGHT BACK! USING QUEER DATA
FOR ACTION

The morning sunlight streamed through the tall windows of my flat in Edinburgh. I sat with a coffee in front of my laptop screen, staring at a reflection of my face, as I waited for the 'ping' to notify me that someone had entered the waiting room of the Zoom call. I have known Kirstie English, a postgraduate researcher in sociology at the University of Glasgow, for a few years through our work together to engage politicians involved in the design of the sex, sexual orientation and trans questions in Scotland's census. I knew our views on gender, sex and sexuality data generally aligned and – as someone who identifies as queer, agender, non-binary and trans – I was keen to hear how Kirstie thought data might positively impact the lives of LGBTQ people in Scotland and the UK. 'Getting a fully-fledged intersectional look at what is currently going on is really important … If a government's purpose is to meet the needs of the people, you need to know who the people are and what their needs are', Kirstie explained. For example, Kirstie continued, 'If you know how many trans and non-binary people there are, you can have an estimate of roughly how many people might need access to a Gender Identity Clinic'. This made a lot of sense to me. Beyond philosophical debates about how to define gender, sex and sexuality, we could not lose sight of the real-world impacts of being counted. 'A lot of people don't know trans people exist', Kirstie admitted. 'If you think of the "trans tipping point" being 2014, that's only when people started getting the idea that this could be something that exists but they might not think of it as something in Scotland'.[1] Kirstie understood the addition of a question

---

[1] In 2014, *Time* magazine published a cover story titled 'The Transgender Tipping Point' that heralded a new generation of public figures who identified as trans, explored how the recognition of issues that face trans people had improved and asked whether this marked 'America's next civil rights frontier', in Katy Steinmetz, 'The Transgender Tipping Point', *Time*, 29 May 2014.

about trans people in the census as 'really significant' as it presented trans as 'just a normal option for how people can be'. I pushed back and probed to what extent increased visibility actually improved the day-to-day lives of LGBTQ people. 'Visibility does help but it's very long term, it takes a while', Kirstie explained. 'For me, it really comes down to who gets to actively say who they are and who gets labels placed upon them. That's the big crux of the issue.'

As two people who identify as LGBTQ and conduct research into LGBTQ topics, I was keen to hear how Kirstie balanced the challenge of investigating issues that resonate personally. 'The big things are energy and resources. A lot of the people I argue against are not personally affected by any of the things they talk about. They have a lot more energy and resources to put into this. Even when I'm not working on it, I'm always thinking about it ... Whereas people who debate trans rights but are not trans themselves, who often have a quite negative view and don't really know any trans people, it's just like a hobby for them for the most part. It's just a thing they do, vent a little bit of anger online'. Kirstie continued, 'There's pointless anger and there's anger that you use. I've stopped arguing with people online because I think that is pointless anger, it is just anger that is going to nothing and not doing anything productive with it ... I feel like pointless anger is just a drain. Whereas if it's anger where you have had it, you've went and you've used it, and you've done some good work then you can rest afterward'.

The role of anger in the use of queer data for action stuck with me. As a productive force, rather than a drain on finite resources, I empathized with Kirstie's navigation of 'academic' and 'activist' pursuits and how the two were ultimately blurred. The overlap between theory and practice encouraged me to think about how to critically challenge dominant approaches to data collection, analysis and presentation in ways that expose problems rather than discourage future activities. Kirstie and I had both personally benefited from the increased recognition of data about LGBTQ people, through the opportunity to undertake a PhD and write a book on the topic, it was therefore vital that our endeavours fostered more opportunities for others to investigate topics related to gender, sex and sexuality data rather than less. We ended our conversation after an hour or so, both feeling refreshed from the exchange of ideas and excited by data's potential to change society for the better. Kirstie had reminded me that, while remaining mindful of the dangers, being counted in the census and other major data collection exercises remains a radical act at a time when many people in Scotland and the UK are unaware that trans people exist. We might not witness the benefits of these actions now but, over time, we will look back and see these data developments as moments of progress.

* * *

Data about LGBTQ experiences, and the *queering* of methods used to collect and analyse data, is a productive force that has positively impacted people's lives. Alongside increased visibility for historically marginalized groups, data provides evidence for the equitable distribution of resources and provision of services. However, rather than create an evidence base for positive action, data can also stall progress and help maintain the status quo. For example, an undercount of lesbian, gay and bisexual people in UK censuses might justify cuts to funding that supports LGB communities or negatively alter the public's attitude towards programmes targeted at sexual minority groups. Furthermore, the requirement that marginalized people use data to prove the existence of problems burns up limited resources that might have a greater impact if they were used to fix issues rather than document their existence. This final chapter critically explores the use of data to serve the interests of the people about whom the data relates. In other words, how does data about LGBTQ people positively impact LGBTQ lives and experiences? Looking to projects in the United States that bring together scholars, activists and artists to disrupt the technological status quo, I share lessons from the misuse of race and ethnicity data that can inform the future relationship between LGBTQ people and data. Critical interventions from the United States, often led by people of colour, call attention to the need for LGBTQ groups in the UK to re-evaluate their approach to data and challenge the assumption that the collection of data is an intrinsic good. Failure to engage with agencies that collect, analyse and use data potentially locks out LGBTQ communities from recognition and access to vital funding and resources. Yet, participation in these practices requires some degree of assimilation with normative approaches to categorization that entails the inclusion and exclusion of particular LGBTQ lives and experiences.

Evidence for action

'When there's no name for a problem, you can't see a problem. When you can't see a problem, you can't solve it', declared Kimberlé Crenshaw at a 2016

TED talk in San Francisco.[2] Data helps name the problem and translate issues that affect many people into a format that becomes an evidence base for action. For groups of people that have been misrepresented, marginalized and oppressed by existing systems of power, data can offer a powerful tool in the fightback against inequality and injustice. When LGBTQ people are presented in a table, graph or data visualization, the general population are reminded of their existence, the inequalities they encounter and what remains unknown about their lives and experiences. The worlds of politics and policymaking run on data, which means that LGBTQ rights organizations are required to engage with existing systems of power and ways of working to bring about change.[3] Activities that use data for action include responding to government consultations and engaging with politicians to change and protect laws; educating and empowering individuals to make a difference; using the media to change narratives about LGBTQ people; and working with institutions to ensure they create spaces that are inclusive and equal.[4] Activities can take many forms. For example, in Scotland the Marriage and Civil Partnership (Scotland) Act, which introduced same-sex marriage in 2014, was preceded by two rounds of public consultation where interested parties were invited to submit evidence to inform decision-making on the issue. In their submission, LGBTI rights organization the Equality Network shared findings from a survey of 427 LGBT people, at that time the largest quantitative exercise to explore the question of same-sex marriage among LGBT people in Scotland, and qualitative data from consultation sessions conducted with 150 LGBT people across different parts of Scotland. 85 per cent of survey respondents argued that marriage should be available to all couples (same-sex and mixed-sex), a sentiment supported by the majority of the Equality Network's consultation participants.[5] Although many factors informed the

[2] Alejandra Vasquez, 'The Urgency of Intersectionality: Kimberlé Crenshaw Speaks at TEDWomen 2016', *TED Blog*, 27 October 2016. In their examination of how housing and homelessness service providers in Scotland use diversity monitoring data, Matthews and Poyner note that 'service providers could say they did not have a problem with homophobic or transphobic harassment, for example, because they simply did not know about it', in Matthews and Poyner, 'Achieving Equality in Progressive Contexts'.
[3] Velte, 'Straightwashing the Census', 111.
[4] Stonewall, the UK's most prominent LGBT rights organization, is well-known for its research into the lives of LGBT people and uses evidence to inform the activities listed, in Stonewall, 'Our Mission and Priorities', Stonewall, 10 August 2015.
[5] Equality Network, 'Response to the Scottish Government's Consultation on the Registration of Civil Partnership and Same Sex Marriage', 2011.

Scottish Parliament's decision to legislate in support of same-sex marriage, this example demonstrates how LGBTQ rights organizations use data to strengthen efforts to introduce or change legislation that impacts the lives of LGBTQ people.

Data about LGBTQ communities can similarly play a key role in the provision of healthcare and housing. In 2021, building work commenced on the UK's first extra-care housing scheme for LGBTQ+ people in Manchester in the North of England.[6] Extra-care housing, sometimes described as assisted living, enables people to live in accommodation where they retain independence but receive support with tasks such as washing, dressing, going to the toilet or taking medication. Data from research conducted by the Manchester-based charity LGBT Foundation reported that 50 per cent of respondents would prefer to receive extra care from an LGBT-specific provider and 74 per cent of respondents expressed interest in moving into LGBT-specific accommodation in the future.[7] Evidence from LGBT Foundation's report informed the design of the new housing scheme in South Manchester, which is overseen by a steering group of LGBTQ+ members and reserves 51 per cent of residential places for people who identify as LGBTQ+, aged over fifty-five and in need of extra physical or mental support. The provision of LGBTQ-specific housing is also found in other sectors. In 2018, the University of Sheffield began to offer students the option to request to stay with other LGBT+ people in the allocation of university accommodation, as some students expressed a preference to live with others who may have shared life experiences.[8] The university's initiative was timely as research conducted by Stonewall that year reported that 42 per cent of LGBT students have hidden their identity at university for fear of discrimination.[9]

Being counted, in a census or other major data collection exercise, can inform how governments and organizations allocate resources and provide services, both now and in the future. The use of data for action is therefore a lucrative business. As discussed in Chapter 6, many of the world's wealthiest companies follow business models based on the extraction of data about people who use their services, the analysis of data to predict future activities and the sale of bespoke advertising. Described as the 'pink pound', LGBTQ

[6] Rachel Pugh, 'The UK's First LGBTQ+ Extra-Care Housing Scheme Gets Go Ahead', The Guardian, 21 October 2020.
[7] LGBT Foundation, 'Housing, Ageing + Care' (Manchester, October 2020).
[8] The University of Sheffield, 'LGBT+ Accommodation', 25 October 2019.
[9] Stonewall, 'LGBT in Britain - University Report' (London, 2018), 9.

people represent sizeable consumer groups in some markets, such as travel and tourism, and are therefore targeted by advertisers and through the commercial sponsorship of events such as Pride festivals.[10] As with other identity-based sectors of commercial markets, the use of data about LGBTQ people to sell products and services risks strengthening rather than weakening inequalities associated with neoliberal practices such as a decrease in real wages, precarious employment and activities that damage the environment. The spending power of LGBTQ people also contributes to 'business case' arguments as to why companies should roll-out EDI initiatives or support anti-discrimination policies: greater access to markets means more LGBTQ people spend more money. Although the use of data for commercial action offers a particular vision of equality – where capitalist markets treat LGBTQ and cis, heterosexual consumers the same – it overlooks the disproportionate harm inflicted on LGBTQ people. Research conducted in 2019 by YouGov and LinkedIn found that LGBT+ employees in the UK earned almost £7,000 less per year than cis, heterosexual colleagues.[11] When at work, research conducted by the Chartered Institute of Personnel and Development has found that LGB+ employees report higher levels of workplace conflict (40 per cent) than heterosexual employees (29 per cent).[12] Data from the GEO also reported that, in 2018, 63 per cent of trans people had worked in paid employment during the past year compared to 83 per cent of cis people.[13] For LGBTQ people that cannot afford international travel, flashy gadgets or enjoy the perks of disposable income, data's role in maximizing the profitability of the pink pound might do more harm than good.

Even when data about LGBTQ individuals is not directly used to inform action that improves the lives of those about whom it relates, its presentation can demonstrate contrast, spotlight potential inequalities in systems and encourage others to respond. The UK Home Office has published experimental statistics on the number of asylum claims where sexual orientation was part of the basis for the claim, which included people who identified as lesbian, gay or bisexual and those at risk in their home country

---

[10] LGBT+ tourism represents more than 1 per cent of some countries' total gross domestic product, in Stephen Little, 'LGBT Great Launches New Survey on LGBT+ Investing', *Investment Week*, 20 October 2020.

[11] Lizzie Edmonds, 'LGBT+ Workers "Paid £7,000 Less than Straight Counterparts"', *Evening Standard*, 2 July 2019.

[12] Chartered Institute of Personnel and Development, 'Inclusion at Work: Perspectives on LGBT+ Working Lives - Executive Summary' (London, February 2021), 1.

[13] Government Equalities Office, 'National LGBT Survey', 133.

due to factors related to sexual orientation.[14] In 2019, sexual orientation was a factor in 3 per cent of all asylum applications lodged in the UK, although this differed by applicant nationality (for example, around two in five claims from Ugandan (43 per cent) and Malaysian (40 per cent) nationals were based on sexual orientation). Applications for asylum where sexual orientation was part of the claim were granted in 46 per cent of cases, slightly lower than the overall grant rate for asylum claims of 52 per cent. Although we must treat experimental statistics with caution, the Home Office's presentation of data encourages us to believe that increased transparency about sexual orientation claims might keep the system in check.[15] Yet, even if future datasets are more robust and further analysis identifies statistically significant differences, will 'evidence' alone change a structure that determines the life chances of some of the most marginalized and vulnerable LGBTQ people in the UK? Data from the Home Office typifies a missing step between the provision of more data about LGBTQ people and the execution of actions that meaningfully address the problems documented. Rather than crunching numbers that detail past events, and faced with limited time and resources, the efforts of LGBTQ rights organizations are better invested in campaigns that seek to overhaul or dismantle immigration services from the bottom-up, stopping harm to people now and in the future. Similar questions emerge when we consider the publication of hate crime data, arguably one of the richest sources of data about LGBTQ people in the UK. For example, the BBC published information that showed that the number of reported homophobic hate crime cases in the UK had almost trebled from 6,655 in 2014–15 to 18,465 in 2019–20, with a 20 per cent rise in homophobic hate crime reports in 2019–20.[16] Although it is hard to tell whether this change reflects increased confidence in reporting, improved collection practices or a shift in the actual number of incidents, it remains equally ambiguous how we might translate data about hate crimes into actions that stop LGBTQ people from experiencing these crimes in the first place. A critical reading of the use of data to alter and/or amplify the visibility

[14] Home Office, 'Experimental Statistics: Asylum Claims on the Basis of Sexual Orientation' (UK Government, 24 September 2020).
[15] Similar arguments are made about open data, where governments publish data so that it is freely available for everyone to use and analyse as they wish. However, as a means to scrutinize government activities, open data is reliant on willing individuals with the skills and resources to make sense of the information published.
[16] Ben Hunte, '"I Thought I Was Going to Die" in Homophobic Attack', *BBC News*, 9 October 2020.

of historically marginalized communities highlights how this can make the situation worse. For trans people, Che Gossett argues, 'One of the traps of trans visibility is that it is premised on invisibility: to bring a select few into view, others must disappear into the background, and this is always a political project that reinforces oppression'.[17] Furthermore, Reina Gossett et al. describe how the 'transgender tipping point' in 2014 occurred at precisely the same political moment when women of colour in the United States, and trans women of colour in particular, experienced increased instances of physical violence.[18] The relationship between visibility and LGBT activism can also differ in contexts outside of the West. Brock and Edenborg, in their account of gay persecution in the Russian republic of Chechnya, conclude that public visibility 'is not a one-way path to liberation but rather a double-edged sword, connected also to insecurity and vulnerability'.[19] Even when improved visibility offers a means to greater recognition and equality, this is often contingent on how people in existing positions of power react to the raised or changed profile of communities previously excluded from public discourse.

Regardless of the accuracy of results from studies of LGBTQ people or the authenticity of categories constructed by response options provided, the act of asking questions about sexual orientation and trans status/history can change lives. In Scotland, for example, the census invites all households to return data on the number of people aged sixteen or over who identify as trans or as someone with a trans history. For many people who complete the census, the concept of trans will be a new idea. Kirstie explained to me, 'If someone sees a word and they're like, "I don't know what the word means", they might look it up. They might look it up and learn something that is applicable to themselves or others in their life'.[20] Asking about individuals' trans status/history in a national data collection exercise might help normalize the concept and depart from sensationalist depictions of trans people. In households where people previously felt unable to speak openly about gender, sex and sexuality, I hope that the inclusion of questions on sexual orientation and trans status/history offers a catalyst for discussion

---

[17] Che Gossett, 'Blackness and the Trouble of Trans Visibility', in *Trap Door: Trans Cultural Production and the Politics of Visibility*, ed. Reina Gossett, Eric A. Stanley, and Johanna Burton, Critical Anthologies in Art and Culture (Cambridge: The MIT Press, 2017), 183.
[18] Gossett, Stanley, and Burton, 'Known Unknowns: An Introduction to Trap Door', xvi.
[19] Brock and Edenborg, '"You Cannot Oppress Those Who Do Not Exist"', 692.
[20] Kirstie English, Interview with Kirstie English, 26 October 2020.

that changes lives for the better. Even though we cannot lose sight of what was lost along the way, such as the normalization and further entrenching of cis/heteronormative values that exclude particular LGBTQ identities, we must also remain attuned to how data practices can open people's minds to new ideas.

Evidence for inaction

Rather than a force to produce something new – whether good or bad – data can also operate as a jam in the system that perpetuates the status quo and protects current ways of working. To gain access to spaces where decisions are made, speak in a language that decision-makers understand and establish credibility, LGBTQ rights organizations often engage methodological approaches and research practices understood by those in existing positions of power. For example, John Grundy and Miriam Smith have argued that mainstream LGBT rights organizations in the United States need to 'assume the existence of a static gay and lesbian population awaiting statistical representation', which can 'limit the boundaries of "legitimate" political grievances to those that can be formulated through modes of quantification'.[21] By adapting the criteria for who is counted so that it meets the needs of the existing system, there is a risk that the attention of LGBTQ rights organizations focuses on the interests of the most 'deserving': affluent, white, cis gay men and lesbians rather than those most in need of support.[22] An appeal to 'deservingness' also assumes that people with power to make change necessarily care about who is and is not represented in data tables or what the results of analysis tell them about inequality in their organization. For example, just because evidence highlights that

---

[21] Grundy and Smith, 'Activist Knowledges in Queer Politics', 301, 312.

[22] A focus on the most privileged within LGBTQ communities is labelled homonormativity, which Lisa Duggan describes as 'a politics that does not contest dominant heteronormative assumptions and institutions, but upholds and sustains them'. In place of upturning traditional structures, a homonormative approach seeks to assimilate with existing white, middle-class values and binary understandings of gender, sex and sexuality. Homonormativity has the effect of further marginalizing, for example, people of colour and trans, bisexual and queer individuals, discussed in Lisa Duggan, *The Twilight of Equality? Neoliberalism, Cultural Politics, and the Attack on Democracy* (Boston: Beacon Press, 2014), 50; Spade, *Normal Life*, 44; Dawne Moon, Theresa W. Tobin, and J. E. Sumerau, 'Alpha, Omega, and the Letters in between: LGBTQI Conservative Christians Undoing Gender', *Gender & Society* 33, no. 4 (August 2019): 591.

LGBTQ staff earn, on average, less than cis, heterosexual staff – there is no obligation for anyone to take action. Data about people's identity characteristics can therefore function as a tool to sustain the status quo and deflect challenges to existing structures of power.[23] Ahmed's account of this danger describes how the practice of diversity work through policies, procedures, networks, events and celebrations can mask the continuation of structural practices that disempower the very people these initiatives claim to support.[24] In the higher education sector, one technique that uses data for inaction is its ability to stall progress: where the collection, analysis and presentation of data are framed, in itself, as work to address the inequalities experienced by LGBTQ staff and students. This critique is present in Ahmed's account of interviews with diversity practitioners in UK universities, who reported their time spent 'doing the document rather than doing the doing' and the distraction of policies and action plans that stopped them 'from just getting stuck in'.[25] During my interview with Kirstie, they also raised the danger of distraction through data accumulation: 'Not asking for information that's not going to go anywhere is important ... Just wanting information for the sake of the information isn't enough. There should be plans for how this is going to filter into policy, how this is going to filter into budgeting, who is considered and in what context'.[26] The misrepresentation of who benefits from the collection of more data chimes with Ahmed's account of diversity work 'as a politics of feeling good, which allows people to relax and feel less threatened, as if we have already "solved it"'.[27] There exists a multitude of projects that organizations could undertake related to the collection and analysis of gender, sex and sexuality data. If every possible project was pursued, no time or resources would remain to implement actions to fix the problems that emerged from these studies.

When data is deployed as a method to stall action, this throws open questions as to why marginalized groups are expected to present this information as a prerequisite for change in the first place. Most LGBTQ people do not require further evidence of their marginalization: the everyday

---

[23] Walcott makes a related point and describes how 'diversity interrupts and delays more radical calls for human transformation', in Walcott, 'The End of Diversity', 405.
[24] Sara Ahmed, 'The Language of Diversity', *Ethnic and Racial Studies* 30, no. 2 (1 March 2007): 235–56.
[25] Ahmed, '"You End up Doing the Document Rather than Doing the Doing"', 599.
[26] English, Interview with Kirstie English.
[27] Ahmed, '"You End up Doing the Document Rather than Doing the Doing"', 605.

experience of inhabiting a body with an LGBTQ identity tells this story. The burden of proof is therefore required for a cis, heterosexual audience who may or may not take action, depending on the quality of the proof provided. Candice Lanius, in the blog post 'Fact Check: Your Demand for Statistical Proof is Racist', discusses how those in positions of power accept anecdotal evidence from people like themselves but demand comprehensive data from minoritized groups about their experiences.[28] Although writing about race, Lanius's claim similarly applies to demands placed upon LGBTQ people, by those in positions of power, to prove (beyond doubt) their oppression before action is taken. This trove of data can compound a deficit narrative of LGBTQ people as the information collected only relates to negative experiences of discrimination and disadvantage.[29] As a result of gathering data to get others to take action, LGBTQ people potentially find themselves swamped in data that neither encapsulates the diversity of LGBTQ experiences nor pays attention to the many positive dimensions of LGBTQ lives.[30]

The need to know the scale of an issue before action is taken articulates a particular type of knowledge that has implications for the count of LGBTQ people in the UK's 2021 and 2022 censuses. When counted at all, LGBTQ people are at risk of being undercounted more than cis, heterosexual people.[31] Although a census is never able to capture data about everyone in the target population, the level of undercount across different groups is spread unequally; a phenomenon described as a differential undercount. This challenge has attracted most attention in relation to the collection of racial and ethnic data in US censuses, where people of colour are less likely to be counted than white people.[32] In the context of UK census questions on sexual orientation, this might mean that 95 per cent of heterosexual respondents disclose their sexual orientation compared to just 85 per cent of lesbian, gay or bisexual respondents. In effect, the presentation of this data would overstate the relative

[28] Candice Lanius, 'Fact Check: Your Demand for Statistical Proof Is Racist', *Cyborgology*, 12 January 2015.

[29] D'Ignazio and Klein, *Data Feminism*.

[30] In their account of large social surveys in the United States, Westbrook et al. identified an over-focus on sexual risk and danger (rather than desire and pleasure) and attributed this to 'funding priorities on disease control and a longstanding culture of sex negativity', in Westbrook, Budnick, and Saperstein, 'Dangerous Data', 26.

[31] Browne, 'Queer Quantification or Queer(y)Ing Quantification', 247.

[32] Margo Anderson and Stephen E. Fienberg, 'Race and Ethnicity and the Controversy Over the US Census', *Current Sociology* 48, no. 3 (July 2000): 87–110; Velte, 'Straightwashing the Census', 119–20.

size of the population who identify as heterosexual and understate the size of those who identify as lesbian, gay or bisexual. The reasons for a differential undercount are multiple and might include disagreement with the design of the question or response options provided, the privileging of those who are 'out' or lack of trust in the state's motivations for data collection. For these reasons, population-level data about LGBTQ people will likely undercount minority groups more so than majority groups. What implications might an undercount have for the provision of government funding or the public's attitude towards targeted programmes that support LGBTQ people? Browne has warned that measurement of LGB populations 'has the potential to render arguments for LGB equality mute, or at least toned down' if results fail to match assumptions, whether accurate or inaccurate, about the size of LGB populations.[33] Writing about efforts to calculate the size of the LGB community in the United States in the early 2010s, Larry Kramer also argued that demographic and statistical analyses that undercount or underrepresent the LGB population can undermine efforts to make political and social advances.[34] For Browne, the use of data about LGB people to inform action must therefore assert the undercount to help ensure the contested decisions made during the collection and analysis of data, which excludes or discourages participation in the exercise, are exposed.[35]

Take control

The use of data to sustain the status quo and deflect challenges to existing structures of power, the burden of proof expected of LGBTQ people before action is taken and the risk of a differential undercount leaves researchers in a bind. In a future that looks increasingly data-driven, the uses of gender, sex and sexuality data pose risks for LGBTQ people that, if left unchecked, might make people's lives worse rather than better. However, these warnings are not a knock-out blow for queer data nor should they discourage researchers from undertaking careful investigations into these themes.

Although the use of data to describe the lives of LGBTQ people does not single-handedly fix structural injustice, stories play a role in bringing about

---

[33] Browne, 'Queer Quantification or Queer(y)Ing Quantification', 247.
[34] For discussion, see Gates and Herman, 'Beyond Academia', 82–3.
[35] Browne, 'Queer Quantification or Queer(y)Ing Quantification', 247.

change. Reina Gossett et al., in their introduction to the edited collection *Trap Door: Trans Cultural Production and the Politics of Visibility*, argue that 'representations do not simply re-present an already existing reality but are also doors into making new futures possible'.[36] They continue, 'If we do not attend to representation and work collectively to bring new visual grammars into existence (while remembering and unearthing suppressed ones), then we will remain caught in the traps of the past'.[37] Writing about the visibility of Black women in digital spaces, Francesca Sobande describes how the expression 'representation matters' can operate in meaningless ways 'when stripped of any scrutiny of connected material conditions, work and labour experiences, media production processes and who is involved in them, and prevailing structural inequalities'.[38] However, as with Gosset et al., Sobande concludes that visual cultures and media depictions have a role to play and an influence on socio-political issues and struggles. With these drivers in mind, queer data goes beyond the collection, analysis and presentation of data about LGBTQ people to also critically examine who is positioned at the centre and who is positioned on the margins in discussions about gender, sex and sexuality. Several scholars have highlighted queer studies' subversion of traditional accounts of the centre and the margins in research projects, which tend to describe the experiences of LGBTQ people (usually positioned on the margins) but overlook the experiences of cis, heterosexual people (usually positioned at the centre).[39] Only examining data about LGBTQ lives and experiences, collected as proof to get others to take action, poses a risk that data foregrounds stories of trauma and disadvantage. In place of a rounded account of the ups and downs of LGBTQ lives and experiences, data can compound a victim narrative. Rather than abandon the collection of data about LGBTQ people, queer data takes revenge on the unmarked categories of cis and heterosexual.[40] Arlene Stein and Ken Plummer describe how a queer approach, 'normalizes homosexuality by making heterosexuality deviant' as 'homosexuality ceases to be the exclusive site of

---

[36] Gossett, Stanley, and Burton, 'Known Unknowns: An Introduction to Trap Door', xvii.
[37] Ibid.
[38] Sobande, *The Digital Lives of Black Women in Britain*, 137.
[39] Stein and Plummer, '"I Can't Even Think Straight" "Queer" Theory and the Missing Sexual Revolution in Sociology', 185; Zosky and Alberts, 'What's in a Name?', 600; Pascoe, 'What to Do with Actual People?', 293.
[40] Pascoe, 'What to Do with Actual People?', 300.

sexual difference.[41] Arguing that the lives of cis, heterosexual people require more attention might seem counter-intuitive, particularly when time and resources are limited. However, a critical examination of the margins, that leaves the centre undiscussed, strengthens the notion of LGBTQ identities as 'other', 'deviant' or 'abnormal' and fails to challenge the relationship between cis/heterosexual genders, sexes and sexualities with dominant systems of power. By exposing the histories of minority *and* majority identity groups, a critical review of gender, sex and sexuality data implicates everyone in these discussions, not just the minority of people who identify as LGBTQ.

To maximize the power of queer data to positively impact the lives of LGBTQ people, we need to assess the motivations behind those currently engaged in work about gender, sex and sexuality data. Rather than return to the same pool of experts and professionals to fix biases and assumptions that cause harm to LGBTQ people, many of whom were responsible for these design failings in the first place, we need to cast the net wider and engage new pools of researchers, practitioners and activists. In their account of how the design of algorithms negatively impacts trans people, Costanza-Chock argues, 'different people experience algorithmic decision support systems differently, and we must redesign these systems based on the lived experience of those they harm'.[42] During our conversation, Kirstie discussed the design of the sex question in Scotland's census and the misguided belief (among trans-exclusionary campaign groups) that, if instructed to do so, trans people would tick their sex assigned at birth: 'That was never going to happen. They're not going to do that. But they assumed that so they just made poor assumptions based on that'.[43] Privilege hazards, discussed in the previous chapter, reappear as a reminder that the effective use of data must pay attention to the approach adopted, who leads this work and whose interests are served.

Before jumping to create something new, we need to trust community experts and see what already works. Leading the charge and putting ideas into practice is a new wave of groups and organizations that fall under the broad umbrella of data justice.[44] A related mixture of university-based,

---

[41] Stein and Plummer, '"I Can't Even Think Straight" "Queer" Theory and the Missing Sexual Revolution in Sociology', 183.

[42] Costanza-Chock, 'Design Justice, AI, and Escape from the Matrix of Domination', 5.

[43] English, Interview with Kirstie English.

[44] See Lina Dencik et al., 'Exploring Data Justice: Conceptions, Applications and Directions', *Information, Communication & Society* 22, no. 7 (7 June 2019): 873–81.

privately funded and community organizations has also been launched that examines the intersection of data, AI, ethics and identity.[45] Although none of these groups exclusively focus on gender, sex and sexuality data as it relates to LGBTQ people, they share an ethos that questions dominant systems of knowledge, destabilizes ideas of the centre and the margins and disrupts the technological status quo.

Participation, reform and abolition

A critical account of the use of data for action problematizes the idea that more data about gender, sex and sexuality is an intrinsic good, an argument that has implications for LGBTQ people in the UK and around the world. Those engaged in data practices, whether as individuals or as groups, need to re-imagine their relationship with data and continually question whose interests are served by the work undertaken. When it comes to participation in data projects, two related questions therefore need to be examined: should LGBTQ people share data about their gender, sex and sexuality? And are there any instances where the provision of data should be mandatory? During our interview, Kirstie expressed their unease about mandatory questions in data collection exercises, such as the census, and the expectation that people should disclose information about their lives and experiences:

> I think mandatory questions are a bit of a problem … The idea that the information is owed to anyone. I think we should be asking very nicely for information, as the information is very helpful, and it would be good if we got information about as many people as possible but I think people should always have the ability to say 'I want as little information about me out in the world as possible'.[46]

The UK General Data Protection Regulation, legislation that oversees data protection and privacy, provides some protection as consent is not understood as freely given if data subjects cannot refuse to disclose data (for whatever

---

[45] Examples of initiatives based in the UK and United States include the Data Justice Lab (Cardiff University), the Ada Lovelace Institute (the Nuffield Foundation), the IDA B WELLS Just Data Lab (Princeton University), Our Data Bodies and Data for Black Lives.
[46] English, Interview with Kirstie English.

reason) without detriment.[47] As something that belongs to us, it makes sense that data should not be taken from us without consent or in ways where we feel coerced to unwillingly share information. However, particularly in regard to the collection of behavioural data, discussed in Chapter 6, this is often not the case. Benjamin has advocated for those engaged in the design of data projects to adopt the idea of 'informed refusal' where the assumption of consent is challenged and an individual's agency to consider the pros and cons of participation is valued.[48] In 2019, a collective of feminist data scholars working across a diversity of disciplines in the United States, Canada and the UK expanded on this vision with the *Feminist Data Manifest-No*, a declaration of refusal and commitment that refuses harmful data regimes and commits to new data futures.[49] The *Manifest-No* includes thirty-two points and challenges data practices based on 'ultimatums, coercive permissions, pervasive cookie collecting, and blocked access' where 'not everyone can safely refuse or opt out without consequence or further harm'.[50] The UK's Open Data Institute has also recommended that those designing digital services need to provide users 'the option to provide or withhold information about their protected characteristics' and stressed that the 'absence of data, where people have opted out, should not be feared. It is valuable data in itself. Data collection is important, but it is not more important than rights and autonomy'.[51] The work of Benjamin, the *Manifest-No* and the Open Data Institute turn on its head current approaches to data collection that assume the participation of data subjects and offer a response to the widespread extraction, exchange and use of gender, sex and sexuality data in ways that often bring little benefit to those about whom the data relates.

Poor consent practices are particularly endemic in terms of service for online platforms where there is no option for negotiation: you either agree to disclose data about yourself or you cannot gain access to the service.[52] The rationale for this blanket approach is perhaps easier to justify in the realm of private companies and social media, where the provision of data is framed as

---

[47] Information Commissioner's Office, 'What Is Valid Consent?', March 2021.
[48] Ruha Benjamin, 'Informed Refusal: Toward a Justice-Based Bioethics', *Science, Technology, & Human Values* 41, no. 6 (November 2016): 969.
[49] Marika Cifor et al., 'Feminist Data Manifest-No', 2019.
[50] Ibid.
[51] Edafe Onerhime, 'Monitoring Equality in Digital Public Services' (Open Data Institute, 2020), 21–2.
[52] See Carissa Véliz, *Privacy Is Power: Why and How You Should Take Back Control of Your Data* (London: Transworld, 2020), chap. Data Vultures.

a form of payment for the service provided. However, this exchange becomes extremely problematic when linked to the provision of public services such as health and social care. Julia Serano uses the expression 'low/nondisclosing' individuals to describe people who would not identify themselves as 'trans' in a data collection exercise but have transitioned in the past.[53] For Serano, these individuals are not masking their identity but, with the transition complete, no longer feel required to identify as part of the trans community. What therefore happens when organizations expect or require individuals to disclose particular data about themselves before they can access services (such as trans-specific mental health services)?[54] Megan M. Rohrer explores this dilemma, particularly its effect on low/nondisclosing people, and questions the meaningfulness of consent in situations where individuals are expected to answer questions about their trans histories as a prerequisite for access to food, housing and other benefits.[55] For Rohrer, 'Just because it may be possible one day to find accurate ways to count trans people, it does not mean that we always should.'[56] As with other negative manifestations of administrative practices, those most likely to experience unjust demands to disclose their data are also those who lack the power to say 'no'.[57]

Those engaged in the use of data for action do not face a binary choice between uncritical participation in data practices and a blanket-call for abolition: the reform of existing systems offers a middle way. For lessons on how to reform data practices that affect LGBTQ people, it is helpful to consider the work of researchers, practitioners and activists engaged in projects about race and ethnicity data. Zuberi, for example, describes how 'racial data are essential if we are to achieve racial equality; however, this does not mean that every statistic should be presented racially'.[58] For Zuberi, the overuse or misuse of racial data 'has only helped aggravate the problem

---

[53] Julia Serano, *Whipping Girl: A Transsexual Woman on Sexism and the Scapegoating of Femininity* (Emeryville: Seal Press, 2007), cited in Megan M. Rohrer, 'The Ethical Case for Undercounting Trans Individuals', *TSQ: Transgender Studies Quarterly* 2, no. 1 (1 January 2015): 177.

[54] Rohrer, 'The Ethical Case for Undercounting Trans Individuals', 177.

[55] Ibid.

[56] Ibid., 175.

[57] The *Feminist Data Manifest-No* notes, 'We refuse to operate under the assumption that risk and harm associated with data practices can be bounded to mean the same thing for everyone, everywhere, at every time. We commit to acknowledging how historical and systemic patterns of violence and exploitation produce differential vulnerabilities for communities', in Cifor et al., 'Feminist Data Manifest-No'.

[58] Zuberi, *Thicker than Blood*, 120.

of racial conflict by making it appear that race causes people to behave or respond in particular ways'.[59] Gillborn et al. also argue that although statistical inquiry might not appear amenable to addressing issues of racism that are complex, fluid and changing, 'in the absence of a critical race-conscious perspective, quantitative analyses will tend to remake and legitimate existing race inequities'.[60] These examples highlight how engagement with existing data practices, and working within systems to bring about change, mean that critical voices are present to call out approaches that cause harm to marginalized communities.

Reform is not without its problems. Spade articulates three concerns about law reform projects that we can apply to the reform of data practices and systems.[61] Firstly, reform only focuses on what systems say they are doing with limited attention to indirect or hidden impacts of data practices. Secondly, reform generally introduces fixes that help the least vulnerable or only temporarily halts the damage inflicted on the most vulnerable. Thirdly, reform provides projects with a rationale for their continued existence and the potential expansion of harmful practices. When reform fails or attempts at reform risk keeping a broken system afloat, the final option for data justice campaigners is abolition. In August 2020, school pupils took to the streets of Glasgow, Scotland to protest about the use of algorithms to adjust awarded grades. In place of regular exams, cancelled due to the Covid-19 pandemic, grades were calculated based on mock exams and teachers' judgements, which were adjusted up or down by an algorithm based on the school's (not the individual's) results from previous years. For example, the adjustment reduced the pass rate for Higher exams, commonly used as entrance qualifications for university, by 15.2 percentage points for pupils in Scotland's least affluent areas and by 6.9 percentage points for pupils in the most affluent areas.[62] Carrying placards such as 'Keep my class out of the classroom', 'Students not stats' and 'Abolish exams', young people put pressure on the government to scrap the algorithm and award grades based on teachers' estimates, a demand that the government ultimately accepted.

Protests in Scotland about the negative impact of algorithms on the life chances of young people present a window into what might lie ahead for

---

[59] Ibid.
[60] Gillborn, Warmington, and Demack, 'QuantCrit', 169.
[61] Spade, Normal Life, 49.
[62] Graeme Esson, 'Scotland's Results 2020: How Grades Were Worked Out for Scottish Pupils', BBC News, 4 August 2020.

the uses of gender, sex and sexuality data. An abolitionist approach opposes tweaks to data practices that, on the surface, appear to make approaches more inclusive but ultimately moves us away from the ultimate goal of using data to improve the lives of the people about whom it relates. As an example, the addition of questions to UK censuses on sexual orientation and trans/ gender identity was generally welcomed by politicians and campaign groups and meant that many LGBTQ people were recognized in the national count for the first time. However, the accommodation of *some* LGBTQ people pre-emptively neutralizes claims that the census presents a cis/heteronormative account of the population. For those with identities not counted in the census, even after the addition of new questions (for example, non-binary people), this development has arguably strengthened the hand of the existing structure and made it easier for census officials to rebuff accusations that the census is exclusionary. The strategic decisions of LGBTQ rights organizations to make accommodations to existing structures of power are nothing new. Writing in 1995, Joshua Gamson decried the gay and lesbian civil rights strategy in the United States as 'for all its gains, does little to attack the political culture that itself makes the denial of and struggle for civil rights necessary and possible'.[63] Gamson identified the strategy's failure to challenge 'the system of meanings that underlies the political oppression: the division of the world into man/woman and gay/straight. On the contrary, they ratify and reinforce these categories.'[64]

Rather than tinker around the edges with question stems, response options and supplementary guidance, an abolitionist approach to the census calls on LGBTQ people to abandon a system designed by cis, heterosexual architects that is beyond repair. In the United States, several data justice groups focused on the collection of data about Black lives and experiences have adopted an abolitionist approach. Most notably, Data for Black Lives, a network of 4,000 researchers and activists engaged in the use of data for social change, have illustrated the radical, productive potential of an abolitionist approach to race data. Yeshi Milner, a Founder and Executive Director of Data for Black Lives, argues that 'abolition is a process, not an end goal' and that calls to abolish big data and end the data-industrial complex are not about stopping the use of data but finding ways to 'put data in the hands of people who need

---

[63] Joshua Gamson, 'Must Identity Movements Self-Destruct? A Queer Dilemma', *Social Problems* 42, no. 3 (1995): 400.
[64] Ibid.

it most'.[65] Drawing links between the abolition of big data and the prison abolition movement, Milner notes, 'How do we dismantle and reimagine industries that concentrate big data into the hands of a few? And how can abolish the structures that turn data into a powerful and deadly weapon?'[66]

To participate, reform or abolish? Systems that collect, analyse and use gender, sex and sexuality data are not set in stone, they require maintenance and upkeep. The ageing of data systems offers flashpoints for change. In the UK, the redesign of censuses every ten years presents opportunities to break from the past that are seized upon by researchers, practitioner and activists. Yet, in many contexts, talk of refusal, reform or abolition is premature as the reality is that LGBTQ people are not counted at all.[67] Across many areas of life, the absence of data about LGBTQ people means that inequalities exist that we are unaware of and therefore unable to mobilize for change or take action.[68] However, even in contexts where data about LGBTQ people is not yet collected, it is never too early to pre-empt the dangers that come through assimilation with existing practices and systems. As we have witnessed with the biases and assumptions designed-into datasets and algorithms, remedial initiatives to fix the errors of the past further deplete limited resources to address inequality. Lessons from data justice groups focused on race and ethnicity, and consideration now of what might lie ahead in the future, can help ensure history is not repeated and the harmful effects of data practices and systems on LGBTQ people are reduced.

* * *

There is nothing intrinsically good or bad about the uses of gender, sex and sexuality data. Even the ethics of loaded terms such as 'surveillance', 'big data' and 'predictive analytics' depend on the motivations behind those executing these actions and for whose interests they serve. This final chapter has explored queer data as a productive force that can bring about positive change in the lives of LGBTQ people. Queer data has radical potential. It has the power to name a problem; which, as Crenshaw notes, is a necessary step in solving a problem. The power of visibility, even when

---

[65] Yeshi Milner, 'Abolish Big Data' (University of California, Irvine, 8 March 2019); Yeshi Milner, 'Abolition Means the Creation of Something New', 31 December 2019.
[66] Ibid.
[67] Schönpflug et al., 'If Queers Were Counted', 22.
[68] Velte, 'Straightwashing the Census', 113.

this representation is not without problems, can reshape conversations and ultimately inform the allocation of resources and services. Being counted can and does change people's lives for the better. However, as articulated in the work of critical trans and race scholars, visibility presents opportunities as well as traps. More data about LGBTQ people does not, on its own, improve people's lives and experiences. The requirement to collect excessive amounts of evidence before those in positions of power take action can stall rather than advance efforts to repair or overhaul broken systems. More worryingly, any data collected might sustain the status quo when it undercounts or misrepresents the extent of the problem, which is itself a reflection of the unfair playing field upon which data practices take place. Although not explicitly focused on the lives of LGBTQ people, data justice projects highlight methods to elevate the voices about whom data relates and ask new questions about how data is constructed. Learning from these initiatives, LGBTQ individuals and groups in the UK need to re-evaluate their relationship with data. Participation, refusal, reform and abolition are possible answers to the problems inherent in the use of gender, sex and sexuality data for action. Although these considerations might appear premature, we should begin to make plans now for how to respond to potential dangers that lie ahead.

CONCLUSION: WHO COUNTS?

Queer data stands in the confluence where identity characteristics meet data practices and systems. A queer approach brings together data *about* gender, sex and sexuality, with particular attention to how this data reflects and shapes the lives of LGBTQ people, and the *queering* of methods used to collect, analyse and present this information. I apply Doan's account of 'queerness-as-being' and 'queerness-as-method', described in the Introduction chapter, to the collection, analysis and use of data to not only ask 'What do we know about LGBTQ people?' but also 'How do we know?' and, most importantly, 'Why do we want to know?' In becoming something more than the sum of its parts, *Queer Data* looks beyond the lives of sexual minority groups to also investigate data's role in the construction of knowledge about *all* identities and question whose stories are positioned at the centre and whose stories sit on the margins. Although the interface between data practices, systems and identity characteristics can expose gaps and absences, methods used to shine a light on what is missing can also ignore, misrepresent or actively exclude those who are most marginalized. Reparative efforts, such as the correction of individual biases or expansion of who is included, can give the impression that past inequalities are in the process of being fixed and grant a second life to practices and systems that continue to cause harm. An illusion of meaningful change means that, in many ways, the counting of *some* LGBTQ people makes the prospect of counting *all* LGBTQ people far harder to achieve.

Queer Data has examined this provocation from multiple viewpoints. Part I provided a historical account of data practices used to capture information about people that transgressed normative ideas about gender, sex or sexuality and examined how the interests of data collectors and the use of particular methods brought to life specific understandings of LGBTQ acts and identities. I continued this examination into the present day to examine the use of surveys, interviews and focus groups to capture quantitative and qualitative data, the role of research methods in constructing the phenomena they claim to describe, and the many impacts of methods on both participants and researchers. Moving from the general to the specific, I considered the design process of questions about sex, sexual orientation and trans status/history in Scotland's 2022 census. To conclude Part I, my exploration of the lines of scrutiny pursued (and not pursued) by figures in positions of power expanded to include the collection of gender, sex and sexuality data in nations and regions outside of the UK.

Part II moved beyond collection methods to investigate how data is shaped during analysis. Techniques such as cleaning, aggregation and disaggregation can erase the efforts of LGBTQ people to subvert data practices or represent the social world in ways that match their everyday realities. When analysis is automated and conducted at scale, for example in big data projects, decision-making can perpetuate existing biases and wrongly imagine the social world as an equal playing field. Data analysis also involves practices that validate or invalidate identity claims, which create issues when a person's self-identified identity (for example, as a woman) does not match data collected from external-identified, biometric or behavioural sources.

Finally, Part III examined how these problems are a product of who is missing from discussions about gender, sex and sexuality data, whose voice matters, and the challenge of communicating ideas about gender, sex and sexuality data in online spaces. I illustrated the need for queer data competence among decision-makers to encourage critical thinking and help ensure data about LGBTQ people is not used in ways that perpetuates harm. Lastly, I showcased the use of data for action and the efforts of scholars, practitioners and activists to deploy data to upset the technological status quo and improve the lives of the people about whom the data relates. For LGBTQ people, a queer approach to data can elevate stories previously excluded from history but also question assumptions about quantitative and qualitative data that naturalize the categories of 'cisgender' and 'heterosexual' as default positions. Building on critical data interventions such as the *Feminist Data Manifest-No* and Data for Black Lives, LGBTQ organizations in the UK need to re-assess their relationship to data and examine whether current practices, systems and the people involved are capable of change. If not, a risk exists that ongoing participation in data projects can shore-up existing inequalities and make the situation worse (particularly for the most marginalized in minority groups) rather than better.

Across eight chapters I have documented how gender, sex and sexuality data has positively impacted the lives and experiences of many LGBTQ people. EDI researchers, practitioners and activists use data to highlight injustices that condition many people's lives and experiences, which were historically excluded from view, and as an evidence base for action. Whether it's lobbying politicians for legislative change or sharing information to shift the hearts and minds of the general public, data exposes people to unfamiliar worlds and draws them into experiences that might sit beyond their own frame of reference. As proof of a problem, data can translate what might seem like individual experiences into something shared and inspire people to mobilize to defend or change the status quo. However, the use of data for action intended to improve the lives and experience of LGBTQ people must also be viewed with caution. Most obviously, biases have influenced the design of collection methods, analytical practices and beliefs as to who is considered a legible data subject and a 'deserving' beneficiary of actions to counter inequality. Yet, a focus on biases only scratches the surface of the problem and ignores how data sustains the requirement that marginalized groups provide evidence of their inequality or, in the case of trans people, proof of their very existence. Participation in data practices, where rules were designed in ways that do not necessarily aid the objectives of LGBTQ liberation, means that LGBTQ organizations risk forever searching for a magic number in the hope this will encourage people in positions of power to take action. But what if this magic number changes or the rules of the game shift yet again? In 2020, the UK Government reported on the results of their 2018 consultation into reform of the GRA: although over 100,000 individuals and organizations responded to the consultation, with the majority backing meaningful reform, the government decided not to proceed with substantial reform of the GRA. Two months after the government decision, the UK Parliament's Women and Equalities Select Committee announced the launch of another inquiry into reform of the GRA, following a similar inquiry conducted by the committee in 2016. By adhering to the demands of the existing system, trans people and allies are invited to accumulate yet more data of injustices experienced by trans people, burning-through finite resources and energy, to provide further proof of the problem. But what if this time, money and energy were used in other ways? What if this labour was spent on the development of mental health services, the provision of community-level legal support and advice, or monetary help with overdue bills and outstanding rent payments? Although the collection, analysis and use of data undoubtedly play an important role in bringing about change, data is only ever one ingredient in a wider mix of approaches to social justice. On its own, data is no substitute for interventions that directly impact people's day-to-day lives.

Where do we go from here?

I wrote *Queer Data* during the Covid-19 global pandemic, which brought into sharp focus the relationship between data and people's identity characteristics. Regular governments briefings presented data on infection rates, the spread of the virus, the number of deaths and the distribution of vaccines via an array of tables, graphs and other visualization techniques. Yet, the virus did not impact everyone equally. Existing inequalities and the economic, psychological and social fallout from measures introduced to curb the spread of the virus meant that women, people of colour, poorer people, disabled people and LGBTQ communities were particularly affected.[1] In addition, the roll-out of data technologies, such as trace and test systems, expanded the powers of state surveillance in many countries, with unforeseen impacts for some LGBTQ people. In South Korea, for example, the spread of Covid-19 in nightclubs and bars in Seoul's Itaewon gay district created a climate of fear among LGBTQ people who worried about being outed to family, friends and employers.[2] South Korea adopted a particularly invasive approach to tracing contacts of those potentially exposed to Covid-19, which involved the capture of location data from multiple sources (including credit card payments) and public disclosure of information about individuals' whereabouts. In a country where LGBTQ people face discrimination and social exclusion, the risk of being publically outed meant that many of the people involved were too scared to contact health services and terrified about what data might reveal about them.[3]

Technologies already exist that can assist states in efforts to identify and manage LGBTQ populations. Whether this involves the analysis of an individual's digital footprints to discern their sexual orientation or the use of facial recognition technologies to identify those present in queer nightclubs or community spaces, surveillance and digital contact tracing invites the

---

[1] For a more detailed account of the impacts of Covid-19 on different identity groups, see Robert Booth, 'Low-Paid Women in UK at "High Risk of Coronavirus Exposure"', *The Guardian*, 29 March 2020; Zubaida Haque, 'Coronavirus Will Increase Race Inequalities' (London: Runnymede Trust, 26 March 2020); Karin Goodwin, 'Crucial Services to Disabled People Cut Due to Coronavirus', *The Ferret*, 26 March 2020; LGBT Foundation, 'Hidden Figures'.
[2] Reuters, 'Tracing of South Korea's New Coronavirus Outbreak Focuses on LGBTQ Clubs', *NBC News*, 11 May 2020.
[3] Nemo Kim, 'South Korea Struggles to Contain New Outbreak Amid Anti-Gay Backlash', *The Guardian*, 11 May 2020.

potential for harm.[4] In spaces where data and identity characteristics intersect, unforeseen outcomes can have devastating consequences, particularly on minoritized or marginalized groups. Those working with data therefore need to rethink their approach and defrost assumptions that have kept ideas about gender, sex and sexuality data frozen in time and space. In opening up new ways to conceptualize the collection, analysis and use of data, we expand the borders of what is considered 'knowledge' and discover ways to count individuals previously understood as 'incomprehensible' by traditional data practices. We already see efforts underway in the UK and around the world to expand understandings of who is considered a legible data subject. For example, approaches to identity categorization that challenge the cis/trans binary (such as Ashley's discussion of gender modality); efforts to expand concepts of gender and sex to include those who identify as non-binary; the provision of write-in boxes in diversity monitoring forms where data is analysed meaningfully and included in the final count; greater attention to data about the lives and experiences of bisexual people; and recognition that an increasing number of young people identify in ways that go beyond the categories of heterosexual/straight, cis, lesbian, gay, bisexual and/or trans.[5]

Queer questions

While writing *Queer Data*, it became clear to me that the book does not go far enough in examining what lies beyond normative ideas about data. By telling the story of how we go to where we are today, it was hard to shake off the value-laden language of 'scales', 'options' and 'characteristics' that presuppose particular ways of knowing, organizing and explaining data about identity. Rather than rip things up and start again, I realized this

---

[4] Catherine D'Ignazio and Lauren F. Klein, 'Seven Intersectional Feminist Principles for Equitable and Actionable COVID-19 Data', *Big Data & Society* 7, no. 2 (1 July 2020): 3; Tomasev et al., 'Fairness for Unobserved Characteristics'.
[5] See Ashley, '"Trans" Is My Gender Modality: A Modest Terminological Proposal'; discussion of a non-binary sex question in Scotland's 2022 census in Chapter 3; Fraser et al., 'Coding Responses to an Open-Ended Gender Measure in a New Zealand National Sample' on the analysis of write-in questions on gender; Breetveld, 'Forms of Bisexual Injustice: Bi, Being, and Becoming a Knower' on bisexual identities and knowledge construction; JJ Garrett-Walker and Michelle J. Montagno, 'Queering Labels: Expanding Identity Categories in LGBTQ + Research and Clinical Practice', *Journal of LGBT Youth* Online (11 March 2021): 3, on identification as 'other' gender and sexual identities.

was not *Queer Data's* story to tell. For readers engaged in work with data, I hope that *Queer Data* is a launch pad for bold and innovative approaches that give precedence to the authenticity of people's identities rather than the requirements of existing data practices and systems. To help guide our navigation of this new data landscape, I present eight queer questions for those engaged in the collection, analysis and use of gender, sex and sexuality data to bring to their work:

1) **What is your end goal?** The collection and analysis of gender, sex and sexuality data is not an objective in itself, nor is the ambition to gather 'good data' or fix the numbers. While paying attention to the potential for methods to misrepresent or exclude, such as strategic essentialism, ensure that data about LGBTQ people is ultimately used to construct a social world that values and improves LGBTQ lives.

2) **Do your methods present an authentic account of LGBTQ lives?** Rather than adopt methods that promise a tidy dataset, recognize that data about identity characteristics is leaky, pluralistic and can change over time. A queer approach involves the use of innovative collection and analysis methods, such as multiple response options and the provision of open-text boxes, to produce a more authentic reflection of lives and experiences.

3) **Who makes decisions about data that impact LGBTQ people?** Decisions that disproportionately affect LGBTQ communities should be made by LGBTQ people. Where this is not practical, or there is a risk of overburdening a small number of people, decision-makers need queer data competence and the ability to recuse themselves when deliberations stretch beyond their capabilities. Use these instances to make space for people with knowledge and experience of the issues under discussion.

4) **Does your project create more good than harm? And for whom?** Assess what your project intends to achieve and its potential to cause harm; only continue when the potential benefits outweigh the potential dangers. Disaggregate the differential impacts *among* LGBTQ people to ensure that the project does not only benefit the least marginalized individuals, for whom sexual orientation is the only characteristics that excludes them from full inclusion.

5) **Do you need more data?** Do not assume the need for more data – enough evidence of a problem might already exist to justify the need

for action. Also explore who is already engaged in data
the topic to see if resources could support existing initia
than create something afresh. The collection, analysis an
data are resource-intensive. Before work begins, you the_ ____u
to ask if this is the best use of time, resources and energy to address
injustices that face LGBTQ people.

6) **Do you elevate LGBTQ lives and critically examine the invisibility
   of majority characteristics?** One of data's strengths is its power to
   tell stories, which can shift hearts and mind and encourage others
   to take action. However, increased visibility alone is not enough.
   A queer approach also problematizes the distinction between the
   centre and the margins so that the invisibility of majority identity
   characteristics, such as cis and heterosexual, are brought into focus
   and critically examined.

7) **Are your ways of working open, accessible and transparent?**
   Traditional approaches to quantitative data collection and analysis
   are misunderstood as an objective account of reality; an assumption
   that masks decisions made throughout the design process. A queer
   approach to data is also influenced by biases and assumptions;
   those engaged in queer data practices therefore need to describe
   how decisions are made, in accessible language, and its effect on
   the results presented. Openness about the limitations of data helps
   ensure that an undercount or misrepresentation of data about
   LGBTQ people is not used to undermine political and social
   advances.

8) **Are damaging data practices and systems capable of reform?**
   Re-evaluate your relationship to data and assess whether existing
   practices and systems are capable of reform. If reform seems
   possible, question who is best placed to undertake this work. When
   reform fails, or efforts to reform risk keeping a damaging system
   alive for longer, consider if an abolitionist approach might put data
   in the hands of those most in need.

Data's power to demonstrate difference has transformed the lives of many
LGBTQ people, whether through its use as evidence to challenge unfair
laws, hold those in positions of power to account or encourage people to
reconsider negative views and attitudes. However, there are limits to the
justice LGBTQ people can achieve through data alone. When enough data

...sts to demonstrate the existence of a problem, yet those with the power to initiate change remain unmoved, how can data help us push harder on this closed door? *Queer Data* presents an alternative account of gender, sex and sexuality data that brings together data *about* LGBTQ people and a *queering* of the foundations that inform how we conceptualize data, determine categories, establish value and use data to change lives. Rather than shore-up EDI initiatives that fail to help those in most need or see the addition of new questions and provision of more response options as mission accomplished, queer data calls on us to fight for something bigger and bolder. Queer data can change the world for the better – we can be part of that change.

BIBLIOGRAPHY

Archive materials

Albany Trust. 'Social Needs Survey: Results'. London, 1970 in *The Hall-Carpenter Archives, London School of Economics and Political Science Library, Archives of Sexuality and Gender* [Albany Trust 10: Surveys and Research, 1960–1983, 10/11].

Interviews

Interview with Kirstie English, 26 October 2020.

Correspondence and materials related to Scotland's 2022 census

Culture, Tourism, Europe and External Affairs Committee. 'Session 5 - Official Report of Meeting'. Edinburgh: The Scottish Parliament, 6 December 2018. http://www.parliament.scot/parliamentarybusiness/report. aspx?r=11836&mode=pdf.

Culture, Tourism, Europe and External Affairs Committee. 'Session 5 - Official Report of Meeting'. Edinburgh: Scottish Parliament, 9 January 2020. https:// www.parliament.scot/parliamentarybusiness/CurrentCommittees/113452.aspx.

Culture, Tourism, Europe and External Affairs Committee. 'Session 5 - Official Report of Meeting'. Edinburgh: Scottish Parliament, 30 January 2020. https:// www.parliament.scot/parliamentarybusiness/report.aspx?r=12495&mode=pdf.

Equality Network and LGBT Youth Scotland. 'Letter to Culture, Tourism, Europe and External Affairs Committee', 1 October 2019. https://archive2021. parliament.scot/S5_European/General%20Documents/CTEEA_2019.10.01Equ alityNetworkCensus(1).pdf.

LGB Alliance. 'Letter to Culture, Tourism, Europe and External Affairs Committee', 26 November 2019. https://www.parliament.scot/S5_European/General%20 Documents/CTEEA_2019.26.11LGBcensus.pdf.

National Records of Scotland. 'Cognitive and Quantitative Testing'. Scotland's Census 2021. Edinburgh, 2017. https://www.scotlandscensus.gov.uk/ documents/census2021/2017_Cognitive_and_Quantitative_Testing_ Methodology_report.pdf.

Bibliography

National Records of Scotland. 'Get Involved'. Scotland's Census, 2020. https://www.scotlandscensus.gov.uk/Get-involved.

National Records of Scotland. 'Letter to Culture, Tourism, Europe and External Affairs Committee', 25 October 2019. https://archive2021.parliament.scot/S5_European/General%20Documents/CTEEA_2019.10.25NRS(1).pdf.

National Records of Scotland. 'Letter to Culture, Tourism, Europe and External Affairs Committee', 18 December 2019. https://www.parliament.scot/S5_European/General%20Documents/CTEEA_2019.12.18_NRSCensus2021.pdf.

National Records of Scotland. 'Letter to Culture, Tourism, Europe and External Affairs Committee', 2 April 2020. https://www.parliament.scot/S5_European/General%20Documents/20200402_NRSToConvener_Census.pdf.

National Records of Scotland. 'Population and Households'. Scotland's Census, 2018. https://www.scotlandscensus.gov.uk/population-households.

National Records of Scotland 'Question Set'. Scotland's Census, 20 July 2020. https://www.scotlandscensus.gov.uk/news/question-set.

National Records of Scotland. 'Sex and Gender Identity Topic Report'. Scotland's Census 2021. Edinburgh, 2018. https://www.scotlandscensus.gov.uk/documents/census2021/Sex_and_Gender_Identity_Topic_Report.pdf.

Scottish Parliament. 'Census (Amendment) (Scotland) Bill', 18 July 2019. https://parliament.scot/bills/census-amendment-scotland-bill.

Scottish Parliament. 'Meeting of the Parliament'. Edinburgh: The Scottish Parliament, 12 June 2019. http://www.parliament.scot/parliamentarybusiness/report.aspx?r=12182&mode=pdf.

Scottish Parliament. 'Stage One Debate on the Census (Amendment) (Scotland) Bill'. Edinburgh, 28 February 2019. https://parliament.scot/bills/census-amendment-scotland-bill.

Scottish Women's Aid, Close the Gap, Rape Crisis Scotland, Engender, and Equate Scotland. 'Scottish Women's Sector Note - Census (Amendment) (Scotland) Bill', December 2018. https://www.engender.org.uk/content/publications/Scottish-womens-sector-submission-to-the-Culture-Tourism-Europe-and-External-Affairs-Committee-on-the-census.pdf.

Other sources

Abrams, Lynn. *Oral History Theory*. Abingdon: Routledge, 2010.

Achiume, Tendayi. 'Report of the Special Rapporteur on Contemporary Forms of Racism, Racial Discrimination, Xenophobia and Related Intolerance'. New York: United Nations Office of the High Commissioner for Human Rights, 10 November 2020. https://www.ohchr.org/EN/newyork/Documents/A-75-590-AUV.docx.

Adebisi, Foluke Ifejola. 'The Only Accurate Part of "BAME" Is the "and"...'. *Foluke's African Skies*, 8 July 2019. https://folukeafrica.com/the-only-acceptable-part-of-bame-is-the-and/.

Advance HE. 'Equality in Higher Education: Student Statistical Report'. London: Advance HE, 2020.

Agar, Jon. *The Government Machine: A Revolutionary History of the Computer.* Cambridge: The MIT Press, 2003.

Age UK. 'Combating Loneliness amongst Older LGBT People: A Case Study of the Sage Project in Leeds'. London: Age UK, 2018.

Ahmed, Maryam. 'UK Passport Photo Checker Shows Bias against Dark-Skinned Women'. *BBC News*, 7 October 2020. https://www.bbc.co.uk/news/technology-54349538.

Ahmed, Sara. 'An Affinity of Hammers'. *TSQ: Transgender Studies Quarterly* 3, no. 1–2 (May 2016): 22–34. https://doi.org/10.1215/23289252-3334151.

Ahmed, Sara. 'Interview with Judith Butler'. *Sexualities* 19, no. 4 (1 June 2016): 482–92. https://doi.org/10.1177/1363460716629607.

Ahmed, Sara. *Queer Phenomenology: Orientations, Objects, Others.* Durham: Duke University Press, 2006.

Ahmed, Sara. 'The Language of Diversity'. *Ethnic and Racial Studies* 30, no. 2 (1 March 2007): 235–56. https://doi.org/10.1080/01419870601143927.

Ahmed, Sara. '"You End up Doing the Document Rather than Doing the Doing": Diversity, Race Equality and the Politics of Documentation'. *Ethnic and Racial Studies* 30, no. 4 (July 2007): 590–609. https://doi.org/10.1080/01419870701356015.

Amnesty International UK. 'Black and Asian Women MPs Abused More Online', 2017. https://www.amnesty.org.uk/online-violence-women-mps.

Anders, Sari M. van. 'Beyond Sexual Orientation: Integrating Gender/Sex and Diverse Sexualities via Sexual Configurations Theory'. *Archives of Sexual Behavior* 44, no. 5 (2015): 1177–213. https://doi.org/10.1007/s10508-015-0490-8.

Anderson, Margo, and Stephen E. Fienberg. 'Race and Ethnicity and the Controversy over the US Census'. *Current Sociology* 48, no. 3 (July 2000): 87–110. https://doi.org/10.1177/0011392100048003007.

Arcas, Blaise Aguera Y., Alexander Todorov, and Margaret Mitchell. 'Do Algorithms Reveal Sexual Orientation or Just Expose Our Stereotypes?' *Medium*, 11 January 2018. https://medium.com/@blaisea/do-algorithms-reveal-sexual-orientation-or-just-expose-our-stereotypes-d998fafdf477.

Ash, Lucy. 'Inside Poland's "LGBT-Free Zones"'. *BBC News*, 20 September 2020. https://www.bbc.com/news/stories-54191344.

Ashley, Florence. 'Recommendations for Institutional and Governmental Management of Gender Information'. *NYU Review of Law & Social Change* 44, no. 4 (2021): 489–528. https://doi.org/10.2139/ssrn.3398394.

Ashley, Florence. 'Trans' Is My Gender Modality: A Modest Terminological Proposal'. In *Trans Bodies, Trans Selves*, edited by Laura Erickson-Schroth, 2nd ed. Oxford: Oxford University Press, 2021.

Australian Institute of Aboriginal and Torres Strait Islander Studies. 'Proof of Aboriginality', 4 September 2020. https://aiatsis.gov.au/family-history/you-start/proof-aboriginality.

Bibliography

Bailkin, Jordanna. *The Afterlife of Empire*. Berkeley: University of California Press, 2017.

Bajracharya, Nasana. 'Still Labelled "Others", Nepal's LGBTQIA+ People Pin Hopes on Census'. *OnlineKhabar*, 31 March 2021. https://english.onlinekhabar.com/still-labelled-others-nepals-lgbtqia-people-pin-hopes-on-census.html.

Bates, Nancy, Yazmín A. García Trejo, and Monica Vines. 'Are Sexual Minorities Hard-to-Survey? Insights from the 2020 Census Barriers, Attitudes, and Motivators Study (CBAMS) Survey'. *Journal of Official Statistics* 35, no. 4 (1 December 2019): 709–29. https://doi.org/10.2478/jos-2019-0030.

Bauer, Heike. *The Hirschfeld Archives: Violence, Death, and Modern Queer Culture*. Philadelphia: Temple University Press, 2017.

Bauer, Heike. 'Theorizing Female Inversion: Sexology, Discipline, and Gender at the Fin de Siècle'. *Journal of the History of Sexuality* 18, no. 1 (2009): 84–102. https://doi.org/10.1353/sex.0.0040.

Baumle, Amanda K. 'The Demography of Sexuality: Queering Demographic Methods'. In *Other, Please Specify: Queer Methods in Sociology*, edited by D'Lane Compton, Tey Meadow, and Kristen Schilt, 277–90. University of California Press, 2018.

BBC News. 'Experts Condemn Asylum DNA Tests'. *BBC News*, 30 September 2009. http://news.bbc.co.uk/1/hi/uk/8282654.stm.

BBC News. 'Row over AI That "Identifies Gay Faces"'. *BBC News*, 11 September 2017. https://www.bbc.co.uk/news/technology-41188560.

BBC News. 'Tasmania Makes It Optional to List Gender on Birth Certificates'. *BBC News*, 10 April 2019. https://www.bbc.co.uk/news/world-australia-47877998.

Beatty, Jack. 'Hitler's Willing Business Partners'. *The Atlantic*, April 2001. https://www.theatlantic.com/magazine/archive/2001/04/hitlers-willing-business-partners/303146/.

Beauchamp, Toby. *Going Stealth: Transgender Politics and US Surveillance Practices*. Durham: Duke University Press, 2019.

Benjamin, Ruha. 'Informed Refusal: Toward a Justice-Based Bioethics'. *Science, Technology, & Human Values* 41, no. 6 (November 2016): 967–90. https://doi.org/10.1177/0162243916656059.

Benjamin, Ruha. *Race after Technology: Abolitionist Tools for the New Jim Code*. Medford: Polity, 2019.

Betts, Peter, Amanda Wilmot, and Tamara Taylor. 'Developing Survey Questions on Sexual Identity: Exploratory Focus Groups'. Office for National Statistics, August 2008. https://www.ons.gov.uk/file?uri=/methodology/classificationsandstandards/sexualidentityguidanceandprojectdocumentation/sexidentfocgrorpt_tcm77-181171.pdf.

Bittner, Amanda, and Elizabeth Goodyear-Grant. 'Sex Isn't Gender: Reforming Concepts and Measurements in the Study of Public Opinion'. *Political Behavior* 39, no. 4 (1 December 2017): 1019–41. https://doi.org/10.1007/s11109-017-9391-y.

Bivens, Rena. 'The Gender Binary Will Not Be Deprogrammed: Ten Years of Coding Gender on Facebook'. *New Media & Society* 19, no. 6 (1 June 2017): 880–98. https://doi.org/10.1177/1461444815621527.

Booth, Robert. 'Low-Paid Women in UK at "High Risk of Coronavirus Exposure"'. *The Guardian*, 29 March 2020. https://www.theguardian.com/world/2020/mar/29/low-paid-women-in-uk-at-high-risk-of-coronavirus-exposure.

Borgesius, Frederik Zuiderveen. 'Discrimination, Artificial Intelligence, and Algorithmic Decision-Making'. Strasbourg: Directorate General of Democracy, Council of Europe, 2018.

Bourne, Emily. 'Before the Passing of the 1967 Sexual Offences Act'. Parliamentary Archives, 8 June 2017. https://archives.blog.parliament.uk/2017/06/08/before-the-passing-of-the-1967-sexual-offences-act/.

Bowker, Geoffrey C., and Susan Leigh Star. *Sorting Things Out: Classification and Its Consequences.* Cambridge: The MIT Press, 1999.

Brammer, Stephen, Andrew Millington, and Stephen Pavelin. 'Gender and Ethnic Diversity among UK Corporate Boards'. *Corporate Governance: An International Review* 15 (1 February 2007): 393–403. https://doi.org/10.1111/j.1467-8683.2007.00569.x.

Breetveld, Robin Rose. 'Forms of Bisexual Injustice: Bi, Being, and Becoming a Knower'. In *Bisexuality in Europe: Sexual Citizenship, Romantic Relationships, and Bi+ Identities*, edited by Emiel Maliepaard and Renate Baumgartner. Abingdon: Routledge, 2020.

Brian, Alastair. 'Claim of 82 per Cent Opposition to Transgender Self-ID Is Mostly False'. *The Ferret*, 2 July 2019. https://theferret.scot/gender-recognition-act-self-identification-fact-check/.

Bridges, Lauren E. 'Digital Failure: Unbecoming the "Good" Data Subject through Entropic, Fugitive, and Queer Data'. *Big Data & Society* 8, no. 1 (1 January 2021): 1–17. https://doi.org/10.1177/2053951720977882.

Brock, Maria, and Emil Edenborg. '"You Cannot Oppress Those Who Do Not Exist"'. *GLQ: A Journal of Lesbian and Gay Studies* 26, no. 4 (1 October 2020): 673–700. https://doi.org/10.1215/10642684-8618730.

Brown, Michael, and Larry Knopp. 'Places or Polygons? Governmentality, Scale, and the Census in the Gay and Lesbian Atlas'. *Population, Space and Place* 12, no. 4 (July 2006): 223–42. https://doi.org/10.1002/psp.410.

Browne, Kath. 'Queer Quantification or Queer(y)Ing Quantification: Creating Lesbian, Gay, Bisexual or Heterosexual Citizens through Governmental Social Research'. In *Queer Methods and Methodologies: Intersecting Queer Theories and Social Science Research*, edited by Kath Browne and Catherine J. Nash, 231–49. Farnham: Ashgate, 2010.

Browne, Kath. 'Selling My Queer Soul or Queerying Quantitative Research?' *Sociological Research Online* 13, no. 1 (January 2008): 200–14. https://doi.org/10.5153/sro.1635.

Browne, Kath, and Catherine J. Nash. 'Queer Methods and Methodologies: An Introduction'. In *Queer Methods and Methodologies: Intersecting Queer Theories and Social Science Research*, edited by Kath Browne and Catherine J. Nash, 1–25. Farnham: Ashgate, 2010.

Browne, Kath, and Catherine J. Nash, eds. *Queer Methods and Methodologies: Intersecting Queer Theories and Social Science Research.* Farnham: Ashgate, 2010.

Buolamwini, Joy, and Timnit Gebru. 'Gender Shades: Intersectional Accuracy Disparities in Commercial Gender Classification'. Edited by Sorelle A Friedler and Christo Wilson. *Proceedings of Machine Learning Research* 81 (2018): 1–15.

Bibliography

Bureau of the Conference of European Statisticians. 'In-Depth Review of Measuring Gender Identity'. Paris: United Nations Economic and Social Council, June 2019. http://www.unece.org/fileadmin/DAM/stats/documents/ece/ces/2019/ECE_CES_2019_19-G1910227E.pdf.

Bureau, US Census. 'Questions Asked on the Form'. 2020Census.gov. Accessed 20 April 2021. https://2020census.gov/en/about-questions.html.

Burns, Christine. *Trans Britain: Our Journey from the Shadows*. Edited by Christine Burns. London: Unbound, 2018.

Butler, Judith. *Bodies That Matter: On the Discursive Limits of 'Sex'*. New York: Routledge, 1993.

Butler, Judith. *Gender Trouble: Feminism and the Subversion of Identity*. New York: Routledge, 1990.

Butler, Judith. *Undoing Gender*. New York: Routledge, 2004.

Cabrera, Nolan. 'When Racism and Masculinity Collide: Some Methodological Considerations from a Man of Colour Studying Whiteness'. *Whiteness and Education* 1, no. 1 (2 January 2016): 15–25. https://doi.org/10.1080/13613324.2015.1122662.

Callis, April S. 'Playing with Butler and Foucault: Bisexuality and Queer Theory'. *Journal of Bisexuality* 9, no. 3–4 (13 November 2009): 213–33. https://doi.org/10.1080/15299710903316513.

Cecco, Leyland. 'Transgender Rights: Ontario Issues First Non-Binary Birth Certificate'. *The Guardian*, 8 May 2018. https://www.theguardian.com/world/2018/may/07/ontario-non-binary-birth-certificate-canada-transgender.

Celis, Karen, Johanna Kantola, Georgina Waylen, and S. Laurel Weldon. 'Introduction: Gender and Politics: A Gendered World, a Gendered Discipline'. In *The Oxford Handbook of Gender and Politics*, edited by Georgina Waylen, Karen Celis, Johanna Kantola, and S. Laurel Weldon, 1–31. Oxford: Oxford University Press, 2013.

Centers for Disease Control and Prevention. 'Fertility, Contraception, and Fatherhood: Data on Men and Women from Cycle 6 (2002) of the National Survey of Family Growth'. 23, 2006.

Centers for Disease Control and Prevention. 'Fertility, Family Planning, and Reproductive Health of US Women: Data from the 2002 National Survey of Family Growth'. 23, 2005.

Channel 4 News Investigations Team. 'Revealed: Trump Campaign Strategy to Deter Millions of Black Americans from Voting in 2016'. *Channel 4 News*, 28 September 2020. https://www.channel4.com/news/revealed-trump-campaign-strategy-to-deter-millions-of-black-americans-from-voting-in-2016.

Chapman, Dennis. *The Home and Social Status*. London: Routledge & Kegan Paul, 1955.

Charlton, James I. *Nothing about Us without Us: Disability Oppression and Empowerment*. Berkeley: University of California Press, 1998.

Chartered Institute of Personnel and Development. 'Inclusion at Work: Perspectives on LGBT+ Working Lives - Executive Summary'. London, February 2021. https://www.cipd.co.uk/Images/inclusion-work-perspectives-exec-summ_tcm18-90360.pdf.

Cifor, M., P. Garcia, T. L. Cowan, J. Rault, T. Sutherland, A. Chan, J. Rode, A. L. Hoffmann, N. Salehi, and L. Nakamura. 'Feminist Data Manifest-No', 2019. https://www.manifestno.com/.

Collett, Clementine, and Sarah Dillon. 'AI and Gender: Four Proposals for Future Research'. Cambridge: The Leverhulme Centre for the Future of Intelligence, 2019. https://doi.org/10.17863/CAM.41459.

Compton, D'Lane, Tey Meadow, and Kristen Schilt, eds. *Other, Please Specify: Queer Methods in Sociology*. University of California Press, 2018.

Connell, Catherine. 'Thank You for Coming Out Today: The Queer Discomfort of In-Depth Interviewing'. In *Other, Please Specify: Queer Methods in Sociology*, edited by D'Lane Compton, Tey Meadow, and Kristen Schilt, 126–39. University of California Press, 2018.

Connell, R. W. *Masculinities*. Berkeley: University of California Press, 1995.

Cook, Matt. *Queer Domesticities: Homosexuality and Home Life in Twentieth-Century London*. New York: Palgrave Macmillan, 2014.

Cooper, Davina, Emily Grabham, and Flora Renz. 'Introduction to the Special Issue on the Future of Legal Gender: Exploring the Feminist Politics of Decertification'. *Feminists@law* 10, no. 2 (8 November 2020). https://doi.org/10.22024/UniKent/03/fal.937.

Costanza-Chock, Sasha. 'Design Justice, AI, and Escape from the Matrix of Domination'. *Journal of Design and Science* Online (16 July 2018). https://doi.org/10.21428/96c8d426.

Couldry, Nick, and Ulises A. Mejias. 'Data Colonialism: Rethinking Big Data's Relation to the Contemporary Subject'. *Television & New Media* 20, no. 4 (2019): 336–49. https://doi.org/10.1177/1527476418796632.

Cowan, Sharon, Harry Josephine Giles, Rebecca Hewer, Becky Kaufmann, Meryl Kenny, Sean Morris, and Katie Nicholl Baines. 'Sex and Gender Equality Law and Policy: A Response to Murray, Hunter Blackburn and Mackenzie'. *Scottish Affairs* Online (22 October 2020): 1–20. https://doi.org/10.3366/scot.2020.0347.

Criado-Perez, Caroline. *Invisible Women: Exposing Data Bias in a World Designed for Men*. London: Chatto & Windus, 2019.

Crown Office and Procurator Fiscal Service. 'Hate Crime in Scotland, 2019-20', 12 June 2020. https://www.copfs.gov.uk/media-site-news-from-copfs/1887-hate-crime-in-scotland-2019-20.

Crowther, Rebecca, Scott Cuthbertson, and Vic Valentine. 'Further Out: The Scottish LGBT Rural Equality Report'. Edinburgh: Equality Network, 2020. https://equality-network.org/wp-content/uploads/2020/10/LGBT-Rural-Report.pdf.

Currah, Paisley, and Lisa Jean Moore. '"We Won't Know Who You Are": Contesting Sex Designations in New York City Birth Certificates'. *Hypatia* 24, no. 3 (2009): 113–35. https://doi.org/10.1111/j.1527-2001.2009.01048.x.

Currah, Paisley, and Susan Stryker. 'Introduction'. *TSQ: Transgender Studies Quarterly* 2, no. 1 (1 January 2015): 1–12. https://doi.org/10.1215/23289252-2848859.

Curtis, Bruce. 'Foucault on Governmentality and Population: The Impossible Discovery'. *The Canadian Journal of Sociology / Cahiers Canadiens de Sociologie* 27, no. 4 (2002): 505–33. https://doi.org/10.2307/3341588.

Dalton, Craig, and Jim Thatcher. 'What Does a Critical Data Studies Look Like, and Why Do We Care?' Society & Space, 12 May 2014. https://www.societyandspace. org/articles/what-does-a-critical-data-studies-look-like-and-why-do-we-care.

Daniels, Jessie. 'Race and Racism in Internet Studies: A Review and Critique'. New Media & Society 15, no. 5 (August 2013): 695–719. https://doi. org/10.1177/1461444812462849.

Dasu, Tamraparni, and Theodore Johnson. Exploratory Data Mining and Data Cleaning. Wiley Series in Probability and Statistics. New York: Wiley, 2003.

Davidson, Gina. 'Scotland's 2021 Census to Have 21 Sexual Orientation Choices for Adults'. The Scotsman, 31 October 2019. https://www.scotsman.com/ news/politics/scotlands-2021-census-have-21-sexual-orientation-choices- adults-823987.

Davis, Angela. 'A Critical Perspective on British Social Surveys and Community Studies and Their Accounts of Married Life c. 1945–70'. Cultural and Social History 6, no. 1 (March 2009): 47–64. https://doi.org/10.2752/147800409X377901.

Day, Abby. Believing in Belonging: Belief and Social Identity in the Modern World. Oxford: Oxford University Press, 2011.

Day, Abby, and Lois Lee. 'Making Sense of Surveys and Censuses: Issues in Religious Self-Identification'. Religion 44, no. 3 (3 July 2014): 345–56. https://doi. org/10.1080/0048721X.2014.929833.

Delgado, Richard, and Jean Stefancic. Critical Race Theory: An Introduction. London: New York University Press, 2001.

Dencik, Lina, Arne Hintz, Joanna Redden, and Emiliano Treré. 'Exploring Data Justice: Conceptions, Applications and Directions'. Information, Communication & Society 22, no. 7 (7 June 2019): 873–81. https://doi.org/10.1080/136911 8X.2019.1606268.

D'Ignazio, Catherine, and Lauren F. Klein. Data Feminism. Cambridge: The MIT Press, 2020.

D'Ignazio, Catherine, and Lauren F. Klein. 'Seven Intersectional Feminist Principles for Equitable and Actionable COVID-19 Data'. Big Data & Society 7, no. 2 (1 July 2020): 1–6. https://doi.org/10.1177/2053951720942544.

Dilley, Patrick. 'Queer Theory: Under Construction'. International Journal of Qualitative Studies in Education 12, no. 5 (October 1999): 457–72. https://doi. org/10.1080/095183999235890.

Doan, Laura. Disturbing Practices: History, Sexuality, and Women's Experience of Modern War. Chicago: The University of Chicago Press, 2013.

Doan, Petra L. 'To Count or Not to Count: Queering Measurement and the Transgender Community'. Women's Studies Quarterly 44, no. 3/4 (2016): 89–110. https://doi.org/10.1353/wsq.2016.0037.

Donoghue, Emma. 'Doing Lesbian History, Then and Now'. Historical Reflections / Réflexions Historiques 33, no. 1 (2007): 15–22. https://www.jstor.org/ stable/41299397.

Drafting Committee. 'Yogyakarta Principles plus 10'. Geneva, 2017. http:// yogyakartaprinciples.org/wp-content/uploads/2017/11/A5_yogyakartaWEB-2. pdf.

Duarte, G., Aguilar, A., Batres, M., and Lanz, A. 'Violence against the LGBTIQ+ Population: Experiences and Dynamics That Sustain It'. Guatemala City: Visibles, 2020. https://visibles.gt/investigacion-violencias-contra-la-poblacion-lgbtiq/.

Duggan, Lisa. *The Twilight of Equality? Neoliberalism, Cultural Politics, and the Attack on Democracy*. Boston: Beacon Press, 2014.

Each One Teach One. 'Welcome to #AfroZensus!' Afrozensus, 2020. https://afrozensus.de.

Edelman, Lee. *No Future: Queer Theory and the Death Drive*. Durham: Duke University Press, 2004.

Edmonds, Lizzie. 'LGBT+ Workers "Paid £7,000 Less than Straight Counterparts"'. *Evening Standard*, 2 July 2019. https://www.standard.co.uk/news/uk/lgbt-workers-paid-7000-less-than-straight-counterparts-a4179996.html.

Elliott, Larry. 'Household Census May Be Scrapped in Favour of Cheaper System'. *The Guardian*, 11 February 2020. https://www.theguardian.com/uk-news/2020/feb/11/household-census-may-be-scrapped-in-favour-of-cheaper-system.

Emmer, Pascal, Caroline Rivas, Brenda Salas Neves, and Chris Schweidler. 'Technologies for Liberation: Toward Abolitionist Futures'. Astraea Lesbian Foundation for Justice and Research Action Design, 2020. https://astraeafoundation.org/FundAbolitionTech/.

Engender. 'Sex/Gender: Gathering and Using Data to Advance Women's Equality and Rights in Scotland'. Engender Submission to the Office of the Chief Statistician, February 2020. https://www.engender.org.uk/content/publications/EgenderSubmission-GatheringandusingdatatoadvancewomensequalityandrightsinScotland-Feb2020-1.pdf.

Equality Act (2010). http://www.legislation.gov.uk/ukpga/2010/15/contents.

Equality and Human Rights Commission. 'Public Sector Equality Duty', 26 March 2021. https://www.equalityhumanrights.com/en/advice-and-guidance/public-sector-equality-duty.

Equality and Human Rights Commission. 'What Is the Equality Act?', 19 June 2019. https://www.equalityhumanrights.com/en/equality-act-2010/what-equality-act.

Equality Network. 'Response to the Scottish Government's Consultation on the Registration of Civil Partnership and Same Sex Marriage', 2011.

Escoffier, Jeffrey. *American Homo: Community and Perversity*. London: Verso, 2018.

Esson, Graeme. 'Scotland's Results 2020: How Grades Were Worked Out for Scottish Pupils'. *BBC News*, 4 August 2020. https://www.bbc.co.uk/news/uk-scotland-53580888.

Eubanks, Virginia. *Automating Inequality: How High-Tech Tools Profile, Police, and Punish the Poor*. New York: St Martin's Press, 2017.

European Parliament and Council of European Union. Regulation (EU) 2016/679 (2016). https://eur-lex.europa.eu/legal-content/EN/TXT/HTML/?uri=CELEX:32016R0679&from=EN.

Faderman, Lillian. *Surpassing the Love of Men: Romantic Friendship and Love between Women from the Renaissance to the Present*. London: The Women's Press, 1997.

Bibliography

Fausto-Sterling, Anne. 'The Five Sexes: Why Male and Female Are Not Enough'. *Sciences* 33 (1 January 1993): 20–4.

Fausto-Sterling, Anne. *Sexing the Body: Gender Politics and the Construction of Sexuality*. New York: Basic Books, 2000.

Fernando, Mayanthi L. 'State Sovereignty and the Politics of Indifference'. *Public Culture* 31, no. 2 (1 May 2019): 261–73. https://doi.org/10.1215/08992363-7286813.

Ferraz, Christina. 'Queerstions: What Does Cisgender Mean?' *Philadelphia Magazine*, 8 July 2014. https://www.phillymag.com/news/2014/07/08/queerstions-cisgender-mean/.

Fetner, Tina, and Melanie Heath. 'Studying the "Right" Can Feel Wrong: Reflection on Anti-LGBT Movements'. In *Other, Please Specify: Queer Methods in Sociology*, edited by D'Lane Compton, Tey Meadow, and Kristen Schilt, 140–53. University of California Press, 2018.

Foucault, Michel. *Discipline and Punish: The Birth of the Prison*. 2nd ed. New York: Vintage Books, 1995.

Fraser, Gloria. 'Evaluating Inclusive Gender Identity Measures for Use in Quantitative Psychological Research'. *Psychology & Sexuality* 9, no. 4 (2 October 2018): 343–57. https://doi.org/10.1080/19419899.2018.1497693.

Fraser, Gloria, Joseph Bulbulia, Lara M. Greaves, Marc S. Wilson, and Chris G. Sibley. 'Coding Responses to an Open-Ended Gender Measure in a New Zealand National Sample'. *The Journal of Sex Research* 57, no. 8 (November 2019): 979–86. https://doi.org/10.1080/00224499.2019.1687640.

Freeman, Elizabeth. *Time Binds: Queer Temporalities, Queer Histories*. Durham: Duke University Press, 2010.

Frisch, Michael. 'A Queer Reading of the United States Census'. In *The Life and Afterlife of Gay Neighborhoods: Renaissance and Resurgence*, edited by Alex Bitterman and Daniel Baldwin Hess, 61–85. The Urban Book Series. Cham: Springer International Publishing, 2021.

Fugard, Andi. 'Should Trans People Be Postmodernist in the Streets but Positivist in the Spreadsheets? A Reply to Sullivan'. *International Journal of Social Research Methodology* 23, no. 5 (25 May 2020): 525–31. https://doi.org/10.1080/1364557 9.2020.1768343.

Gair, Susan. 'Feeling Their Stories: Contemplating Empathy, Insider/Outsider Positionings, and Enriching Qualitative Research'. *Qualitative Health Research* 22, no. 1 (2012): 134–43. https://doi.org/10.1177/1049732311420580.

Gamson, Joshua. 'Must Identity Movements Self-Destruct? A Queer Dilemma'. *Social Problems* 42, no. 3 (1995): 390–407. https://doi.org/10.2307/3096854.

Garcia-Navarro, Lulu. 'For Affirmative Action, Brazil Sets Up Controversial Boards to Determine Race'. *NPR*, 29 September 2016. https://www.npr.org/sections/parallels/2016/09/29/495665329/for-affirmative-action-brazil-sets-up-controversial-boards-to-determine-race.

Garrett-Walker, J. J., and Michelle J. Montagno. 'Queering Labels: Expanding Identity Categories in LGBTQ + Research and Clinical Practice'. *Journal of LGBT Youth* Online (11 March 2021): 1–17. https://doi.org/10.1080/19361653.2021.18 96411.

Gates, Gary J. 'Brief of Gary J. Gates as Amicus Curiae on the Merits in Support of Respondent Windsor', 2013.

Gates, Gary J. 'How Many People Are Lesbian, Gay, Bisexual, and Transgender?' Los Angeles: The Williams Institute, April 2011. https://williamsinstitute.law. ucla.edu/wp-content/uploads/How-Many-People-LGBT-Apr-2011.pdf.

Gates, Gary J., and Jody L. Herman. 'Beyond Academia: Strategies for Using LGBT Research to Influence Public Policy'. In *Other, Please Specify: Queer Methods in Sociology*, edited by D'Lane Compton, Tey Meadow, and Kristen Schilt, 80–94. Berkeley: University of California Press, 2018.

Geary, Rebecca S., Clare Tanton, Bob Erens, Soazig Clifton, Philip Prah, Kaye Wellings, Kirstin R. Mitchell, et al. 'Sexual Identity, Attraction and Behaviour in Britain: The Implications of Using Different Dimensions of Sexual Orientation to Estimate the Size of Sexual Minority Populations and Inform Public Health Interventions'. *PLOS ONE* 13, no. 1 (2 January 2018). https://doi.org/10.1371/journal.pone.0189607.

Gelman, Andrew, Gregor Mattson, and Daniel Simpson. 'Gaydar and the Fallacy of Objective Measurement'. *Unpublished*, 2018. http://www.stat.columbia. edu/~gelman/research/unpublished/gaydar2.pdf.

Gender Identity in US Surveillance Group. 'Best Practices for Asking Questions to Identify Transgender and Other Gender Minority Respondents on Population-Based Surveys'. Los Angeles: The Williams Institute, 2014. https://williamsinstitute.law.ucla.edu/publications/geniuss-trans-pop-based-survey/.

Ghaziani, Amin, and Matt Brim, eds. *Imagining Queer Methods*. New York: New York University Press, 2019.

Giddens, Anthony. *Modernity and Self-Identity: Self and Society in the Late Modern Age*. Stanford: Stanford University Press, 1991.

Gieseking, Jen Jack. 'Size Matters to Lesbians, Too: Queer Feminist Interventions into the Scale of Big Data'. *The Professional Geographer* 70, no. 1 (January 2018): 150–6. https://doi.org/10.1080/00330124.2017.1326084.

Gillborn, David, Paul Warmington, and Sean Demack. 'QuantCrit: Education, Policy, "Big Data" and Principles for a Critical Race Theory of Statistics'. *Race Ethnicity and Education* 21, no. 2 (4 March 2018): 158–79. https://doi.org/10.1080/13613324.2017.1377417.

Glick, Jennifer L., Katherine Theall, Katherine Andrinopoulos, and Carl Kendall. 'For Data's Sake: Dilemmas in the Measurement of Gender Minorities'. *Culture, Health & Sexuality* 20, no. 12 (2 December 2018): 1362–77. https://doi.org/10.1080/13691058.2018.1437220.

Gluck, Sherna Berger, and Daphne Patai, eds. *Women's Words: The Feminist Practice of Oral History*. New York: Routledge, 1991.

Goodwin, Karin. 'Crucial Services to Disabled People Cut Due to Coronavirus'. *The Ferret*, 26 March 2020. https://theferret.scot/social-care-disabled-people-cut-coronavirus/.

Gossett, Che. 'Blackness and the Trouble of Trans Visibility'. In *Trap Door: Trans Cultural Production and the Politics of Visibility*, edited by Reina Gossett, Eric A. Stanley, and Johanna Burton. Critical Anthologies in Art and Culture. Cambridge: The MIT Press, 2017.

Bibliography

Gossett, Reina, Eric A. Stanley, and Johanna Burton. 'Known Unknowns: An Introduction to Trap Door'. In *Trap Door: Trans Cultural Production and the Politics of Visibility*, edited by Reina Gossett, Eric A. Stanley, and Johanna Burton. Critical Anthologies in Art and Culture. Cambridge: The MIT Press, 2017.

Government Digital Services. 'Using Authenticators to Protect an Online Service'. GOV.UK, 14 May 2020. https://www.gov.uk/government/publications/authentication-credentials-for-online-government-services/giving-users-access-to-online-services.

Government Equalities Office. 'LGBT Action Plan: Improving the Lives of Lesbian, Gay, Bisexual and Transgender People'. London: Government Equalities Office, 2018. https://nls.ldls.org.uk/welcome.html?ark:/81055/vdc_100062711857.0x000001.

Government Equalities Office. 'National LGBT Survey: Research Report'. Manchester: Government Equalities Office, 2018. https://assets.publishing.service.gov.uk/government/uploads/system/uploads/attachment_data/file/721704/LGBT-survey-research-report.pdf.

Greaves, Lara M., Fiona Kate Barlow, Carol H. J. Lee, Correna M. Matika, Weiyu Wang, Cinnamon-Jo Lindsay, Claudia J. B. Case, et al. 'The Diversity and Prevalence of Sexual Orientation Self-Labels in a New Zealand National Sample'. *Archives of Sexual Behavior* 46, no. 5 (2016): 1325–36. https://doi.org/10.1007/s10508-016-0857-5.

Green, Adam Isaiah. 'Gay but Not Queer: Toward a Post-Queer Study of Sexuality'. *Theory and Society* 31, no. 4 (2002): 521–45. https://doi.org/10.1023/A:1020976902569.

Griffiths, Sian. 'Stonewall's New Boss Nancy Kelley Let Census Expert Be No-Platformed'. *The Times*, 24 May 2020. https://www.thetimes.co.uk/article/stonewalls-new-boss-nancy-kelley-let-census-expert-be-no-platformed-ljsnw6v3r.

Grundy, John, and Miriam Smith. 'Activist Knowledges in Queer Politics'. *Economy and Society* 36, no. 2 (May 2007): 294–317. https://doi.org/10.1080/03085140701254324.

Grzanka, Patrick R. 'Queer Survey Research and the Ontological Dimensions of Heterosexism'. *WSQ: Women's Studies Quarterly* 44, no. 3 (7 October 2016): 131–49. https://doi.org/10.1353/wsq.2016.0039.

Haber, Benjamin. 'The Queer Ontology of Digital Method'. *Women's Studies Quarterly* 44, no. 3/4 (2016): 150–69. https://doi.org/10.1353/wsq.2016.0040.

Hacking, Ian. 'Biopower and the Avalanche of Printed Numbers'. *Humanities in Society* 5 (1982): 279–95.

Hacking, Ian. 'Making Up People'. *London Review of Books*, 17 August 2006. https://www.lrb.co.uk/the-paper/v28/n16/ian-hacking/making-up-people.

Hammonds, Evelynn. 'Black (W)Holes and the Geometry of Black Female Sexuality'. *Differences: A Journal of Feminist Cultural Studies* 6, no. 2–3 (1994): 126–45.

Haque, Zubaida. 'Coronavirus Will Increase Race Inequalities'. London: Runnymede Trust, 26 March 2020. https://www.runnymedetrust.org/blog/coronavirus-will-increase-race-inequalities.

Harding, Sandra G., ed. *The Feminist Standpoint Theory Reader: Intellectual and Political Controversies*. New York: Routledge, 2004.

Hartley-Parkinson, Richard. 'Anyone "Should Be Allowed to Identify as Black, Regardless of Their Skin Colour"'. *Metro*, 18 November 2019. https://metro.co.uk/2019/11/18/anyone-allowed-identify-black-regardless-skin-colour-11173537/.

Haseldon, Lucy, and Theodore Joloza. 'Measuring Sexual Identity: A Guide for Researchers'. Newport: Office for National Statistics, 2009. http://www.ons.gov.uk/ons/guide-method/measuring-equality/equality/sexual-identity-project/guidance/measuring-sexual-identity--a-guide-for-researchers.pdf.

Hashim, Asad. 'Pakistan Passes Landmark Transgender Rights Law'. *Aljazeera*, 9 May 2018. https://www.aljazeera.com/news/2018/5/9/pakistan-passes-landmark-transgender-rights-law.

Hassein, Nabil. 'Against Black Inclusion in Facial Recognition'. *Digital Talking Drum*, 15 August 2017. https://digitaltalkingdrum.com/2017/08/15/against-black-inclusion-in-facial-recognition/.

Hellen, Nicholas. 'BBC Films Teach Children of "100 Genders, or More"'. *The Times*. Accessed 9 May 2021. https://www.thetimes.co.uk/article/bbc-films-teach-children-of-100-genders-or-more-7xfhbg97p.

Hern, Alex. 'Cambridge Analytica: How Did It Turn Clicks into Votes?' *The Guardian*, 6 May 2018. https://www.theguardian.com/news/2018/may/06/cambridge-analytica-how-turn-clicks-into-votes-christopher-wylie.

Hines, Sally. 'Counting the Cost of Difference: A Reply to Sullivan'. *International Journal of Social Research Methodology* 23, no. 5 (2 September 2020): 533–8. https://doi.org/10.1080/13645579.2020.1768344.

Hiramori, Daiki, and Saori Kamano. 'Asking about Sexual Orientation and Gender Identity in Social Surveys in Japan: Findings from the Osaka City Residents' Survey and Related Preparatory Studies'. *Journal of Population Problems* 76, no. 4 (2020): 443–6. https://doi.org/10.31235/osf.io/w9mjn.

Historic England. 'Anne Lister and Shibden Hall'. Pride of Place: England's LGBTQ Heritage. Accessed 4 March 2021. http://historicengland.org.uk/research/inclusive-heritage/lgbtq-heritage-project/love-and-intimacy/anne-lister-and-shibden-hall/.

Hoffmann, Anna Lauren. 'Terms of Inclusion: Data, Discourse, Violence'. *New Media & Society* Online (16 September 2020). https://doi.org/10.1177/1461444820958725.

Holzer, Lena. 'Non-Binary Gender Registration Models in Europe'. Brussels: ILGA-Europe, 2018.

Home Office. 'Experimental Statistics: Asylum Claims on the Basis of Sexual Orientation'. UK Government, 24 September 2020. https://www.gov.uk/government/statistics/immigration-statistics-year-ending-june-2020/experimental-statistics-asylum-claims-on-the-basis-of-sexual-orientation.

Hornsey, Richard. *The Spiv and the Architect: Unruly Life in Postwar London*. Minneapolis: University of Minnesota Press, 2010.

Houlbrook, Matt. *Queer London: Perils and Pleasures in the Sexual Metropolis, 1918-1957*. Chicago: University of Chicago Press, 2006.

Bibliography

Human Rights Watch. "'Every Day I Live in Fear": Violence and Discrimination against LGBT People in El Salvador, Guatemala, and Honduras, and Obstacles to Asylum in the United States', October 2020. https://www.hrw.org/report/2020/10/07/every-day-i-live-fear/violence-and-discrimination-against-lgbt-people-el-salvador.

Hunte, Ben. "'I Thought I Was Going to Die" in Homophobic Attack'. *BBC News*, 9 October 2020. https://www.bbc.co.uk/news/uk-54470077.

Hunter Blackburn, Lucy. 'Sex Question Should Stick to Birth Certificate'. *The Scotsman*, 15 September 2019. https://www.scotsman.com/news/opinion/columnists/lucy-hunter-blackburn-sex-question-should-stick-birth-certificate-1407711.

Information Commissioner's Office. 'What Is Valid Consent?', March 2021. https://ico.org.uk/for-organisations/guide-to-data-protection/guide-to-the-general-data-protection-regulation-gdpr/consent/what-is-valid-consent.

Inter-American Commission on Human Rights. 'Violence against LGBTI Persons', 12 November 2015. http://www.oas.org/en/iachr/reports/pdfs/ViolenceLGBTIPersons.pdf.

International Civil Aviation Organisation. 'A Review of the Requirement to Display the Holder's Gender on Travel Documents'. Montreal, 2012.

Jackson, Mike. 'Who We Are'. London Lesbians and Gays Support the Miners, 2015. http://lgsm.org/about-lgsm.

Jernigan, Carter, and Behram Mistree. 'Gaydar: Facebook Friendships Expose Sexual Orientation'. *First Monday* 14, no. 10 (5 October 2009). https://doi.org/10.5210/fm.v14i10.2611.

Johnson, Jeffrey Alan. 'Information Systems and the Translation of Transgender'. *TSQ: Transgender Studies Quarterly* 2, no. 1 (1 January 2015): 160–5. https://doi.org/10.1215/23289252-2848940.

Johnson, Joy L., Joan L. Bottorff, Annette J. Browne, Sukhdev Grewal, B. Ann Hilton, and Heather Clarke. 'Othering and Being Othered in the Context of Health Care Services'. *Health Communication* 16, no. 2 (April 2004): 255–71. https://doi.org/10.1207/S15327027HC1602_7.

Jones, Jane Clare, and Lisa MacKenzie. 'The Political Erasure of Sex: Sex and the Census', 2020. https://thepoliticalerasureofsex.org/wp-content/uploads/2020/10/The-Political-Erasure-of-Sex_Full-Report.pdf.

Judson, Ellen, Asli Atay, Alex Krasodomski-Jones, Rose Lasko-Skinner, and Josh Smith. 'Engendering Hate: The Contours of State-Aligned Gendered Disinformation Online'. London: DEMOS, October 2020. https://demos.co.uk/wp-content/uploads/2020/10/Engendering-Hate-Report-FINAL.pdf.

Keyes, Os. 'Counting the Countless'. *Real Life*, 8 April 2019. https://reallifemag.com/counting-the-countless/.

Keyes, Os. 'The Misgendering Machines: Trans/HCI Implications of Automatic Gender Recognition'. *Proceedings of the ACM on Human-Computer Interaction* 2, *Interaction* 2 (November 2018): 1–22. https://doi.org/10.1145/3274357.

Kim, Nemo. 'South Korea Struggles to Contain New Outbreak Amid Anti-Gay Backlash'. *The Guardian*, 11 May 2020. https://www.theguardian.com/world/2020/may/11/south-korea-struggles-to-contain-new-outbreak-amid-anti-lgbt-backlash.

Kitchin, Rob. *The Data Revolution: Big Data, Open Data, Data Infrastructures & Their Consequences*. Los Angeles: SAGE Publications, 2014.

Kłonkowska, Anna. 'Making Transgender Count in Poland: Disciplined Individuals and Circumscribed Populations'. *TSQ: Transgender Studies Quarterly* 2, no. 1 (1 January 2015): 123–35. https://doi.org/10.1215/23289252-2848931.

Knight, Kyle G., Andrew Flores, and Sheila J. Nezhad. 'Surveying Nepal's Third Gender: Development, Implementation, and Analysis'. *TSQ: Transgender Studies Quarterly* 2, no. 1 (1 January 2015): 101–22. https://doi.org/10.1215/23289252-2848904.

Kwakye, Chelsea, and Ọrẹ Ogunbiyi. *Taking up Space: The Black Girl's Manifesto for Change*. London: #Merky Books, 2019.

Lachance, Marc, Kaveri Mechanda, and Alice Born. 'Gender – Developing a Statistical Standard'. New York: United Nations Department of Economic and Social Affairs Statistics Division, 30 August 2017. https://unstats.un.org/unsd/classifications/expertgroup/egm2017/ac340-21.PDF.

Langhamer, Claire. 'Love and Courtship in Mid-Twentieth Century England'. *The Historical Journal* 50, no. 1 (March 2007): 173–96. https://doi.org/10.1017/S0018246X06005966.

Langhamer, Claire. 'The Meanings of Home in Postwar Britain'. *Journal of Contemporary History* 40, no. 2 (2005): 341–62. https://doi.org/10.1177/0022009405051556.

Lanius, Candice. 'Fact Check: Your Demand for Statistical Proof Is Racist'. *Cyborgology*, 12 January 2015. https://thesocietypages.org/cyborgology/2015/01/12/fact-check-your-demand-for-statistical-proof-is-racist/.

Laqueur, Thomas. *Making Sex: Body and Gender from the Greeks to Freud*. Cambridge: Harvard University Press, 1990.

Law, John. 'On Sociology and STS'. *The Sociological Review* 56, no. 4 (1 November 2008): 623–49. https://doi.org/10.1111/j.1467-954X.2008.00808.x.

Law, John. 'Seeing Like a Survey'. *Cultural Sociology* 3, no. 2 (July 2009): 239–56. https://doi.org/10.1177/1749975509105533.

Leachman, Gwendolyn. 'Institutionalizing Essentialism: Mechanisms of Intersectional Subordination within the LGBT Movement'. *Legal Studies Research Paper Series*, 1383 (2016). https://ssrn.com/abstract=2799371.

Leonardo, Zeus. 'Through the Multicultural Glass: Althusser, Ideology and Race Relations in Post-Civil Rights America'. *Policy Futures in Education* 3, no. 4 (1 December 2005): 400–12. https://doi.org/10.2304/pfie.2005.3.4.400.

Lewin, Ellen, and William L. Leap, eds. *Out in the Field: Reflections of Lesbian and Gay Anthropologists*. Urbana: University of Illinois Press, 1996.

Lewis, Brian, ed. *British Queer History: New Approaches and Perspectives*. Manchester: Manchester University Press, 2013.

LGB Alliance. 'Schools Crisis? Which Crisis?' LGB Alliance. Accessed 3 March 2021. https://lgballiance.org.uk/schools-campaign/.

LGBT Foundation. 'Hidden Figures: The Impact of the Covid-19 Pandemic on LGBT Communities in the UK'. Manchester, May 2020. www.lgbt.foundation/coronavirus/hiddenfigures.

Bibliography

LGBT Foundation. 'Housing, Ageing + Care'. Manchester, October 2020. https://s3-eu-west-1.amazonaws.com/lgbt-website-media/Files/8f229162-0589-4d8f-be67-cee5c610edc5/Housing%2c%2520Ageing%2520%2b%2520Care%2520(4).pdf.

LGBT Youth Scotland. 'Life in Scotland for LGBT Young People: Analysis of the 2017 Survey for Lesbian, Gay, Bisexual and Transgender Young People'. Edinburgh, 2018. https://www.lgbtyouth.org.uk/media/1354/life-in-scotland-for-lgbt-young-people.pdf.

Lindqvist, Anna, Marie Gustafsson Sendén, and Emma A. Renström. 'What Is Gender, Anyway: A Review of the Options for Operationalising Gender'. *Psychology & Sexuality* Online (18 February 2020): 1–13. https://doi.org/10.1080/19419899.2020.1729844.

Little, Stephen. 'LGBT Great Launches New Survey on LGBT+ Investing'. *Investment Week*, 20 October 2020. https://www.investmentweek.co.uk/news/4021957/lgbt-great-launches-new-survey-on-lgbt-investing.

Lloyd, Moya. *Beyond Identity Politics: Feminism, Power & Politics*. London: SAGE Publications, 2005.

Loewy, Karen L. 'Erasing LGBT People from Federal Data Collection: A Need for Vigilance'. *American Journal of Public Health* 107, no. 8 (August 2017): 1217–18. https://doi.org/10.2105/AJPH.2017.303914.

Lombardi, Emilia. 'Trans Issues in Sociology: A Trans-Centred Perspective'. In *Other, Please Specify: Queer Methods in Sociology*, edited by D'Lane Compton, Tey Meadow, and Kristen Schilt, 67–79. University of California Press, 2018.

Lopez, Oscar. 'El Salvador Police Sentenced in Nation's First Trans Murder Convictions'. *Reuters*, 31 July 2020. https://www.reuters.com/article/us-el-salvador-lgbt-murder-trfn-idUSKCN24W00P.

Lorber, Judith. 'Believing Is Seeing: Biology as Ideology'. *Gender and Society* 7, no. 4 (1993): 568–81. https://doi.org/10.1177/089124393007004006.

Lugones, María. 'Heterosexualism and the Colonial/Modern Gender System'. *Hypatia* 22, no. 1 (2007): 186–219. https://doi.org/10.1111/j.1527-2001.2007.tb01156.x.

Lyons, Anthony, Joel Anderson, Mary Lou Rasmussen, and Edith Gray. 'Toward Making Sexual and Gender Diverse Populations Count in Australia'. *Australian Population Studies* 4, no. 2 (16 November 2020): 14–29. https://doi.org/10.37970/aps.v4i2.69.

Macaulay, Cecilia, and Nora Fakim. '"Don't Call Me BAME": Why Some People Are Rejecting the Term'. *BBC News*. 30 June 2020. https://www.bbc.com/news/uk-53194376.

Magliozzi, Devon, Aliya Saperstein, and Laurel Westbrook. 'Scaling Up: Representing Gender Diversity in Survey Research'. *Socius* 2 (1 January 2016): 2378023116664352. https://doi.org/10.1177/2378023116664352.

Mantha, Yoan, and Simon Hudson. 'Estimating the Gender Ratio of AI Researchers around the World'. Element AI Lab, 2018. https://medium.com/element-ai-research-lab/estimating-the-gender-ratioof-ai-researchers-around-the-world-81d2b8dbe9c3.

Matthews, Peter, and Chris Poyner. 'Achieving Equality in Progressive Contexts: Queer(y)Ing Public Administration'. *Public Administration Quarterly* 44, no. 4 (15 November 2020): 545–77. https://doi.org/10.37808/paq.44.4.3.

McConnell, Elizabeth, Bálint Néray, Bernie Hogan, Aaron Korpak, Antonia Clifford, and Michelle Birkett. '"Everybody Puts Their Whole Life on Facebook": Identity Management and the Online Social Networks of LGBTQ Youth'. *International Journal of Environmental Research and Public Health* 15, no. 6 (26 May 2018): 1078. https://doi.org/10.3390/ijerph15061078.

McDermott, Elizabeth. '"Counting" for Equality: Youth, Class and Sexual Citizenship'. In *Sexualities Research: Critical Interjections, Diverse Methodologies, and Practical Applications*, edited by Andrew King, Ana Cristina Santos, and Isabel Crowhurst. Routledge Advances in Critical Diversities. London: Routledge, 2017.

McDonald, Cece, Miss Major Griffin-Gracy, and Toshio Meronek. 'Cautious Living: Black Trans Woman and the Politics of Documentation'. In *Trap Door: Trans Cultural Production and the Politics of Visibility*, edited by Reina Gossett, Eric A. Stanley, and Johanna Burton. Critical Anthologies in Art and Culture. Cambridge: The MIT Press, 2017.

McGlotten, Shaka. 'Black Data'. In *No Tea, No Shade: New Writings in Black Queer Studies*, edited by E. Patrick Johnson, 262–86. Durham: Duke University Press, 2016.

McManus, Sally. 'Sexual Orientation Research Phase 1: A Review of Methodological Approaches'. Scottish Executive Social Research, 2003. https://www.webarchive.org.uk/wayback/archive/20160120173945mp_/http://www.gov.scot/Resource/Doc/47034/0013850.pdf.

McQuater, Katie. 'Census Sex Question Guidance Could "Undermine Data Reliability", Say Academics'. *Research Live*, 16 December 2019. http://www.research-live.com/article/news/census-sex-question-guidance-could-undermine-data-reliability-say-academics/id/5062952.

Meadow, Tey. '"A Rose Is a Rose": On Producing Legal Gender Classifications'. *Gender & Society* 24, no. 6 (December 2010): 814–37. https://doi.org/10.1177/0891243210385918.

Medeiros, Mike, Benjamin Forest, and Patrik Öhberg. 'The Case for Non-Binary Gender Questions in Surveys'. *PS: Political Science & Politics* 53, no. 1 (January 2020): 128–35. https://doi.org/10.1017/S1049096519001203.

Meek, Jeffrey. *Queer Voices in Post-War Scotland: Male Homosexuality, Religion and Society*. London: Palgrave Macmillan, 2015.

Meschitti, Viviana. 'Being an Early Career Academic: Is There Space for Gender Equality in the Neoliberal University?' In *Gender, Science and Innovation: New Perspectives*, edited by Helen Lawton Smith, Colette Henry, Henry Etzkowitz, and Alexandra Poulovassilis. Northampton: Edward Elgar Publishing, 2020.

Michaels, Stuart, Carolina Milesi, Michael Stern, Melissa Heim Viox, Heather Morrison, Paul Guerino, Christina N. Dragon, and Samuel C. Haffer. 'Improving Measures of Sexual and Gender Identity in English and Spanish to Identify

LGBT Older Adults in Surveys'. *LGBT Health* 4, no. 6 (1 December 2017): 412–18. https://doi.org/10.1089/lgbt.2016.0168.

Milner, Yeshi. 'Abolish Big Data'. University of California, Irvine, 8 March 2019. https://www.youtube.com/watch?v=26lM2RGAdlM.

Milner, Yeshi. 'Abolition Means the Creation of Something New', 31 December 2019. https://medium.com/@YESHICAN/abolition-means-the-creation-of-something-new-72fc67c8f493.

Mishel, Emma. 'Intersections between Sexual Identity, Sexual Attraction, and Sexual Behavior among a Nationally Representative Sample of American Men and Women'. *Journal of Official Statistics* 35, no. 4 (1 December 2019): 859–84. https://doi.org/10.2478/jos-2019-0036.

Mishel, Emma, Tristan Bridges, and Mònica L. Caudillo. 'Google, Tell Me. Is He Gay?: Masculinity, Homophobia, and Gendered Anxieties in Google Search Queries about Sexuality'. *SocArXiv* Online (8 November 2018): 1–21. https://doi.org/10.31235/osf.io/4se75.

Monro, Surya, Sally Hines, and Antony Osborne. 'Is Bisexuality Invisible? A Review of Sexualities Scholarship 1970–2015'. *The Sociological Review* 65, no. 4 (1 November 2017): 663–81. https://doi.org/10.1177/0038026117695488.

Moon, Dawne, Theresa W. Tobin, and J. E. Sumerau. 'Alpha, Omega, and the Letters in Between: LGBTQI Conservative Christians Undoing Gender'. *Gender & Society* 33, no. 4 (August 2019): 583–606. https://doi.org/10.1177/0891243219846592.

Moran, Marie. '(Un)Troubling Identity Politics: A Cultural Materialist Intervention'. *European Journal of Social Theory* 23, no. 2 (May 2020): 258–77. https://doi.org/10.1177/1368431018819722.

Murray, Kath, and Lucy Hunter Blackburn. 'Losing Sight of Women's Rights: The Unregulated Introduction of Gender Self-Identification as a Case Study of Policy Capture in Scotland'. *Scottish Affairs* 28, no. 3 (31 July 2019): 262–89. https://doi.org/10.3366/scot.2019.0284.

Murray, Kath, Lucy Hunter Blackburn, and Lisa Mackenzie. '2021 Census: Assessment of the Guidance Proposed by the UK Census Authorities to Accompany the Sex Question', 7 February 2020. https://mbmpolicy.files.wordpress.com/2020/02/mbm-briefing-on-2021-census-guidance-february-2020.pdf.

Musson, Chris, and Ben Archibald. 'Scots Face List of 21 Sexualities to Choose from in 2021 Census Such as Gynephilic'. *The Scottish Sun*, 29 October 2019. https://www.thescottishsun.co.uk/news/4894324/sexualities-scotland-census-list/.

Nagarajan, Rema. 'First Count of Third Gender in Census: 4.9 Lakh'. *Times of India*, 30 May 2014. https://timesofindia.indiatimes.com/india/First-count-of-third-gender-in-census-4-9-lakh/articleshow/35741613.cms.

Namaste, Ki. 'The Politics of Inside/Out: Queer Theory, Poststructuralism, and a Sociological Approach to Sexuality'. *Sociological Theory* 12, no. 2 (1994): 220–31. https://doi.org/10.2307/201866.

Nelson, Katie G. '"Intersex" Is Counted in Kenya's Census — but Is This a Victory?' *Public Radio Exchange*, 10 September 2019. https://www.pri.org/stories/2019-09-10/intersex-counted-kenyas-census-victory.

Newburn, Tim. *Permission and Regulation: Law and Morals in Post-War Britain.* London: Routledge, 1992.

Nicholson, Linda. 'Interpreting Gender'. *Signs* 20, no. 1 (1994): 79–105. https://doi. org/10.1086/494955.

Noble, Safiya Umoja. *Algorithms of Oppression: How Search Engines Reinforce Racism.* New York: New York University Press, 2018.

Noor, Poppy. 'White US Professor Jessica Krug Admits She Has Pretended to Be Black for Years'. *The Guardian*, 3 September 2020. https://www.theguardian. com/world/2020/sep/03/jessica-krug-white-professor-pretended-black.

Oakley, Ann. 'Paradigm Wars: Some Thoughts on a Personal and Public Trajectory'. *International Journal of Social Research Methodology* 2, no. 3 (January 1999): 247–54. https://doi.org/10.1080/136455799295041.

Obergefell v. Hodges, 14 556 (US 2015).

O'Connell, Martin, and Sarah Feliz. 'Same-Sex Couple Household Statistics from the 2010 Census'. US Census Bureau, September 2011. https://www.census.gov/ library/working-papers/2011/demo/SEHSD-WP2011-26.html.

Office for National Statistics. 'About the Census and Data Collection Transformation Programme', 16 September 2020. https://www.ons.gov.uk/aboutus/whatwedo/ programmesandprojects/censusanddatacollectiontransformationprogramme/ aboutthecensusanddatacollectiontransformationprogrammecdctp.

Office for National Statistics. 'Age Groups'. Ethnicity Facts and Figures, 22 August 2018. https://www.ethnicity-facts-figures.service.gov.uk/uk-population-by-ethnicity/demographics/age-groups/latest#.

Office for National Statistics. 'Final Guidance for the Question "What Is Your Sex?"' Census 2021, 12 February 2021. https://www.ons.gov.uk/census/ censustransformationprogramme/questiondevelopment/genderidentity/ census2021finalguidanceforthequestionwhatisyoursex.

Office for National Statistics. 'Sex and Gender Identity Question Development for Census 2021', 26 June 2020. https://www.ons.gov.uk/census/ censustransformationprogramme/questiondevelopment/sexandgenderidentityq uestiondevelopmentforcensus2021#questions-recommended-for-census-2021.

Oliveira, Cleuci de. 'Brazil's New Problem with Blackness'. *Foreign Policy*, 5 April 2017. https://foreignpolicy.com/2017/04/05/brazils-new-problem-with-blackness-affirmative-action/.

Oltermann, Philip, and Jon Henley. 'France and Germany Urged to Rethink Reluctance to Gather Ethnicity Data'. *The Guardian*, 16 June 2020. https://www. theguardian.com/world/2020/jun/16/france-and-germany-urged-to-rethink-reluctance-to-gather-ethnicity-data.

O'Neil, Cathy. *Weapons of Math Destruction: How Big Data Increases Inequality and Threatens Democracy.* New York: Crown, 2016.

Onerhime, Edafe. 'Monitoring Equality in Digital Public Services'. Open Data Institute, 2020. http://theodi.org/wp-content/uploads/2020/01/OPEN-ODI-2020-01_Monitoring-Equality-in-Digital-Public-Services-report.pdf.

Oppenheim, Maya. 'Chechen Leader Ramzan Kadyrov Claims No Gay People Exist in Region Just Fake Chechens'. *The Independent*, 7 May 2017. http://www.

independent.co.uk/news/world/europe/ramzan-kadyrov-chechen-leader-no-gay-people-just-fake-chechens-a7722246.html.

Oppenheim, Maya. 'Germany Introduces Third Gender for People Who Identify as Intersex'. *The Independent*, 1 January 2019. https://www.independent.co.uk/news/world/europe/germany-intersex-third-gender-identity-passport-lgbt-rights-a8706696.html.

Oppenheim, Maya. 'Hungarian Prime Minister Viktor Orban Bans Gender Studies Programmes'. *The Independent*, 24 October 2018. https://www.independent.co.uk/news/world/europe/hungary-bans-gender-studies-programmes-viktor-orban-central-european-university-budapest-a8599796.html.

Organisation for Economic Co-operation and Development. *Society at a Glance 2019: OECD Social Indicators*. Paris: OECD Publishing, 2019. https://doi.org/10.1787/soc_glance-2019-en.

O'Sullivan, Kyle. 'Piers Morgan Identifies as Penguin and Demands to Live in Aquarium in Furious Rant'. *Daily Mirror*, 11 September 2019. https://www.mirror.co.uk/tv/tv-news/piers-morgan-identifies-penguin-demands-20005622.

Owen, Glen. 'Anyone Should Be Allowed to "Identify" as Black Regardless of the Colour of Their Skin or Background, Says the University Lecturers' Union'. *Mail Online*, 17 November 2019. https://www.dailymail.co.uk/news/article-7693927/Anyone-allowed-identify-black-according-Left-wing-university-lecturers.html.

Parsons, Vic. 'There Were More Responses to the Gender Recognition Act Consultation from an Anti-Trans Group Than Actual Trans People'. *Pink News*, 22 September 2020. https://www.pinknews.co.uk/2020/09/22/gender-recognition-act-reform-announcement-fair-play-for-women-liz-truss-trans/.

Pascoe, C. J. 'What to Do with Actual People?: Thinking through a Queer Social Science Method'. In *Other, Please Specify: Queer Methods in Sociology*, edited by D'Lane Compton, Tey Meadow, and Kristen Schilt, 291–303. Berkeley: University of California Press, 2018.

Pasquale, Frank. *The Black Box Society: The Secret Algorithms That Control Money and Information*. Cambridge: Harvard University Press, 2015.

Peart, John. 'LGBT MP'. LGBT MP, 2021. https://mps.whoare.lgbt/.

Phipps, Alison. *Me, Not You: The Trouble with Mainstream Feminism*. Manchester: Manchester University Press, 2020.

Pieters, Janene. 'Amsterdam Municipality Goes Gender-Neutral in Speeches, Letters'. *NL Times*, 26 July 2017. https://nltimes.nl/2017/07/26/amsterdam-municipality-goes-gender-neutral-speeches-letters.

Plummer, Ken. 'Critical Humanism and Queer Theory: Living with the Tensions'. In *The SAGE Handbook of Qualitative Research*, edited by Norman K. Denzin and Yvonna S. Lincoln. Thousand Oaks: Sage Publications, 2005.

Plummer, Ken. 'Introduction to the Albany Trust Archive'. The Albany Trust and Hall-Carpenter Archives in Archives of Sexuality & Gender, Part I: LGBTQ History and Culture Since 1940, November 2001. https://www.gale.com/intl/essays/merrington-plummer-albany-trust-hall-carpenter-archives.

Pugh, Rachel. 'The UK's First LGBTQ+ Extra-Care Housing Scheme Gets Go Ahead'. *The Guardian*, 21 October 2020. https://www.theguardian.com/society/2020/oct/21/uks-first-extra-care-housing-lgbtq-manchester.

Reed, Terry. 'Written Evidence Submitted by GIRES to the Transgender Equality Inquiry', 2015. http://data.parliament.uk/writtenevidence/committeeevidence.svc/evidencedocument/women-and-equalities-committee/transgender-equality/written/19292.pdf.

Reuters. 'Tracing of South Korea's New Coronavirus Outbreak Focuses on LGBTQ Clubs'. *NBC News*, 11 May 2020. https://www.nbcnews.com/feature/nbc-out/tracing-s-korea-s-new-coronavirus-outbreak-focuses-lgbtq-clubs-n1204321.

Richardson, Elsa. 'New Queer Histories: Laura Doan's Disturbing Practices and the Constance Maynard Archive'. *Women's History Review* 25, no. 1 (2 January 2016): 161–8. https://doi.org/10.1080/09612025.2015.1047249.

Ridolfo, Heather, Kristen Miller, and Aaron Maitland. 'Measuring Sexual Identity Using Survey Questionnaires: How Valid Are Our Measures?' *Sexuality Research and Social Policy* 9, no. 2 (June 2012): 113–24. https://doi.org/10.1007/s13178-011-0074-x.

Rogers, Adam. 'Actually, Gender-Neutral Pronouns Can Change a Culture'. *Wired*, 15 August 2019. https://www.wired.com/story/actually-gender-neutral-pronouns-can-change-a-culture/.

Rohrer, Megan M. 'The Ethical Case for Undercounting Trans Individuals'. *TSQ: Transgender Studies Quarterly* 2, no. 1 (1 January 2015): 175–8. https://doi.org/10.1215/23289252-2848958.

Rooke, Alison. 'Queer in the Field: On Emotions, Temporality and Performativity in Ethnography'. In *Queer Methods and Methodologies*, edited by Kath Browne and Catherine J. Nash, 25–40. Farnham: Ashgate, 2010.

Rosiecka, Helena. 'Methodology for Decision Making on the 2021 Census Sex Question Concept and Associated Guidance'. Office for National Statistics, 10 February 2021. https://uksa.statisticsauthority.gov.uk/publication/methodology-for-decision-making-on-the-2021-census-sex-question-concept-and-associated-guidance/.

Roth, Andrew. 'Chechnya: Two Dead and Dozens Held in LGBT Purge, Say Activists'. *The Guardian*, 14 January 2019. https://www.theguardian.com/world/2019/jan/14/chechnya-two-dead-and-dozens-held-in-lgbt-purge-reports.

Rowling, J. K. 'JK Rowling Writes about Her Reasons for Speaking Out on Sex and Gender Issues'. *JK Rowling*, 10 June 2020. https://www.jkrowling.com/opinions/j-k-rowling-writes-about-her-reasons-for-speaking-out-on-sex-and-gender-issues/.

Ruberg, Bonnie, and Spencer Ruelos. 'Data for Queer Lives: How LGBTQ Gender and Sexuality Identities Challenge Norms of Demographics'. *Big Data & Society* 7, no. 1 (January 2020): 205395172093328. https://doi.org/10.1177/2053951720933286.

Ruppert, Evelyn. '"I Is; Therefore I Am": The Census as Practice of Double Identification'. *Sociological Research Online* 13, no. 4 (July 2008): 69–81. https://doi.org/10.5153/sro.1778.

Bibliography

Ruppert, Evelyn. 'Population Objects: Interpassive Subjects'. *Sociology* 45, no. 2 (April 2011): 218–33. https://doi.org/10.1177/0038038510394027.

Ryan, J. Michael. 'Born Again?: (Non-) Motivations to Alter Sex/Gender Identity Markers on Birth Certificates'. *Journal of Gender Studies* 29, no. 3 (2 April 2020): 269–81. https://doi.org/10.1080/09589236.2019.1631148.

Ryan, J. Michael. 'Expressing Identity: Toward an Understanding of How Trans Individuals Navigate the Barriers and Opportunities of Official Identity'. *Journal of Gender Studies* 29, no. 3 (2 April 2020): 349–60. https://doi.org/10.1080/0958 9236.2019.1570841.

Sadowski, Jathan. 'When Data Is Capital: Datafication, Accumulation, and Extraction'. *Big Data & Society* 6, no. 1 (1 January 2019). https://doi. org/10.1177/2053951718820549.

Saini, Angela. *Superior: The Return of Race Science*. London: 4th Estate, 2019.

Saperstein, Aliya, and Laurel Westbrook. 'Categorical and Gradational: Alternative Survey Measures of Sex and Gender'. *European Journal of Politics and Gender* 4, no. 1 (February 2021): 11–30. https://doi.org/10.1332/25151082 0X15995647280686.

Savage, Michael. *Identities and Social Change in Britain Since 1940: The Politics of Method*. Oxford: Oxford University Press, 2010.

Scheel, Stephan. 'Biopolitical Bordering: Enacting Populations as Intelligible Objects of Government'. *European Journal of Social Theory* 23, no. 4 (26 January 2020): 571–90. https://doi.org/10.1177/1368431019900096.

Schilt, Kristen, Tey Meadow, and D'Lane Compton. 'Introduction: Queer Work in a Straight Discipline'. In *Other, Please Specify: Queer Methods in Sociology*, edited by Kristen Schilt, Tey Meadow, and D'Lane Compton, 1–34. Berkeley: University of California Press, 2018.

Schofield, Michael. *A Minority: A Report on the Life of the Male Homosexual in Great Britain*. London: Longmans, 1960.

Schofield, Michael. *Society and the Homosexual*. London: Gollancz, 1952.

Schofield, Michael. *Sociological Aspects of Homosexuality*. London: Prentice Hall Press, 1965.

Schönpflug, Karin, Christine M. Klapeer, Roswitha Hofmann, and Sandra Müllbacher. 'If Queers Were Counted: An Inquiry into European Socioeconomic Data on LGB(TI)QS'. *Feminist Economics* 24, no. 4 (October 2018): 1–30. https://doi.org/10.1080/13545701.2018.1508877.

Schotel, Anne Louise, and Liza M. Mügge. 'Towards Categorical Visibility? The Political Making of a Third Sex in Germany and the Netherlands'. *JCMS: Journal of Common Market Studies* Online (28 January 2021): 1–44. https://doi. org/10.1111/jcms.13170.

Scott, James C. *Seeing Like a State: How Certain Schemes to Improve the Human Condition Have Failed*. New Haven: Yale University Press, 1998.

Scottish Government. 'Marriage and Civil Partnership (Scotland) Bill - Policy Memorandum'. Edinburgh: Scottish Government, 2013. https://archive2021. parliament.scot/S4_Bills/Marriage%20and%20Civil%20Partnership%20 (Scotland)%20Bill/b36s4-introd-pm.pdf.

Scottish Government. 'Review of the Gender Recognition Act 2004: Analysis of Responses to the Public Consultation Exercise'. Edinburgh: Scottish Government, 2018. https://www.gov.scot/publications/review-gender-recognition-act-2004-analysis-responses-public-consultation-exercise-report/.

Scottish Government. 'Scotland's People Annual Report 2019'. Edinburgh, September 2020. https://www.gov.scot/binaries/content/documents/govscot/publications/statistics/2020/09/scottish-household-survey-2019-annual-report/documents/scotlands-people-annual-report-2019/scotlands-people-annual-report-2019/govscot%3Adocument/scotlands-people-annual-report-2019.pdf.

Scottish Government. 'Scottish Social Attitudes 2015: Attitudes to Discrimination and Positive Action'. Social Research. Edinburgh: Scottish Government, 2016. http://www.gov.scot/Publications/2016/09/3916/0.

Scottish Government. 'Sex and Gender in Data Working Group'. Accessed 4 April 2021. https://www.gov.scot/groups/sex-and-gender-in-data-working-group/.

Secretary of the State for the Home Department and Secretary of State for Scotland. 'Report of the Committee on Homosexual Offences and Prostitution'. London: Her Majesty's Stationery Office, 1957.

Seidman, Steven, ed. *Queer Theory/Sociology*. Twentieth-Century Social Theory. Cambridge: Blackwell, 1996.

Serano, Julia. *Whipping Girl: A Transsexual Woman on Sexism and the Scapegoating of Femininity*. Emeryville: Seal Press, 2007.

Shrestha, Manesh. 'Nepal Census Recognises "Third Gender"'. *CNN*, 31 May 2011. http://www.cnn.com/2011/WORLD/asiapcf/05/31/nepal.census.gender/index.html.

Siegel, Reeva. 'Why Equal Protection No Longer Protects: The Evolving Forms of Status-Enforcing State Action'. *Stanford Law Review* 49 (May 1997). https://doi.org/10.2307/1229249.

Sin Violencia LGBTI. 'Prejudice Knows No Bounds: Executive Summary'. Sin Violencia LGBTI, 2019. https://sinviolencia.lgbt/wp-content/uploads/2019/09/Executive-Summary-Prejudice-knows-no-bounds.pdf.

Sin Violencia LGBTI. 'Sin Violencia LGBTI'. Accessed 8 May 2021. https://sinviolencia.lgbt/non-violence-lgbti/.

Sobande, Francesca. *The Digital Lives of Black Women in Britain*. Palgrave Studies in (Re)Presenting Gender. Cham: Springer International Publishing, 2020.

Spade, Dean. *Normal Life: Administrative Violence, Critical Trans Politics, and the Limits of Law*. Durham: Duke University Press, 2015.

Spivak, Gayatri Chakravorty. 'Subaltern Studies: Deconstructing Historiography [1985]'. In *The Spivak Reader: Selected Works of Gayatri Chakravorty Spivak*, edited by Donna Landry and Gerald M. MacLean. New York: Routledge, 1996.

Statistics Netherlands. 'The Dutch Virtual Census'. Youtube, 22 November 2012. https://www.youtube.com/watch?v=SLpDkcyenf0&feature=youtu.be.

Stats NZ. 'Sex and Gender Identity Statistical Standards: Consultation'. Stats NZ, 2 July 2020. https://www.stats.govt.nz/consultations/sex-and-gender-identity-statistical-standards-consultation.

Stats NZ. 'Sex and Gender Identity Statistical Standards: Findings from Public Consultation, July - August 2020', 2020. https://www.stats.govt.nz/reports/sex-and-gender-identity-statistical-standards-findings-from-public-consultation-julyaugust-2020.

Stein, Arlene, and Ken Plummer. '"I Can't Even Think Straight" "Queer" Theory and the Missing Sexual Revolution in Sociology'. *Sociological Theory* 12, no. 2 (1994): 178–87. https://doi.org/10.2307/201863.

Steinmetz, Katy. 'The Transgender Tipping Point'. *Time*, 29 May 2014. https://time.com/magazine/us/135460/june-9th-2014-vol-183-no-22-u-s/.

Stonewall. 'LGBT in Britain - Health Report'. London, November 2018. https://www.stonewall.org.uk/system/files/lgbt_in_britain_health.pdf.

Stonewall. 'LGBT in Britain - Home and Communities'. London, 2018. https://www.stonewall.org.uk/sites/default/files/lgbt_in_britain_home_and_communities.pdf.

Stonewall. 'LGBT in Britain - University Report'. London, 2018. https://www.stonewall.org.uk/system/files/lgbt_in_britain_universities_report.pdf.

Stonewall. 'Our Mission and Priorities'. Stonewall, 10 August 2015. https://www.stonewall.org.uk/about-us/our-mission-and-priorities.

Stonewall Scotland. 'School Report Scotland: The Experiences of Lesbian, Gay, Bi and Trans Young People in Scotland's Schools in 2017', 2017. https://www.stonewallscotland.org.uk/system/files/school_report_scotland_2017.pdf.

Stryker, Susan, Paisley Currah, and Lisa Jean Moore. 'Introduction: Trans-, Trans, or Transgender?' *Women's Studies Quarterly* 36, no. 3/4 (2008): 11–22. https://doi.org/10.1353/wsq.0.0112.

Suen, Leslie W., Mitchell R. Lunn, Katie Katuzny, Sacha Finn, Laura Duncan, Jae Sevelius, Annesa Flentje, et al. 'What Sexual and Gender Minority People Want Researchers to Know about Sexual Orientation and Gender Identity Questions: A Qualitative Study'. *Archives of Sexual Behavior* 49, no. 7 (October 2020): 2301–18. https://doi.org/10.1007/s10508-020-01810-y.

Sullivan, Alice. 'Sex and the Census: Why Surveys Should Not Conflate Sex and Gender Identity'. *International Journal of Social Research Methodology* 23, no. 5 (2 September 2020): 517–24. https://doi.org/10.1080/13645579.2020.1768346.

Szulc, Łukasz. 'Digital Gender Disidentifications: Beyond the Subversion versus Hegemony Dichotomy and toward Everyday Gender Practices'. *International Journal of Communication* 14 (13 October 2020): 19. https://ijoc.org/index.php/ijoc/article/view/15396.

Tahir, Tariq. 'BBC Films Used in Schools Teach Children There Are "100 Genders or More" Despite GPs Only Recognising Six'. *The Sun*, 8 September 2019. https://www.thesun.co.uk/news/9886252/bbc-schools-children-100-genders/.

Task Force on Communicating Gender Statistics. 'Guidance on Communicating Gender Statistics'. United Nations Economic Commission for Europe Conference of European Statisticians, 2020.

Tavits, Margit, and Efrén O. Pérez. 'Language Influences Mass Opinion toward Gender and LGBT Equality'. *Proceedings of the National Academy of Sciences* 116, no. 34 (20 August 2019): 16781–86. https://doi.org/10.1073/pnas.1908156116.

Taylor, Mark. 'UK Games Industry Census: Understanding Diversity in the UK Games Industry Workforce'. Ukie, February 2020. https://ukie.org.uk/resources/uk-games-industry-census-2021.

Tomasev, Nenad, Kevin R. McKee, Jackie Kay, and Shakir Mohamed. 'Fairness for Unobserved Characteristics: Insights from Technological Impacts on Queer Communities'. *ArXiv:2102.04257* Online (2021). http://arxiv.org/abs/2102.04257.

Tooth Murphy, Amy. 'Listening In, Listening Out: Intersubjectivity and the Impact of Insider and Outsider Status in Oral History Interviews'. *Oral History* 48, no. 1 (2020). https://www.ohs.org.uk/scripts/journal-search.php?parameter=issue&searchkey=101#listing1486.

Topping, Alexandra. 'Guidance on Sex Question in Census Must Be Changed, High Court Rules'. *The Guardian*, 9 March 2021. http://www.theguardian.com/uk-news/2021/mar/09/guidance-on-sex-question-in-uk-census-must-be-changed-high-court-rules.

Towle, Evan B., and Lynn Marie Morgan. 'Romancing the Transgender Native: Rethinking the Use of the "Third Gender" Concept'. *GLQ: A Journal of Lesbian and Gay Studies* 8, no. 4 (2002): 469–97. https://doi.org/10.1215/10642684-8-4-469.

Treharne, Gareth, and Chris Brickell. 'Editorial: Accessing Queer Data in a Multidisciplinary World: Where Do We Go from Queer?' *Gay and Lesbian Issues and Psychology Review* 7, no. 2 (2011): 83–8.

Tsika, Noah. 'CompuQueer: Protocological Constraints, Algorithmic Streamlining, and the Search for Queer Methods Online'. *Women's Studies Quarterly* 44, no. 3/4 (2016): 111–30. https://doi.org/10.1353/wsq.2016.0038.

University of Sheffield. 'LGBT+ Accommodation', 25 October 2019. https://www.sheffield.ac.uk/accommodation/prospective/lgbt.

US Government Accountability Office. '2020 Decennial Census', 6 March 2019. https://www.gao.gov/highrisk/2020_decennial_census/why_did_study.

Ushie, Boniface. 'Recognising Intersex People Opens Access to Fundamental Rights in Kenya'. *The Conversation*, 28 August 2019. http://theconversation.com/recognising-intersex-people-opens-access-to-fundamental-rights-in-kenya-122413.

Valentine, Vic. 'Non-Binary People's Experiences in the UK'. Edinburgh: Scottish Trans Alliance, Equality Network, 2015. https://www.scottishtrans.org/wp-content/uploads/2016/11/Non-binary-report.pdf.

Vasquez, Alejandra. 'The Urgency of Intersectionality: Kimberlé Crenshaw Speaks at TEDWomen 2016'. *TED Blog*, 27 October 2016. https://blog.ted.com/the-urgency-of-intersectionality-kimberle-crenshaw-speaks-at-tedwomen-2016/.

Vaughan, Adam. 'UK Launched Passport Photo Checker It Knew Would Fail with Dark Skin'. *New Scientist*, 9 October 2019. https://www.newscientist.com/article/2219284-uk-launched-passport-photo-checker-it-knew-would-fail-with-dark-skin/.

Veale, Michael, and Reuben Binns. 'Fairer Machine Learning in the Real World: Mitigating Discrimination without Collecting Sensitive Data'. *Big Data & Society* 4, no. 2 (2017): 1–17. https://doi.org/10.1177/2053951717743530.

Bibliography

Véliz, Carissa. *Privacy Is Power: Why and How You Should Take Back Control of Your Data*. London: Transworld, 2020.

Velte, Kyle. 'Straightwashing the Census'. *Boston College Law Review* 61, no. 1 (29 January 2020): 69–127. https://doi.org/10.2139/ssrn.3358453.

Vicinus, Martha. '"They Wonder to Which Sex I Belong": The Historical Roots of the Modern Lesbian Identity'. *Feminist Studies* 18, no. 3 (1992): 467–97. https://doi.org/10.2307/3178078.

Vickers, Emma. *Queen and Country: Same-Sex Desire in the British Armed Forces, 1939–45*. Gender in History. Manchester: Manchester University Press, 2012.

Vincent, James. 'Facebook Introduces More than 70 New Gender Options to the UK: "We Want to Reflect Society"'. *The Independent*, 24 June 2014. https://www.independent.co.uk/life-style/gadgets-and-tech/facebook-introduces-more-than-70-new-gender-options-to-the-uk-we-want-to-reflect-society-9567261.html.

Walcott, Rinaldo. 'The End of Diversity'. *Public Culture* 31, no. 2 (1 May 2019): 393–408. https://doi.org/10.1215/08992363-7286885.

Walker, Shaun. 'Polish President Issues Campaign Pledge to Fight "LGBT Ideology"'. *The Guardian*, 12 June 2020. https://www.theguardian.com/world/2020/jun/12/polish-president-issues-campaign-pledge-to-fight-lgbt-ideology.

Walter, Maggie, and Chris Andersen. *Indigenous Statistics: A Quantitative Research Methodology*. Walnut Creek: Routledge, 2013.

Wang, Yilun, and Michal Kosinski. 'Deep Neural Networks Are More Accurate than Humans at Detecting Sexual Orientation from Facial Images'. *Journal of Personality and Social Psychology* 114, no. 2 (February 2018): 246–57. https://doi.org/10.1037/pspa0000098.

Ward, Sarah. 'Academics Criticise Scotland's 2021 Census for Allowing Sex to Be Self-Identified'. *The Scotsman*, 26 December 2019. https://www.scotsman.com/news/uk-news/academics-criticise-scotlands-2021-census-allowing-sex-be-self-identified-1398949.

Waters, Chris, Frank Mort, and Becky Conekin. 'Introduction'. In *Moments of Modernity: Reconstructing Britain, 1945–1964*, edited by Becky Conekin, Frank Mort, and Chris Waters. London: Rivers Oram Press, 1999.

Weeks, Jeffrey. *Coming Out: Homosexual Politics in Britain from the Nineteenth Century to the Present*. London: Quartet Books, 1977.

Weinrich, James D., Peter J. Snyder, Richard C. Pillard, Igor Grant, Denise L. Jacobson, S. Renée Robinson, and J. Allen Mccutchan. 'A Factor Analysis of the Klein Sexual Orientation Grid in Two Disparate Samples'. *Archives of Sexual Behavior* 22, no. 2 (1 April 1993): 157–68. https://doi.org/10.1007/BF01542364.

West, Donald J. *Homosexuality*. London: Gerald Duckworth and Company, 1955.

Westbrook, Laurel, and Aliya Saperstein. 'New Categories Are Not Enough: Rethinking the Measurement of Sex and Gender in Social Surveys'. *Gender & Society* 29, no. 4 (1 August 2015): 534–60. https://doi.org/10.1177/0891243215584758.

Westbrook, Laurel, Jamie Budnick, and Aliya Saperstein. 'Dangerous Data: Seeing Social Surveys through the Sexuality Prism'. *Sexualities* Online (10 February 2021): 1–33. https://doi.org/10.1177/1363460720986927.

Whittle, Stephen, Lewis Turner, and Maryam Al-Alami. 'Engendered Penalties: Transgender and Transsexual People's Experiences of Inequality and Discrimination'. Press for Change, 2007. https://www.ilga-europe.org/sites/default/files/trans_country_report_-_engenderedpenalties.pdf.

Williams, Martin. 'Academics Urge MSPs Not to Change Census Sex Question'. *The Herald*, 20 September 2019. https://www.heraldscotland.com/news/17917647.academics-urge-msps-not-change-census-sex-question/.

YouGov. 'How Brits Describe Their Sexuality', 21 January 2021. https://yougov.co.uk/topics/relationships/trackers/how-brits-describe-their-sexuality.

Young, Eris. *They/Them/Their: A Guide to Nonbinary and Genderqueer Identities*. London: Jessica Kingsley Publishers, 2020.

Young, Michael, and Peter Willmott. *Family and Kinship in East London*. London: Routledge and Kegan Paul, 1957.

Zosky, Diane L., and Robert Alberts. 'What's in a Name? Exploring Use of the Word Queer as a Term of Identification within the College-Aged LGBT Community'. *Journal of Human Behavior in the Social Environment* 26, no. 7–8 (16 November 2016): 597–607. https://doi.org/10.1080/10911359.2016.1238803.

Zuberi, Tukufu. *Thicker than Blood: How Racial Statistics Lie*. Minneapolis: University of Minnesota Press, 2001.

Zweig, Ferdynand. *The Worker in an Affluent Society: Family Life and Industry*. London: Heinemann, 1961.

INDEX

Index

Index